SONGS OF FELLOWSHIP

MUSIC EDITION

KINGSWAY MUSIC
EASTBOURNE

Most of the songs in this publication
are covered by the Church Copyright Licence

United Kingdom	United States
CCL UK Ltd	CCL Inc
PO Box 1339	6130 NE 78th Court
Eastbourne	Suite C11
East Sussex	Portland
BN21 4YF	Oregon 97218

ISBN 0 86065 935 6
Words edition ISBN 0 86065 936 4
Large Print Words edition ISBN 0 86065 937 2

Scripture quotations adjacent to some of the songs
in this volume are from the Holy Bible: New International Version,
copyright © International Bible Society 1973, 1978, 1984.
Published by Hodder & Stoughton and
used by permission.

North American distributors:
Kingsway Music Inc., c/o Alexendria House Inc
468 McNally Drive, Nashville, TN 37211

Produced by Bookprint Creative Services
P.O. Box 827, BN23 6NX, England for
KINGSWAY MUSIC LTD
Lottbridge Drove, Eastbourne, E. Sussex BN23 6NT
Printed in Great Britain by The Bath Press Ltd, Bath, Avon.

Contents

Acknowledgements

Our grateful thanks to the editorial team who have contributed over the last two years to this marvellous musical resource for the Church through the nineties.

Dave Bankhead	Heartbeat – New Generation Ministries
Dave Bilbrough	Songwriter and Worship Leader
Chris Bowater	Lifestyle Ministries
Chris Cartwright	Music Director, Kensington Temple
Frank Fortunato	International Music Director – Operation Mobilisation
Rob Frost	National Methodist Evangelist
Wynne Goss	Pastor, Songwriter, Worship Leader – Living Vine Mid Glamorgan
Phil Lawson–Johnston	Songwriter and Worship Leader
Andrew Maries	Music Director, St. Michael-le-Belfrey Church, York
David Peacock	Jubilate
Noel Richards	Worship Leader, Songwriter – Pioneer
Ian Smale (Ishmael)	Songwriter, Worship Leader – The Glorie Company
Ian Traynar	Lifesong Ministries – Christian Musicians' and Artists' Trust
Ian Watson	Music Director, Praise Gathering, Glasgow –
Ian White	Songwriter, Worship Leader – Little Misty Music
Jackie Williams	Worship Leader, Arranger – JAW Music, Sheffield
Nigel Coltman	Executive Editor, Project Co-ordinator
Stuart Townend	Editor and Arranger

Our thanks to all those who have contributed to *Songs of Fellowship* over the years, including Margaret Evans, Geoff Shearn, Pat Herridge, Gary Wilson, Les Moir and the songwriters, without whom there would be no songbook.

Important notes

Order of songs

The songs appear in alphabetical order by first line (letter by letter), not necessarily by author's title, for easy use in praise and worship meetings. An index of titles and first lines is included at the back, along with other useful indexes and chord charts (see Contents page).

To further facilitate the use of this book, all two-page songs and hymns appear on facing pages to avoid turning over, while maintaining the alphabetical order.

Scripture references

References – listed in biblical order – are to the key Bible passages quoted or echoed in the songs, and to some passing references. In many cases the whole Bible passage will repay further exploration, beyond the verses listed. A full index to the Scripture references is provided at the back of the book.

1.

Abba Father

Mt 26:39, 42; Mk 14:36; Lk 22:42;
Rom 8:15; Gal 4:6

Capo 3 (G)

Dave Bilbrough

Thoughtfully

2.

Abide with me

Mt 28:20; Lk 24:29; Rom 8:37–39;
1 Cor 15:55

Capo 3 (C)
EVENTIDE

William Henry Monk (1823-89)

Peacefully

1. A - bide with me, fast falls the e - ven -
tide; the dark - ness deep - ens,
Lord, with me a - bide; when o - ther
help - ers fail and com - forts flee,
Help of the help-less, O a - bide with me.

2. Swift to its close ebbs out life's little day;
   Earth's joys grow dim, its glories pass away;
   Change and decay in all around I see;
   O Thou who changest not, abide with me.

3. I need Thy presence every passing hour;
   What but Thy grace can foil the tempter's power?
   Who like Thyself my guide and stay can be?
   Through cloud and sunshine, O abide with me.

4. I fear no foe, with Thee at hand to bless;
   Ills have no weight, and tears no bitterness.
   Where is death's sting? Where, grave, thy victory?
   I triumph still, if Thou abide with me.

5. Reveal Thyself before my closing eyes;
   Shine through the gloom, and point me to the skies,
   Heaven's morning breaks, and earth's vain shadows flee;
   In life, in death, O Lord, abide with me.

Henry Francis Lyte (1793-1847)

3. Ah Lord God

Jer 32:17–19

Kay Chance

Capo 2 (C)

Ah Lord God, Thou ___ hast made the hea-vens and the

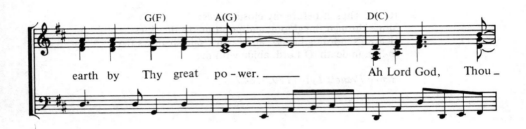

earth by Thy great po-wer. ___ Ah Lord God, Thou ___

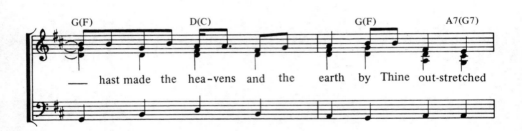

___ hast made the hea-vens and the earth by Thine out-stretched

arm. No-thing is too dif-fi-cult for

4.

Alleluia

Jerry Sinclair

1. Al – le – lu – ia, al – le – lu – ia, al – le – lu – ia, al – le – lu – ia. Al – le – lu – ia, al – le – lu – ia, al – le – lu – ia, al – le – lu – ia.

2. He's my Saviour . . .

3. He is worthy . . .

4. I will praise Him . . .

5.

Alleluia! Alleluia!
(Jesus is our King)

Capo 4 (C)

Ps 51:10; Mt 26:26–27; Mk 14:22–23;
Lk 22:19–20; 1 Cor 11:23–26

Sherrell Prebble & Howard Clark

With joyful dignity

Chorus

Al - le -lu -ia! Al - le - lu - ia! O -pen-ing our hearts to Him, sing-ing al - le -lu -ia! Al - le - lu - ia! Je - sus is our King!

Fine

Verse

1. Cre - ate in us, O God a hum - ble heart that sets us free to pro- claim the won-drous ma - jes -ty of our Fa - ther in hea - ven.

D.C.

2. We bear the name of Christ,
   Justified, we meet with Him.
   His words and presence calm our fear,
   Revealing God our Father here.

3. Let kindred voices join,
   Honouring the Lamb of God
   Who teaches us by bread and wine
   The mystery of His body.

4. Pour out Your Spirit on us,
   Empowering us to live as one,
   To carry Your redeeming love
   To a world enslaved by sin.

6. Alleluia, Alleluia, give thanks to the risen Lord

Mt 28:6; Mk 16:6; Lk 24:6; Jn 21:14; Gal 2:20; Heb 12:22, 24

Capo 5 (C)

Triumphantly

Donald Fishel

2. Spread the good news o'er all the earth,
   Jesus has died and has risen.

3. We have been crucified with Christ,
   Now we shall live for ever.

4. God has proclaimed the just reward,
   Life for all men, Alleluia!

5. Come let us praise the living God,
   Joyfully sing to our Saviour.

7. All hail King Jesus!

1 Tim 6:15; Rev 17:14; 19:16

Dave Moody

All hail King Je-sus! All hail Em-man-u-el! ___

— King of kings, Lord of lords, bright morning star. ___

— And through-out e-ter-ni-ty I'll sing Your prai-ses, ___

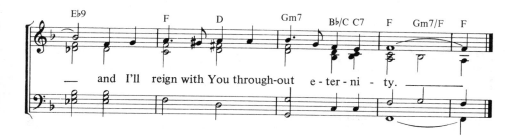

— and I'll reign with You through-out e-ter-ni-ty. ___

8.

All hail the Lamb

Rev 5:12

Dave Bilbrough

All hail the Lamb, en-throned on high; His praise shall __ be our __ bat-tle cry; He reigns vic-tor-i-ous, for-e-ver glo-ri-ous, His name is Je - sus, He is the Lord. ___

9. All hail the power of Jesus' name!

Heb 2:9;
Rev 4:10–11

MILES LANE

With vigour

William Shrubsole (1760-1806)

1. All hail the pow'r of Je - sus' name! Let an - gels prostrate fall; bring forth the roy - al di - a - dem, and crown Him, crown Him, crown Him, crown Him Lord of all.

2. Crown Him, ye martyrs of your God,
   Who from His altar call;
   Extol Him in whose path ye trod,
   And crown Him Lord of all.

3. Ye seed of Israel's chosen race,
   Ye ransomed of the fall,
   Hail Him who saves you by His grace,
   And crown Him Lord of all.

4. Sinners, whose love can ne'er forget
   The wormwood and the gall,
   Go, spread your trophies at His feet,
   And crown Him Lord of all.

5. Let every kindred, every tribe
   On this terrestrial ball,
   To Him all majesty ascribe,
   And crown Him Lord of all.

6. O that, with yonder sacred throng,
   We at His feet may fall,
   Join in the everlasting song,
   And crown Him Lord of all!

Edward Perronet (1726-92)
Revised by John Rippon (1751-1836)

In the beginning was the Word, and the Word was with God, and the Word was God. He was with God in the beginning.

Through him all things were made; without him nothing was made that has been made. In him was life, and that life was the light of men.
The light shines in the darkness, but the darkness has not understood it.

JOHN 1:1–5

10.

All heaven declares

Ps 19:1; Rev 5:12

Noel and Tricia Richards

1. All heav'n de-clares the glo-ry of the ri - sen Lord.
Who can com-pare with the beau-ty of the Lord?
For-e-ver He will be the Lamb up-on the throne.
I glad-ly bow the knee and wor-ship Him a - lone.

2. I will proclaim
The glory of the risen Lord.
Who once was slain
To reconcile man to God.
Forever You will be
The Lamb upon the throne.
I gladly bow the knee
And worship You alone.

11.

All heaven waits

Mt 6:10; Rom 8:34; Eph 4:4;
1 Thess 4:16–17; 2 Thess 2:8;
Heb 7:25

Capo 5(Am)

Graham Kendrick & Chris Rolinson

1. All heav-en waits with ba-ted breath, for saints on earth to pray. Ma-jes-tic an-gels rea-dy stand with swords of fi-ery blade. A-stound-ing power a-waits a word from God's re-splen-dent throne.

2. Awake, O church, arise and pray
   Complaining words discard.
   The Spirit comes to fill your mouth
   With truth, His mighty sword.
   Go place your feet on Satan's ground
   And there proclaim Christ's name,
   In step with heaven's armies march
   To conquer and to reign!

(Ladies)
3. Now in our hearts and on our lips
   The word of faith is near,
   Let heaven's will on earth be done,
   Let heaven flow from here.
   (Men)
   Come blend your prayers with Jesus' own
   Before the Father's throne
   And as the incense clouds ascend
   God's holy fire rains down.

4. Soon comes the day when with a shout
   King Jesus shall appear
   And with Him all the church,
   From every age, shall fill the air.
   The brightness of His coming shall
   Consume the lawless one,
   As with a word the breath of God
   Tears down his rebel throne.

5. One body here, by heav'n inspired,
   We seek prophetic power;
   In Christ agreed, one heart and voice,
   To speak this day, this hour,
   In every place where chaos rules
   And evil forces brood;
   Let Jesus' voice speak like the roar
   Of a great multitude.

12. All over the world

Is 11:9

Roy Turner

2. All over His church God's Spirit is moving,
   All over His church as the prophet said it would be;
   All over His church there's a mighty revelation
   Of the glory of the Lord, as the waters cover the sea.

3. Right here in this place the Spirit is moving,
   Right here in this place as the prophet said it would be;
   Right here in this place there's a mighty revelation
   Of the glory of the Lord, as the waters cover the sea.

13. All people that on earth do dwell *Ps 100*

OLD 100th   *French Psalter* (1551)

1. All peo-ple that on earth do dwell, sing to the Lord with
cheer - ful voice; Him serve with mirth, His praise forth -
tell, come ye be - fore Him and re - joice.

2. Know that the Lord is God indeed,
   Without our aid He did us make:
   We are His flock, He doth us feed,
   And for His sheep He doth us take.

3. O enter then His gates with praise,
   Approach with joy His courts unto:
   Praise, laud, and bless His name always,
   For it is seemly so to do.

4. For why, the Lord our God is good;
   His mercy is for ever sure;
   His truth at all times firmly stood,
   And shall from age to age endure.

5. Praise God from whom all blessings flow,
   Praise Him all creatures here below,
   Praise Him above, ye heavenly hosts:
   Praise Father, Son and Holy Ghost.

William Kethe (d. 1594)

14. All things bright and beautiful

(First tune)

ALL THINGS BRIGHT AND BEAUTIFUL

W.H. Monk (1823-89)

Brightly

1. All things bright and beau-ti-ful, all crea-tures great and small,
all things wise and won-der-ful, the Lord God made them all.

1. Each lit-tle flower that op — ens, each lit-tle bird that sings, He
made their glow-ing col — ours, He made their ti-ny wings.

2. The purple-headed mountain,
   The river running by,
   The sunset, and the morning
   That brightens up the sky:

3. The cold wind in the winter,
   The pleasant summer sun,
   The ripe fruits in the garden,
   He made them every one.

4. He gave us eyes to see them,
   And lips that we might tell
   How great is God Almighty,
   Who has made all things well.

Cecil F. Alexander (1818-95)

All things bright and beautiful
(Second tune)

ROYAL OAK
Brightly

Traditional English melody
arranged by Martin Shaw (1875-1958)

Chorus
All things bright and beau-ti-ful, all crea-tures great and _ small,
all things wise and won-der-ful, the Lord God made them all.

Verse
1. Each lit-tle flower that op-ens, each lit-tle bird_that sings, He _
made their glow-ing _ col - ours, He _ made their ti-ny _ wings.

2. The purple-headed mountain,
The river running by
The sunset, and the morning
That brightens up the sky:

3. The cold wind in the winter,
The pleasant summer sun,
The ripe fruits in the garden,
He made them every one.

4. He gave us eyes to see them,
And lips that we might tell
How great is God Almighty,
Who has made all things well.

Cecil F. Alexander (1818-95)

15.
All you angels round His throne
(Give Him praise)

Ps 103:20–22;
148:2, 7, 9–11

Capo 2 (G)

Marc Nelson

2. All the angels round Your throne praise You! . . .

We give You praise . . .

16. Almighty God

Jn 1:3; 2 Pet 1:19; Rev 22:16

Austin Martin

Worshipfully

Al-might-y God, _____ we bring You praise _____ for Your Son, _____ the Word of God, _____ by whose power _____ the world was made, _____ by whose blood _____ we are re-deemed. Mor-ning star, _____ the Fath-er's glo-ry, _____ we now wor-ship _____ and a-dore You. _____ In our hearts _____ Your light has ri-sen; _____ Je-sus, Lord, _____ we worship You.

17. Almighty God, our heavenly Father
Ps 51:1–2

(Confession)

Chris Rolinson

With feeling

Al-migh-ty God, our hea-ven-ly Fa-ther, we have sinned a-gainst __ You, and a-gainst our fel - low men. __ In thought and word _and deed, through neg - li-gence,_through weak-ness, through our own de -

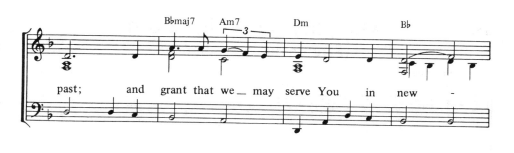

past; and grant that we — may serve You in new -

ness of life. _____ To the glo - ry of your

name, to the glo - ry of your name, to the

glo - ry of your name, to the glo - ry of your name, to the

glo - ry of your name. _____ A - men, a - men.

18. Almighty Sovereign Lord
(Stretch out Your hand)

Mt 3:2; 4:17; 10:7;
Mk 1:15; Lk 4:43;
8:1; 9:2, 11, 60

Phil Lawson Johnston

1. Al - might - y Sov' - reign Lord, Cre - a - tor God, You made the hea-vens and the earth. You're spo - ken to the world, Your - self the liv - ing Word, You give us eyes to see Your king - dom. So stretch out Your hand, O God, in signs and

wonders, we rest our faith on Your al-might-y power.

Stretch out Your hand, O God, to heal and de-

-liv-er, we de-clare, we de-clare Your

king-dom is here.

Last time only

2. Stir up Your people like a mighty wind,
   Come shake us, wake us from our sleep.
   Give us compassion, Lord,
   Love for Your holy word,
   Give us the courage of Your kingdom.

3. Why do so many stand against You now,
   Bringing dishonour to Your name?
   Consider how they mock,
   But we will never stop
   Speaking with boldness of Your kingdom.

19.

Amazing grace!

Ps 142:5; Mt 18:13; Lk 15:4;
Jn 1:16; Rom 5:2;
2 Cor 4:8–9; Rev 14:3

AMAZING GRACE

With feeling

Early American melody

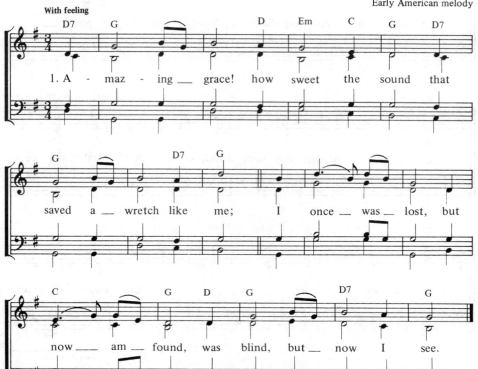

1. A - maz - ing __ grace! how sweet the sound that saved a __ wretch like me; I once __ was __ lost, but now __ am __ found, was blind, but __ now I see.

2. 'Twas grace that taught my heart to fear,
   And grace my fears relieved;
   How precious did that grace appear,
   The hour I first believed!

3. Through many dangers, toils and snares
   I have already come:
   'Tis grace that brought me safe thus far,
   And grace will lead me home.

4. The Lord has promised good to me,
   His word my hope secures;
   He will my shield and portion be
   As long as life endures.

5. Yes, when this heart and flesh shall fail,
   And mortal life shall cease,
   I shall possess within the veil
   A life of joy and peace.

6. When we've been there a thousand years,
   Bright shining as the sun,
   We've no less days to sing God's praise
   Then when we first begun.

John Newton (1725-1807)

———— □ ▢ □ -————

The Lord does not look at the things man looks at. Man looks at the outward appearance, but the Lord looks at the heart.

1 SAMUEL 16:7

———— □ ▢ □ ————

20. An army of ordinary people

Rom 9:8

Dave Bilbrough

1. An ar-my of or-di-na-ry people, _____ a kingdom where love is the key, _____ a ci-ty, a light to the na-tions, _ heirs to the pro-mise _ are we. _____ A people _ whose life is in Je - sus, _____ a nation to-geth-er we stand. On-ly through grace are we worth-y, _ in-he-ri-tors of the land. _ A new day is dawn-ing, _

2. A people without recognition,
But with Him a destiny sealed,
Called to a heavenly vision:
His purpose shall be fulfilled.
Come let us stand strong together,
Abandon ourselves to the King.
His love shall be ours for ever,
This victory song we shall sing.

21.

And can it be?

Rom 8:1; Phil 2:6–8

Thomas Campbell (1825-76)

SAGINA
With strength

1. And can it be that I should gain an in - t'rest in the Sav - iour's blood? Died He for me, who caused His pain? For me, who Him to death pur - sued? A - maz - ing love! how can it be that

Thou, — my God, — shouldst die — for me?

A- maz-ing love! How can it be that

A - maz-ing love! How can it be

Thou, my God, shouldst — die for me?

that Thou, my God, shouldst die for me?

2. 'Tis mystery all! The Immortal dies:
Who can explore His strange design?
In vain the first-born seraph tries
To sound the depths of love divine!
'Tis mercy all! let earth adore,
Let angel minds inquire no more.

3. He left His Father's throne above,
So free, so infinite His grace;
Emptied Himself of all but love,
And bled for Adam's helpless race;
'Tis mercy all, immense and free;
For, O my God, it found out me.

4. Long my imprisoned spirit lay
Fast bound in sin and nature's night;
Thine eye diffused a quickening ray,
I woke, the dungeon flamed with light;
My chains fell off, my heart was free;
I rose, went forth, and followed Thee.

5. No condemnation now I dread;
Jesus, and all in Him, is mine!
Alive in Him, my living Head,
And clothed in righteousness divine,
Bold I approach the eternal throne,
And claim the crown, through Christ my own.

Charles Wesley (1707-88)

22. A new commandment

Jn 13:34–35

Author unknown
Arr. Margaret Evans

Capo 2(C)

Smoothly

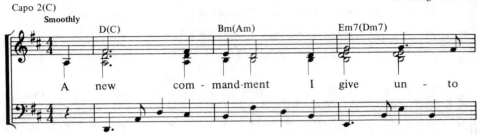

A new com-mand-ment I give un-to

you, that you love one an-oth-er as

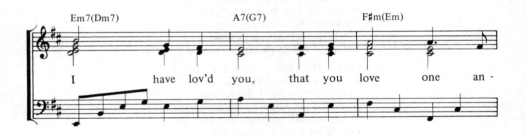

I have lov'd you, that you love one an-

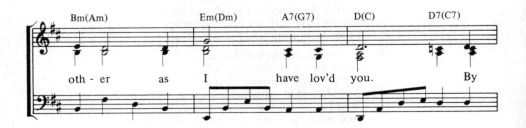

oth-er as I have lov'd you. By

23. Angels from the realms of glory

Mt 2:1, 10;
Lk 2:8, 13

French carol melody

IRIS

Jubilantly

1. An - gels, from the ____ realms of glo - ry,

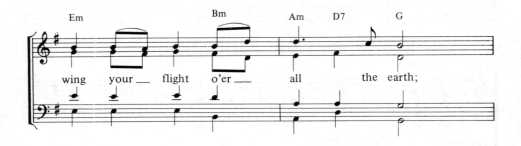

wing your ____ flight o'er ____ all the earth;

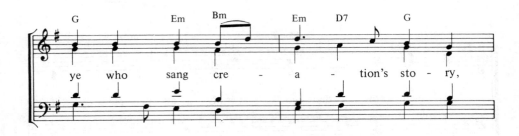

ye who sang cre - a - tion's sto - ry,

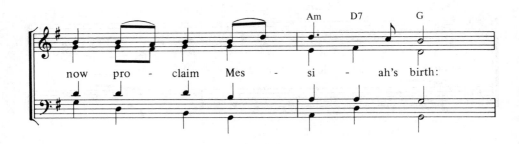

now pro - claim Mes - si - ah's birth:

2. Shepherds, in the field abiding,
   Watching o'er your flocks by night,
   God with man is now residing,
   Yonder shines the infant-light:

3. Sages, leave your contemplations,
   Brighter visions beam afar;
   Seek the great desire of nations,
   Ye have seen His natal star:

4. Saints, before the altar bending,
   Watching long in hope and fear,
   Suddenly the Lord descending
   In His temple shall appear:

James Montgomery (1771-1854)

― □ ▢ □ ―

*Therefore, since we have been
justified through faith, we have peace
with God through our Lord Jesus
Christ, through whom we have gained
access by faith into this grace in
which we now stand. And we rejoice in
the hope of the glory of God.*

ROMANS 5:1–2

― □ ▢ □ ―

24. Angel voices ever singing

ANGEL VOICES

Ps 8:4; Rev 5:11; 14:2

Edwin George Monk (1819-1900)

2. Thou who art beyond the farthest
Mortal eye can scan,
Can it be that Thou regardest
Songs of sinful man?
Can we know that Thou art near us
And wilt hear us?
Yes, we can.

3. Yes, we know that Thou rejoicest
O'er each work of Thine;
Thou didst ears and hands and voices
For Thy praise design;
Craftsman's art and music's measure
For Thy pleasure
All combine.

4. In Thy house, great God, we offer
Of Thine own to Thee,
And for Thine acceptance proffer,
All unworthily,
Hearts and minds and hands and voices
In our choicest
Psalmody.

5. Honour, glory, might, and merit
Thine shall ever be,
Father, Son, and Holy Spirit,
Blessèd Trinity.
Of the best that Thou hast given
Earth and heaven
Render Thee.

Francis Pott (1832-1909)

25.   A safe stronghold our God is still

Eph 6:10–12;
Jas 4:7;
1 Pet 5:8; 1 Jn 3:8;
Rev 20:10

EIN' FESTE BURG
With strength

Martin Luther (1483-1546)

1. A safe strong-hold_ our God_ is still, a trust-y shield and_
   help us clear_ from all_ the ill that hath us now o'er_

wea - pon; He'll tak - en. The an - cient prince of

hell hath ris'n with pur - pose fell; strong

mail of craft and pow'r he wear - eth in ___ this

hour; on earth is not his ___ fel - low.

2. With force of arms we nothing can,
   Full soon were we down-ridden;
   But for us fights the proper Man,
   Whom God Himself hath bidden.
   Ask ye: Who is this same?
   Christ Jesus is His name,
   The Lord Sabaoth's Son;
   He, and no other one,
   Shall conquer in the battle.

3. And were this world all devils o'er,
   And watching to devour us,
   We lay it not to heart so sore;
   Not they can overpower us.
   And let the prince of ill
   Look grim as e'er he will,
   He harms us not a whit:
   For why? his doom is writ;
   A word shall quickly slay him.

4. God's word, for all their craft and force,
   One moment will not linger;
   But, spite of hell, shall have its course;
   'Tis written by His finger.
   And though they take our life,
   Goods, honour, children, wife,
   Yet is their profit small:
   These things shall vanish all;
   The city of God remaineth.

Martin Luther (1483-1546)
Tr. Thomas Carlyle (1795-1881)

26.

Ascribe greatness

Deut 32:3–4

Peter West
Mary Lou Locke
& Mary Kirkbride

Capo 2 (G)

27.

As the deer

Ps 8:10; 42:1–2; Jn 15:15

Martin Nystrom

Capo 2 (C)

1. As the deer pants _ for the wa-ter, so my soul longs af - ter You.

You a -lone are my heart's de-sire _ and I long to wor - ship You.

Chorus

You a -lone are my strength, my shield, to You a-lone may my spi - rit yield.

You a-lone are my heart's de-sire _ and I long to wor - ship You.

2. I want You more than gold or silver,
   Only You can satisfy.
   You alone are the real joy-giver
   And the apple of my eye.

3. You're my Friend and You are my Brother,
   Even though You are a King.
   I love You more than any other,
   So much more than anything.

28.

As we are gathered

Mt 18:20

John Daniels

As we are gath-ered Je - sus is here; one with each oth-er, Je - sus is here; joined by the Spi-rit, washed in the blood, part of the bo-dy, — the church of God. As we are gath-ered Je - sus is here; one with each oth - er, Je - sus is here.

——————— □ ☐ □ ———————

Praise the Lord, you his angels,
you mighty ones who do his
bidding,
who obey his word.
Praise the Lord, all his heavenly
hosts,
you his servants who do his will.
Praise the Lord, all his works
everywhere in his dominion.

PSALM 103:20–22

——————— □ ☐ □ ———————

29.

As we come with praise

(Come with praise)

Ps 149:6–9

Dale Garratt

Capo 3 (Am)

With a strong beat

As we come with praise _ be-fore His maj - es-ty, __ we will

cel - e-brate_with joy and vic - to-ry,__ for the Lord has come_and set His

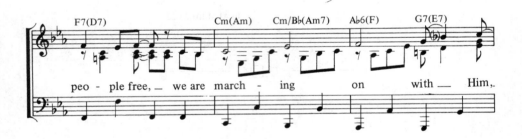

peo - ple free, _ we are march - ing on with __ Him,_

He's our de-liv - er-er __ (He's)

30.

As we seek Your face

Ps 27:8; Rev 1:17; 4:8

Dave Bilbrough

Capo 3 (D)

1. As we seek Your face, may we know Your heart, feel Your pre - sence, ac - cept - ance, as we seek Your face.

2. Move among us now,
   Come reveal Your power,
   Show Your presence, acceptance,
   Move among us now.

3. At Your feet we fall,
   Sovereign Lord,
   We cry "holy, holy"
   At Your feet we fall.

31.

As with gladness

Mt 2:1, 10–11; Rev 21:23

Capo 2 (G)

DIX   Steadily

Adapted from a chorale by Conrad Kocher (1786-1872)

1. As with gladness men of old did the guiding star behold;
as with joy they hailed its light, leading onward, beaming bright,
so, most gracious God, may we evermore be led by Thee.

2. As with joyful steps they sped,
Saviour, to Thy lowly bed,
There to bend the knee before
Thee whom heaven and earth adore,
So may we with willing feet
Ever seek Thy mercy-seat.

3. As they offered gifts most rare
At Thy cradle rude and bare,
So may we with holy joy,
Pure, and free from sin's alloy,
All our costliest treasures bring,
Christ, to Thee, our heavenly King.

4. Holy Jesus, every day
Keep us in the narrow way;
And, when earthly things are past,
Bring our ransomed souls at last
Where they need no soul to guide,
Where no clouds Thy glory hide.

5. In the heavenly country bright
Need they no created light;
Thou its light, its joy, its crown,
Thou its sun, which goes not down.
There for ever may we sing
Hallelujahs to our King.

W.C. Dix (1837-98)

32.

At the name of Jesus
(First tune)

Mt 24:30–31; Mk 13:26–27;
Jn 1:1; 1 Cor 10:13;
Phil 2:8–11; Rev 19:12–13, 16

CAMBERWELL

John Michael Brierley (1932 -)

With strength

1. At the name of Je - sus ev - 'ry knee shall bow,
ev - 'ry tongue con - fess Him King of glo - ry __ now;
'tis the Fa-ther's pleasure we should call Him Lord,
who from the be - gin -ning was the migh - ty
Word. now.

2. Humbled for a season,
   To receive a name
   From the lips of sinners
   Unto whom He came;
   Faithfully He bore it
   Spotless to the last,
   Brought it back victorious,
   When from death He passed.

3. Bore it up triumphant
   With its human light,
   Through all ranks of creatures
   To the central height,
   To the throne of Godhead,
   To the Father's breast,
   Filled it with the glory
   Of that perfect rest.

4. In your hearts enthrone Him;
   There let Him subdue
   All that is not holy,
   All that is not true:
   Crown Him as your captain
   In temptation's hour,
   Let His will enfold you
   In its light and power.

5. Brothers, this Lord Jesus
   Shall return again,
   With His Father's glory,
   With His angel-train;
   For all wreaths of empire
   Meet upon His brow,
   And our hearts confess Him
   King of glory now.

Caroline Maria Noel (1817-77)

At the name of Jesus
(Second tune)

Capo 2(C)
EVELYNS
William Henry Monk (1823-89)

1. At the name of Je - sus ev - 'ry knee shall bow,

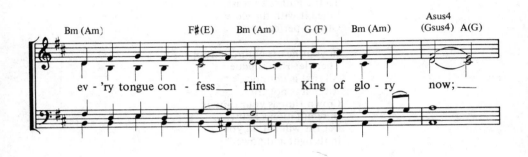

ev - 'ry tongue con - fess___ Him King of glo - ry now; ___

'tis the Fa - ther's plea - sure we should call Him Lord,

who from the be - gin - ning was the migh - ty Word.

2. Humbled for a season,
   To receive a name
   From the lips of sinners
   Unto whom He came;
   Faithfully He bore it
   Spotless to the last,
   Brought it back victorious,
   When from death He passed.

3. Bore it up triumphant
   With its human light,
   Through all ranks of creatures
   To the central height,
   To the throne of Godhead,
   To the Father's breast,
   Filled it with the glory
   Of that perfect rest.

4. In your hearts enthrone Him;
   There let Him subdue
   All that is not holy,
   All that is not true:
   Crown Him as your captain
   In temptation's hour,
   Let His will enfold you
   In its light and power.

5. Brothers, this Lord Jesus
   Shall return again,
   With His Father's glory,
   With His angel-train;
   For all wreaths of empire
   Meet upon His brow,
   And our hearts confess Him
   King of glory now.

Caroline Maria Noel (1817-77)

33.

At this time of giving

Mt 2:11; 1 Cor 12:4

(The giving song)

Graham Kendrick

Accelerating with each verse

2. May His tender love surround you
   At this Christmastime;
   May you see His smiling face
   That in the darkness shines.

3. But the many gifts He gives
   Are all poured out from one;
   Come receive the greatest gift,
   The gift of God's own Son.

Last two choruses and verses:
   Lai, lai, lai . . . (etc.)

———————— □ ▢ □ ————————

May the God of hope fill you with all joy and peace as you trust in him, so that you may overflow with hope by the power of the Holy Spirit.

ROMANS 15:13

———————— □ ▢ □ ————————

34.

At Your feet we fall

Rev 1:14–18

Capo 2 (G)

David Fellingham

With steady strength

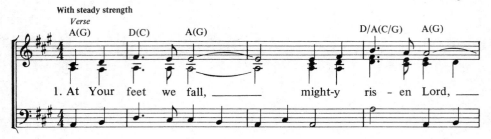

1. At Your feet we fall, _____ might-y ris - en Lord, ____

____ as we come be-fore Your throne to wor-ship You. _____

____ By Your Spi - rit's power ____ You now draw our hearts, ____

____ and we hear Your voice in tri-umph ring-ing clear. _____

I am He that liv - eth, that liv - eth and was dead._____ Be-

-hold, I am a - live for ev - er - more. _____

2. There we see You stand, mighty risen Lord,
   Clothed in garments pure and holy, shining bright.
   Eyes of flashing fire, feet like burnished bronze,
   And the sound of many waters is Your voice.

3. Like the shining sun in its noonday strength,
   We now see the glory of Your wondrous face.
   Once that face was marred, but now You're glorified,
   And Your words like a two-edged sword have mighty power.

35. Awake, awake, O Zion

Is 52:1, 7, 9

David J. Hadden

Triumphantly

Chorus

A - wake, a - wake, O Zi - on, come clothe your-
self with strength. _____ A- _____

1st time *2nd time* *Last time* *Fine*

Verse

1. Put on your gar - ments of splen - dour, O Je-
ru - sa - lem. _____ Come sing your songs of joy and
tri - umph, see that your God reigns. _____ A-

D.C.

2. Burst into songs of joy together,
O Jerusalem.
The Lord has comforted His people,
The redeemed Jerusalem.

36.

Away in a manger

Lk 2:7

Capo 3 (D)

CRADLE SONG

W.J. Kirkpatrick (1838-1921)

1. A - way in a __ man - ger, no __ crib for a bed, the __
lit - tle Lord Je - sus laid __ down His sweet head; the
stars in the __ bright sky looked __ down where He lay, the __
lit - tle Lord Je - sus a - sleep on the hay.

2. The cattle are lowing, the Baby awakes,
But little Lord Jesus, no crying He makes;
I love You, Lord Jesus! Look down from the sky
And stay by my side until morning is nigh.

3. Be near me, Lord Jesus; I ask You to stay
Close by me for ever and love me, I pray.
Bless all the dear children in Your tender care,
And fit us for heaven to live with You there.

Verses 1 and 2 unknown, verse 3 J. T. McFarland. (c. 1906)

37. Be bold, be strong

Josh 1:9

Morris Chapman

Be bold, — be strong, — for the Lord, your God, is with — you. — Be bold, be strong, — for the Lord, your God, is with — you. — I am not a - fraid, —

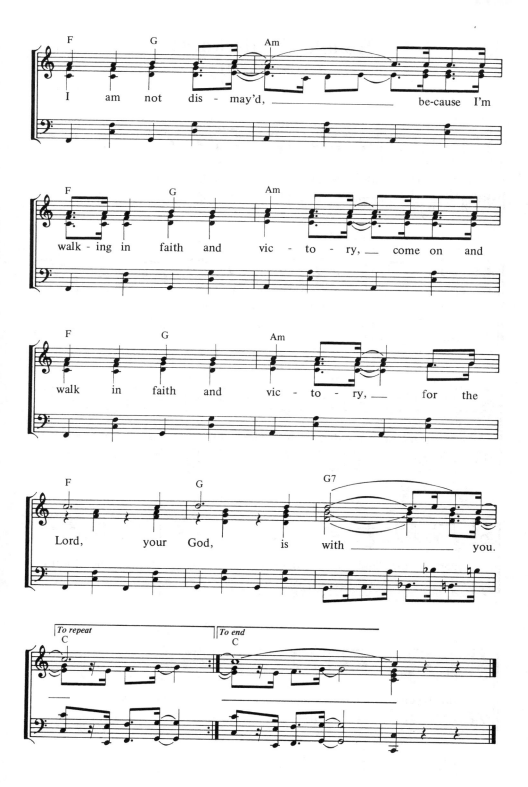

38.

Behold the darkness
(Arise, shine)

Is 60:1–5, 14, 19–20

Eric Glass

Joyfully

1. Be - hold the dark - ness shall co - ver the earth, __ and gross dark - ness the people, but the Lord shall a - rise up - on thee and His glory shall be seen up - on thee. So a - rise, shine, for thy light is come, __ and the glory of the Lord is ri - sen; __ so a - rise, shine, for thy light is come, __ and the glory of the Lord is up - on thee. __

2. The Gentiles shall come to thy light,
   And Kings to the brightness of thy rising;
   And they shall call thee the city of the Lord,
   The Zion of the Holy One of Israel.

3. Lift up thine eyes round about and see,
   They gather themselves together;
   And they shall come, thy sons from afar,
   And thy daughters shall be nursed at thy side.

4. Then shalt thou see and flow together,
   And thy heart shall be enlarged;
   The abundance of the sea is converted unto thee,
   And the nations shall come unto thee.

5. The sun shall no more go down,
   Neither shall the moon withdraw itself;
   But the Lord shall be thine everlasting light,
   And the days of thy mourning shall be ended.

39. Beneath the cross of Jesus

Gen 28:12; Ezek 33:7;
Mt 27:55; Mk 15:40;
Lk 23:49; Jn 19:25; Rom 3:25;
Gal 6:14; Heb 12:2

ST CHRISTOPHER
With feeling

Frederick Charles Maker (1844-1927)

1. Be - neath the cross of Je - sus I fain would take my stand, the sha - dow of a migh - ty rock with - in a wear - y land; a home with - in the wild - er - ness, a rest up - on the way, from the burn - ing of the noon - tide heat, and the bur - den of the day.

2. O safe and happy shelter!
   O refuge tried and sweet!
   O trysting place where heaven's love
   And heaven's justice meet!
   As to the holy patriarch
   That wondrous dream was given,
   So seems my Saviour's cross to me
   A ladder up to heaven.

3. There lies, beneath its shadow,
   But on the farther side,
   The darkness of an awful grave
   That gapes both deep and wide;
   And there between us stands the cross,
   Two arms outstretched to save;
   Like a watchman set to guard the way
   From that eternal grave.

4. Upon that cross of Jesus
   Mine eye at times can see
   The very dying form of One
   Who suffered there for me;
   And from my smitten heart, with tears,
   Two wonders I confess —
   The wonders of His glorious love,
   And my own worthlessness.

5. I take, O cross, thy shadow,
   For my abiding place;
   I ask no other sunshine than
   The sunshine of His face;
   Content to let the world go by,
   To know no gain nor loss —
   My sinful self my only shame,
   My glory all the cross.

Elizabeth Cecilia Clephane (1830-69)

40.

Be still

Ex 3:5; Jer 32:17; Heb 12:28;
1 Jn 3:5; Rev 1:14, 16

David J. Evans

Reverently

1. Be still, for the pre-sence of the Lord, the Ho-ly One is here.

Come, bow be - fore Him now, with rev-er-ence and fear.

In Him no sin is found, we stand on ho-ly ground.

Be still, for the pre-sence of the Lord, the Ho-ly One is here.

2. Be still, for the glory of the Lord is shining all around;
   He burns with holy fire, with splendour He is crowned.
   How awesome is the sight, our radiant King of light!
   Be still, for the glory of the Lord is shining all around.

3. Be still, for the power of the Lord is moving in this place,
   He comes to cleanse and heal, to minister His grace.
   No work too hard for Him, in faith receive from Him;
   Be still, for the power of the Lord is moving in this place.

41.

Be still and know

Ps 46:10

Author unknown
Arr. Margaret Evans

2. I am the Lord that healeth thee. . . (*etc*).

3. In Thee, O Lord, do I put my trust. . . (*etc*).

42.

Be Thou my vision

Capo 3 (C)

SLANE

Josh 13:33; Prov 29:18;
1 Cor 1:30; Eph 6:11, 14

Ancient Irish melody

1. Be Thou my___ vi - O___ Lord of my
heart, be___ all else but naught to me,
save that Thou art; be Thou my___ best___
thought in the day and the night, both
wak - ing and sleep - ing, Thy___ pre - sence my light.

2. Be Thou my wisdom, be Thou my true word,
   Be Thou ever with me, and I with Thee, Lord;
   Be Thou my great Father, and I Thy true son;
   Be Thou in me dwelling, and I with Thee one.

3. Be Thou my breastplate, my sword for the fight;
   Be Thou my whole armour, be Thou my true might;
   Be Thou my soul's shelter, be Thou my strong tower:
   O raise Thou me heavenward, great Power of my power.

4. Riches I need not, nor man's empty praise:
   Be Thou mine inheritance now and always;
   Be Thou and Thou only the first in my heart:
   O Sovereign of heaven, my treasure Thou art.

5. High King of heaven, Thou heaven's bright Sun,
   O grant me its joys after victory is won;
   Great Heart of my own heart, whatever befall,
   Still be Thou my vision, O Ruler of all.

Ancient Irish
Tr Mary Elizabeth Byrne (1880-1931) & Eleanor Henrietta Hull (1860-1935)

43.

Bind us together

1 Cor 13:13; Col 3:14

Bob Gillman

Easy waltz feel
Chorus

Bind us   to - ge - ther,   Lord,   Bind   us   to - ge - ther   with

cords   that   can - not   be   bro - ken.

Bind   us   to - ge - ther,   Lord,   Bind   us   to - ge - ther,—

Bind   us   to - ge - ther   with   love.

Verse

1. There is on-ly one God. ____

There is on-ly one King. ____

There is on-ly one Bo-dy. ____

D.C. al Fine

That is why we sing. ____

2.   Made for the glory of God,
    Purchased by His precious Son.
    Born with the right to be clean,
    For Jesus the victory has won. . . .

3.   You are the family of God.
    You are the promise divine.
    You are God's chosen desire.
    You are the glorious new wine. . . .

44

Blessèd assurance

Mt 24:42; Mk 13:35; Lk 21:36;
Eph 1:14; Heb 10:22;
Rev 1:5; 7:14

BLESSÈD ASSURANCE

Worshipfully
Verse

Phoebe Palmer Knapp (1839-1908)

1. Bless-èd as - sur - ance, Je - sus is mine: ___ O what a

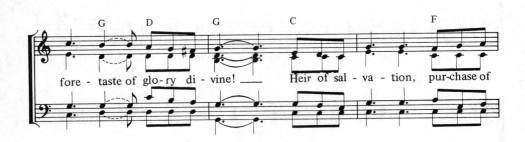

fore - taste of glo - ry di - vine! ___ Heir of sal - va - tion, pur-chase of

God; ___ born of His Spi - rit, wash'd in His blood. ___ This is my

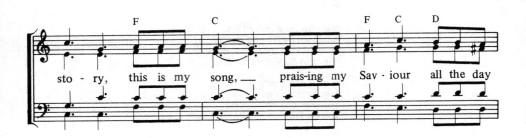

sto - ry, this is my song, ___ prais-ing my Sav - iour all the day

long. _____ This is my sto - ry, this is my song, _____ prais-ing my Sav - iour all the day long. _____

2. Perfect submission, perfect delight,
   Visions of rapture burst on my sight;
   Angels descending bring from above
   Echoes of mercy, whispers of love.

3. Perfect submission, all is at rest,
   I in my Saviour am happy and blessed;
   Watching and waiting, looking above,
   Filled with His goodness, lost in His love.

Fanny J. Crosby (1820-1915)

45.

Blessèd be

Eph 1:3–5

Capo 1 (G)

David Fellingham

Bless - ed be _____ the God _ and Fa - ther _____

_ of our _____ Lord Je - sus Christ _

_ who has blessed us ____ with ev'ry spi-ri-tual bless-ing _____

_ in heav'n-ly pla - ces ____ in Christ. _____

46.   Blessed be the name of the Lord
Ps 18:2

Kevin Prosch
and Danny Daniels

1. Bless-ed be the name __ of the Lord. __
Bless-ed be the name __ of the Lord. __ For
He   is   our   rock,   for He   is   our
Rock, __ He is the Lord. __ For

2. Jesus reigns on high in all the earth.
    Jesus reigns on high in all the earth.
    Jesus reigns on high in all the earth.
    Jesus reigns on high in all the earth.
    The universe is in the hands
    Of the Lord.
    The universe is in the hands
    Of the Lord.

———————— □ ▢ □ ————————

I will praise you, O Lord, among the
    nations;
I will sing of you among the peoples.
For great is your love, reaching to the
    heavens;
    your faithfulness reaches to the
    skies.
Be exalted, O God, above the heavens;
    let your glory be over all the earth.

PSALM 57:9–11

———————— □ ▢ □ ————————

47.

Bless the Lord, O my soul

Ps 103:1–4

Phil Rogers

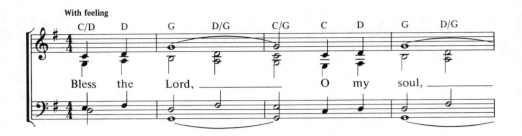

Bless the Lord, _____ O my soul, _____

_____ and let all that is with - in _____ me bless His

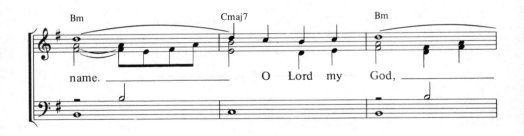

name. _____ O Lord my God, _____

_____ You are so great, _____ for You are

48.
Bless the Lord, O my soul
(King of kings)

Ps 103:1; 1 Tim 6:15;
Rev 17:14; 19:16

Author unknown
Arr. Margaret Evans

* The 2nd Part singers can divide into altos, tenors and basses if prefered.

49.
Blest be the tie

Gal 6:2

DENNIS

J.G. Nägeli (1768-1836)

Steadily

1. Blest be the tie that binds our hearts in Christ-ian love; the fel-low-ship of kin-dred minds is like to that a-bove.

2. Before our Father's throne
   We pour our ardent prayers;
   Our fears, our hopes, our aims are one,
   Our comforts and our cares.

3. We share our mutual woes,
   Our mutual burdens bear,
   And often for each other flows
   The sympathising tear.

4. When for a while we part,
   This thought will soothe our pain,
   That we shall still be joined in heart,
   And hope to meet again.

5. This glorious hope revives
   Our courage by the way
   While each in expectation lives,
   And longs to see the day.

6. From sorrow, toil, and pain,
   And sin we shall be free;
   And perfect love and friendship reign
   Through all eternity.

John Fawcett (1740-1817) alt.

50. Break Thou the Bread of Life

Mt 14:19; 15:35;
Mk 6:41; 8:6;
Lk 9:16; Jn 6:11, 35

Capo 3(C)
LATHBURY

William F. Sherwin (1826-88)

Peacefully

1. Break Thou the Bread of Life, dear Lord, to me, as Thou didst break the bread be - side the sea; be - yond the sa - cred page I seek Thee, Lord, my spi - rit longs for Thee, Thou Liv - ing Word.

2. Thou art the Bread of Life,
   O Lord, to me,
   Thy holy Word the truth
   That saveth me;
   Give me to eat and live
   With Thee above,
   Teach me to love Thy truth,
   For Thou art love.

3. O send Thy Spirit, Lord,
   Now unto me,
   That He may touch my eyes
   And make me see;
   Show me the truth concealed
   Within Thy Word,
   And in Thy Book revealed.
   I see Thee, Lord.

4. Bless Thou the Bread of Life
   To me, to me,
   As Thou didst bless the loaves
   By Galilee;
   Then shall all bondage cease,
   All fetters fall,
   And I shall find my peace,
   My all in all.

Mary A. Lathbury (1841-1913)
vv. 2 & 3 Alexander Groves (1843-1909)

51. Breathe on me, Breath of God

Gen 2:7;
Job 33:4; Is 42:5;
Ezek 37:5; Jn 3:8

Robert Jackson (1842-1914)

Capo 3(D)
TRENTHAM
Prayerfully

1. Breathe on me, Breath of God, fill me with

life a - new; that I may love what

Thou dost love and do __ what Thou wouldst do.

2. Breathe on me, Breath of God,
    Until my heart is pure;
    Until my will is one with Thine
    To do and to endure.

3. Breathe on me, Breath of God,
    Till I am wholly Thine;
    Until this earthly part of me
    Glows with Thy fire divine.

4. Breathe on me, Breath of God,
    So shall I never die,
    But live with Thee the perfect life
    Of Thine eternity.

Edwin Hatch (1835-89)

—— □ ▢ □ ——

And we, who with unveiled faces all reflect the Lord's glory, are being transformed into his likeness with ever-increasing glory, which comes from the Lord, who is the Spirit.

2 CORINTHIANS 3:18

—— □ ▢ □ ——

52.

Bring a psalm

1 Cor 14:26

Brent Chambers

Bring a psalm to the Lord, from the Spirit and from His word. Lift your voice and re-joice, for our God is a migh-ty King, so come and clap your hands, raise a shout, as we stand before the Lord, for the

53.

Broken for me

Mt 26:26–27; Mk 14:22–23;
Lk 22:19–20; 1 Cor 11:23–26

Janet Lunt

Capo 2 (D)

Bro-ken for me, _____ bro-ken for

you, the bo-dy of Je - sus, _____

_____ bro-ken for you. 1. He of-fered His

bo - dy, _____ He poured out His soul;

Je - sus was bro - ken, that we might be whole. bro - ken for you.

2. Come to My table and with Me dine;
   Eat of My bread and drink of my wine.

3. This is My body given for you;
   Eat it remembering I died for you.

4. This is My blood I shed for you,
   For your forgiveness, making you new.

54.
Brother, let me be your servant
(The servant song)

Mt 20:27–28;
Mk 10:44–45;
Jn 13:14–15;
Rom 12:15; Gal 6:2

Capo 1 (D)

Richard Gillard
arranged by Betty Pulkingham

1. Bro-ther, let me be your ser-vant, let me be as Christ to you; pray that I may have the grace to let you be my ser - vant, too.

2. We are pilgrims on a journey,
   We are brothers on the road;
   We are here to help each other
   Walk the mile and bear the load.

3. I will hold the Christ light for you
   In the night-time of your fear;
   I will hold my hand out to you,
   Speak the peace you long to hear.

4. I will weep when you are weeping,
   When you laugh I'll laugh with you;
   I will share your joy and sorrow
   Till we've seen this journey through.

5. When we sing to God in heaven
   We shall find such harmony,
   Born of all we've known together
   Of Christ's love and agony.

6. (As verse 1)

*Shout for joy to the Lord, all the
earth.
Serve the Lord with gladness;
come before him with joyful songs.*

PSALM 100:1–2

55.

By Your side

Noel and Tricia Richards

Capo 3 (G)

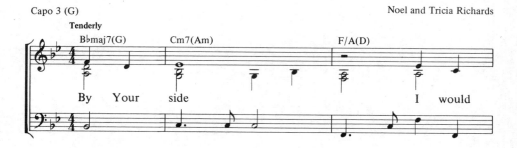

By Your side   I would

stay;   in Your arms

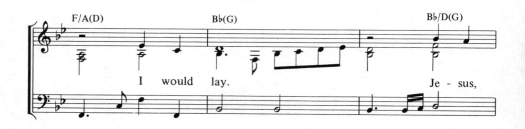

I would lay.   Je - sus,

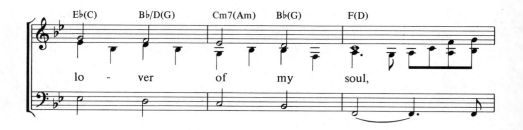

lo - ver of my soul,

———————— □ ▢ □ ————————

*I pray also that the eyes of your
heart may be enlightened in order that
you may know the hope to which he has
called you, the riches of his glorious
inheritance in the saints, and his
incomparably great power for us who
believe.*

EPHESIANS 1:18–19

———————— □ ▢ □ ————————

56.

Cause me to come

Ps 36:8

R. Edward Miller

Capo 2 (C)

Thoughtfully

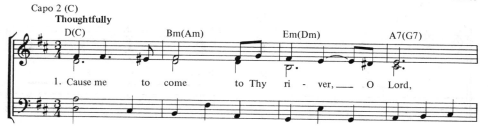

1. Cause me to come to Thy ri - ver, —— O Lord,

Cause me to come to Thy ri - ver, ———— O Lord,

Cause me to come to Thy ri - ver, —— O Lord, Cause me to

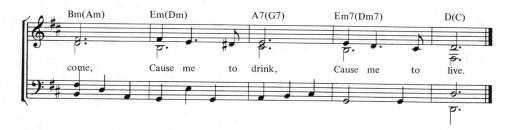

come, Cause me to drink, Cause me to live.

2. Cause me to drink from Thy river, O Lord, *(three times)*
   Cause me to come, cause me to drink, cause me to live.

3. Cause me to live by Thy river, O Lord, *(three times)*
   Cause me to come, cause me to drink, cause me to live.

57.

Celebrate Jesus

Mt 28:6; Mk 16:6; Lk 24:6; Jn 21:14

Capo 3 (D)

Gary Oliver

58. Change my heart, O God

Ps 51:10; Jer 18:6; Rom 9:21

Eddie Espinosa

———————— □ ⬜ □ ————————

Shout for joy to the Lord, all the
    earth,
    burst into jubilant song with
      music;
make music to the Lord with the
    harp,
    with the harp and the sound of
      singing,
with trumpets and the blast of the
    ram's horn –
    shout for joy before the Lord, the
      King.

PSALM 98:4–6

———————— □ ⬜ □ ————————

59.   Christians awake!

Lk 2:8–11, 13–14

John Wainwright (1723-68)

YORKSHIRE

With strength

1. Christ - ians a - wake! Sa - lute the hap - py morn, where - on the Sa - viour of man - kind was born; rise to a - dore the mys - te - ry of love which hosts of an - gels chant - ed from a - bove; with them the joy - ful ti - dings first be - gun of

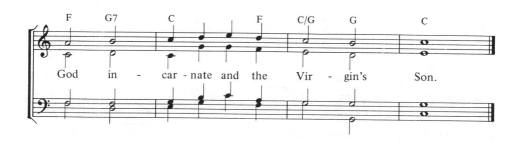

God in - car - nate and the Vir - gin's Son.

2. Then to the watchful shepherds it was told,
   Who heard the angelic herald's voice "Behold,
   I bring good tidings of a Saviour's birth
   To you and all the nations upon earth:
   This day hath God fulfilled His promised word,
   This day is born a Saviour, Christ the Lord."

3. He spake; and straightway the celestial choir
   In hymns of joy unknown before conspire;
   High praise of God's redeeming love they sang,
   And heaven's whole orb with hallelujahs rang;
   God's highest glory was their anthem still,
   "On earth be peace, and unto men goodwill."

4. O may we keep and ponder in our mind
   God's wondrous love in saving lost mankind;
   Trace we the Babe who hath retrieved our loss,
   From His poor manger to His bitter cross;
   Tread in His steps, assisted by His grace,
   Till man's first heavenly state again takes place.

5. Then may we hope, the angelic hosts among,
   To sing, redeemed, a glad triumphant song:
   He that was born upon this joyful day
   Around us all His glory shall display;
   Saved by His love, incessant we shall sing
   Eternal praise to heaven's almighty King.

John Byrom (1692-1763) altd.

60. Christ is risen

Mt 28:6; Mk 16:6; Lk 24:6; Jn 21:14;
1 Cor 15:55; Phil 2:10–11

Chris Rolinson

Christ is ri-sen! Hal-le-lu-jah, hal-le-lu-jah! Christ is

ri-sen, ri-sen in-deed, hal-le-lu - jah! 1. Love's work is done, the

bat-tle is won; where now, O death, is your sting? He rose a-gain, to

rule and to reign, Je-sus our con-quer-ing King.

2. Lord over sin,
Lord over death,
At His feet Satan must fall!
Every knee bow,
All will confess
Jesus is Lord over all!

3. Tell it abroad
"Jesus is Lord!"
Shout it and let your praise ring!
Gladly we raise
Our songs of praise,
Worship is our offering.

—— □ ▢ □ ——

God exalted him to the highest
place
and gave him the name that is
above every name,
that at the name of Jesus every knee
should bow,
in heaven and on earth and under
the earth.

PHILIPPIANS 2:9–10

—— □ ▢ □ ——

61. Christt the Lord is risen today

Mt 28:6; Mk 16:6;
Lk 24:6; Jn 21:14;
1 Cor 15:55
R. Williams (1781-1812)

Triumphantly

1. Christ the Lord is ris'n to-day: Hal - le - lu - jah!

Sons of men and an-gels say: Hal - le - lu - jah!

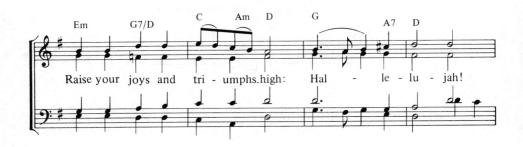

Raise your joys and tri - umphs.high: Hal - le - lu - jah!

Sing, ye heav'ns, and earth re - ply: Hal - le - lu - jah!

2. Love's redeeming work is done: Hallelujah!
   Fought the fight, the battle won: Hallelujah!
   Vain the stone, the watch, the seal: Hallelujah!
   Christ hath burst the gates of hell: Hallelujah!

3. Lives again our glorious King: Hallelujah!
   Where, O death, is now thy sting? Hallelujah!
   Once He died, our souls to save: Hallelujah!
   Where thy victory, O grave? Hallelujah!

4. Soar we now where Christ hath led: Hallelujah!
   Following our exalted Head: Hallelujah!
   Made like Him, like Him we rise: Hallelujah!
   Ours the cross, the grave, the skies: Hallelujah!

5. Hail the Lord of earth and heaven: Hallelujah!
   Praise to Thee by both be given: Hallelujah!
   Thee we greet, in triumph sing: Hallelujah!
   Hail our resurrected King: Hallelujah!

Charles Wesley (1707-88)

62.

Christ triumphant

Is 53:3; Jn 1:14; Heb 4:14

Capo 3 (D)

Words: Michael Saward
Music: Michael Baughen

With vigour

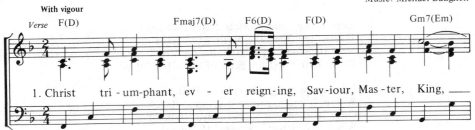

1. Christ tri-um-phant, ev-er reign-ing, Sav-iour, Mas-ter, King, ___

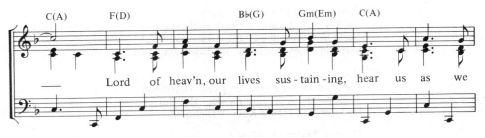

___ Lord of heav'n, our lives sus-tain-ing, hear us as we

Chorus

sing: ___ Yours the glo-ry and the crown, ___ the high

re - nown, ___ the e-ter - nal name. ___

2. Word incarnate, truth revealing,
   Son of Man on earth!
   Power and majesty concealing
   By Your humble birth:

3. Suffering servant, scorned, ill-treated,
   Victim crucified!
   Death is through the cross defeated,
   Sinners justified:

4. Priestly King, enthroned for ever
   High in heaven above!
   Sin and death and hell shall never
   Stifle hymns of love:

5. So, our hearts and voices raising
   Through the ages long,
   Ceaselessly upon You gazing,
   This shall be our song:

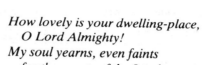

How lovely is your dwelling-place,
  O Lord Almighty!
My soul yearns, even faints
  for the courts of the Lord;
my heart and my flesh cry out
  for the living God.

PSALM 84:1–2

63.

Clear the road
(Prepare the way)

Is 40:3; Mt 3:3; Mk 1:3; Lk 3:4; Jn 1:14, 23

Capo 2 (C)

Graham Kendrick

1. Clear the road, make wide the _ way.

(Clear the road, make wide the _ way.) Wel-come now the God _ who saves.

(Wel-come now the God _ who saves.) Fill the streets with shouts of _ joy.

(Fill the streets with shouts of _ joy.) *(Cheers, etc.)*

Pre - pare the way of the

Pre - pare the way of the Lord! _____

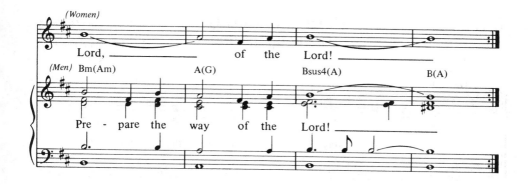

2. Raise Your voice and join the song, *(echo)*
   God made flesh to us has come. *(echo)*
   Welcome Him, your banners wave. *(echo)*
   (Cheers, shouts, wave banners, etc.)

3. For all sin the price is paid, *(echo)*
   All our sins on Jesus laid. *(echo)*
   By His blood we are made clean. *(echo)*
   (Cheers, shouts of thanksgiving)

4. At His feet come humbly bow, *(echo)*
   In your lives enthrone Him now. *(echo)*
   See, your great Deliverer comes. *(echo)*
   (Cheers, shouts welcoming Jesus)

   (Chorus twice to end)

64.

Colours of day
(Light up the fire)

Jn 8:12; 1 Jn 2:8

Sue McClellan, John Pac,
Keith Ryecroft

1. Col - ours of day dawn in - to the mind, the

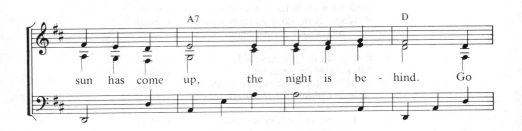

sun has come up, the night is be - hind. Go

down in the ci - ty, in - to the street, and

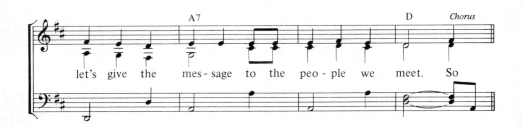

let's give the mes - sage to the peo - ple we meet. So

light up the fire and let the flame burn,
op - en the door, let Je - sus re - turn. Take
seeds of His Spi - rit, let the fruit grow, tell the
peo - ple of Je - sus, let His love show.

2. Go through the park, on into the town;
   The sun still shines on, it never goes down.
   The light of the world is risen again;
   The people of darkness are needing a friend.

3. Open your eyes, look into the sky,
   The darkness has come, the sun came to die.
   The evening drawn on, the sun disappears,
   But Jesus is living, His Spirit is near.

65. Come and praise Him, royal priesthood

1 Pet 2:9

Andy Carter

66. Come and praise the living God

Heb 12:22

Capo 2 (Am)

Mike Kerry

Triumphantly

Chorus

Come and praise the li-ving God, — come and wor-ship, come and wor-ship.

He has made you priest and king, — come and wor-ship the li-ving God. —

Verse / *Last time Fine* / *Verse*

— 1. We — come not to a moun-tain of fire and smoke, —

not to gloom and dark-ness or trum-pet sound; we come to the new Je-

-ru - sa - lem, the ho - ly ci - ty of God. —

2. By His voice He shakes the earth,
     His judgements known throughout the world.
     But we have a city that for ever stands,
     The holy city of God.

67.

Come and see
(We worship at Your feet)

Is 53:5–6; Mt 27:28–31; Mk 15:17–20;
Lk 22:63; 23:34; Jn 19:2, 5, 17;
2 Cor 5:21; Rev 5:12

Graham Kendrick

Worshipfully

1. Come and see, come and see, come and see the King of love; see the purple robe and crown of thorns He wears. Sol-diers mock, ru-lers sneer as He lifts the cru - el cross; lone and friend-less now, He climbs to-wards the hill.

Chorus

We wor-ship at Your feet, where wrath and mer - cy meet, and a

2. Come and weep, come and mourn
   For your sin that pierced Him there;
   So much deeper than the wounds of thorn and nail.
   All our pride, all our greed,
   All our fallenness and shame;
   And the Lord has laid the punishment on Him.

3. Man of heaven, born to earth
   To restore us to Your heaven.
   Here we bow in awe beneath Your searching eyes.
   From Your tears comes our joy,
   From Your death our life shall spring;
   By Your resurrection power we shall rise.

68.

Come bless the Lord

Ps 134:1–2

Capo 1 (E)

With warmth and pace

arranged Margaret Evans

Come bless the Lord, _____ all ye serv - ants of the

Lord, _____ who stand by night _____

_ in the house of the Lord, _____ Lift up your

hands _____ in the ho - ly place, _____ Come bless the

Lord, _____ Come bless the Lord. _____

───── □ ▢ □ ─────

He is the head of the body, the church; he is the beginning and the firstborn from among the dead, so that in everything he might have the supremacy.

COLOSSIANS 1:18

───── □ ▢ □ ─────

69. Come into the Holy of Holies

Heb 6:19–20; 9:12

Capo 1(G)

John Sellers

Worshipfully

Come in-to the Ho-ly of Ho - lies; ___

en - ter by the blood of the Lamb. ___

Come in - to His pre-sence with sing - ing, ___

wor - ship at the throne ___ of God. ___

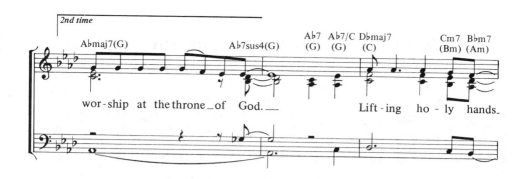

2nd time

A♭maj7(G)   A♭7sus4(G)   A♭7 A♭7/C D♭maj7   Cm7 B♭m7
                           (G) (G) (C)   (Bm) (Am)

wor-ship at the throne_of God.___   Lift-ing ho-ly hands_

E♭(D)   D♭(C)   Cm7(Bm)   Cm7/F(Bm) F7(E)

___   to the King___ of kings,

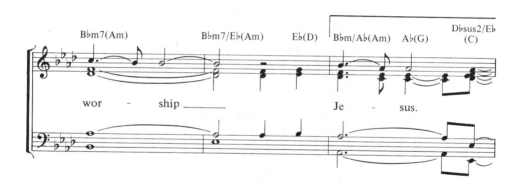

B♭m7(Am)   B♭m7/E♭(Am)   E♭(D)   B♭m/A♭(Am)   A♭(G)   D♭sus2/E♭
                                                           (C)

wor - ship _____   Je - sus.

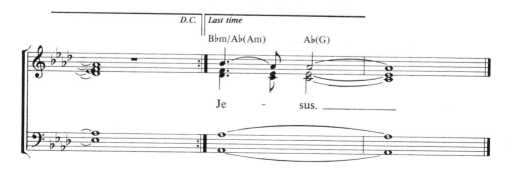

D.C. | *Last time*
        B♭m/A♭(Am)   A♭(G)

Je - sus. _____

Capo 3 (G)

NATIVITY

Henry Lahee (1826-1912)

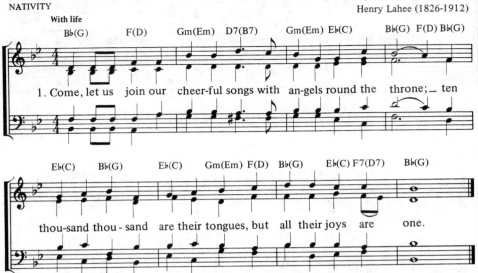

1. Come, let us join our cheer-ful songs with an-gels round the throne; ten thou-sand thou - sand are their tongues, but all their joys are one.

Alternative tune: LYNGHAM

2. 'Worthy the Lamb that died,' they cry,
   'To be exalted thus.'
   'Worthy the Lamb,' our lips reply,
   'For He was slain for us.'

3. Jesus is worthy to receive
   Honour and power divine:
   And blessings, more than we can give,
   Be, Lord, for ever Thine.

4. Let all that dwell above the sky,
   And air, and earth, and seas,
   Conspire to lift Thy glories high,
   And speak Thine endless praise.

5. The whole creation join in one
   To bless the sacred name
   Of Him that sits upon the throne,
   And to adore the Lamb.

Isaac Watts (1674-1748)

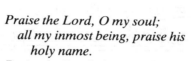

Praise the Lord, O my soul;
  all my inmost being, praise his
    holy name.
Praise the Lord, O my soul,
  and forget not all his benefits.

PSALM 103:1–2

71.

Come, let us sing

Ps 95: 1–3, 6–7

Lively

Intro

Brent Chambers

Come, let us sing ____ for joy ____ to the Lord, ____

come, let us sing ____ for joy ____ to the Lord, ____ come, let us sing ____ for joy

____ to the Lord, ____ come, let us sing ____ for joy ____ to the Lord. ____

Chorus

Come, let us sing ____ for joy __ to the Lord, ____ let us shout

Last time to Coda ⊕

____ a - loud ____ to the Rock __ of our ____ sal - va - tion. ____

2. Let us bow before Him in our worship,
   Let us kneel before God, our great King;
   For He is our God and we are His people
   That's why we shout and sing.

72. Come, let us sing of a wonderful love

Lk 15:4; 1 Jn 4:10

Capo 3(C)
WONDERFUL LOVE
With a gentle lilt

Frederick Luke Wiseman (1858-1944)

1. Come, let us sing of a won - der - ful love, ten - der and true;___ out of the heart of the Fa - ther a - bove,___ stream-ing to me and to you:___ won - der - ful love___ dwells in the heart of the Fa - ther a - bove.

2. Jesus, the Saviour, this gospel to tell,
   Joyfully came;
   Came with the helpless and hopeless to dwell,
   Sharing their sorrow and shame;
   Seeking the lost,
   Saving, redeeming at measureless cost.

3. Jesus is seeking the wanderers yet;
   Why do they roam?
   Love only waits to forgive and forget;
   Home, weary wanderer, home!
   Wonderful love
   Dwells in the heart of the Father above.

4. Come to my heart, O Thou wonderful love,
   Come and abide,
   Lifting my life, till it rises above
   Envy and falsehood and pride,
   Seeking to be
   Lowly and humble, a learner of Thee.

   Robert Walmsley (1831-1905)

73.

Come on and celebrate
(Celebrate)

Patricia Morgan
Dave Bankhead

Come on and cel - e - brate_ His gift of love, we will

cel - e - brate_ the Son of God who loved_ us _____

_ and gave us life. _____ We'll shout Your

praise, O King, _ You give us joy no-thing else can bring,_

74. Come see the beauty of the Lord

Ps 27:4; Is 53:6; Mt 27:29;
Mk 15:17; Jn 19:2; Rev 5:12

Graham Kendrick

and on His brow He bears our pride; a crown of thorns.

Come see the beauty of the Lord, come see the beauty of His face.

This song is sung as a call and response throughout, the congregation copying the leader or the ladies following the men.

2. But only love pours from His heart
As silently He takes the blame.
He has my name upon His lips,
My condemnation falls on Him.
This love is marvellous to me,
His sacrifice has set me free
And now I live.

75.   Come, ye thankful people, come

Mt 9:37–38;
13:30, 37–42;
Lk 10:2; Jn 4:35; Rev 14:15

ST. GEORGE'S, WINDSOR

C.J. Elvey (1816-93)

1. Come, ye thank-ful peo-ple, come, raise the song of
har-vest home! All is safe-ly gath-ered in ere the win-ter
storms be-gin; God, our Ma-ker, doth pro-vide
for our needs to be sup-plied; come to God's own
tem-ple, come, raise the song of har-vest home.

2. All the world is God's own field,
   Fruit unto His praise to yield;
   Wheat and tares together sown,
   Unto joy or sorrow grown;
   First the blade, and then the ear,
   Then the full corn shall appear:
   Lord of harvest, grant that we
   Wholesome grain and pure may be.

3. For the Lord our God shall come
   And shall take His harvest home,
   From His field shall in that day
   All offences purge away,
   Give His angels charge at last
   In the fire the tares to cast,
   But the fruitful ears to store
   In His garner evermore.

4. Even so, Lord, quickly come,
   Bring Thy final harvest home;
   Gather Thou Thy people in,
   Free from sorrow, free from sin;
   There, for ever purified,
   In Thy garner to abide:
   Come, with all Thine angels, come,
   Raise the glorious harvest-home.

Henry Alford (1810-71)

76. Create in me

Ps 51:7, 10

David Fellingham

Create in me a clean heart, O God, and re - new a right spi - rit in me. Create in me a clean heart, O God, and re - new a right spi - rit in me.

77. Crown Him with many crowns

Rev 5:13; 19:12

Capo 2(C)

DIADEMATA

George J. Elvey (1816-93)

Triumphantly

1. Crown Him with ma - ny crowns, the Lamb up - on His
throne; hark, how the heav'n - ly an - them drowns all
mu - sic but its own! A - wake, my soul, and
sing of Him who died for thee and
hail Him as thy match-less King, through all e - ter - ni - ty.

2. Crown Him the Lord of life,
   Who triumphed o'er the grave,
   And rose victorious in the strife
   For those He came to save:
   His glories now we sing,
   Who died and rose on high;
   Who died eternal life to bring,
   And lives that death may die.

3. Crown Him the Lord of love;
   Behold His hands and side,
   Those wounds yet visible above
   In beauty glorified:
   No angel in the sky
   Can fully bear that sight,
   But downward bends His burning eye
   At mysteries so bright.

4. Crown Him the Lord of peace,
   Whose power a sceptre sways
   From pole to pole, that wars may cease,
   And all be prayer and praise:
   His reign shall know no end,
   And round His piercèd feet
   Fair flowers of paradise extend
   Their fragrance ever sweet.

5. Crown Him the Lord of years,
   The Potentate of time,
   Creator of the rolling spheres,
   Ineffably sublime!
   All hail, Redeemer, hail!
   For Thou hast died for me;
   Thy praise shall never, never fail
   Throughout eternity.

Matthew Bridges (1800-94) & Godfrey Thring (1823-1903)

78.
Darkness like a shroud
(Arise shine!)

Capo 4 (C)

Ps 119:105; Is 60:1–3;
Mt 5:14; Jn 8:12;
Eph 6:10, 17; Rev 21:23

Graham Kendrick

2. Children of the light,
   Be clean and pure.
   Rise, you sleepers,
   Christ will shine on you.
   Take the Spirit's flashing two-edged sword
   And with faith declare God's mighty word;
   Stand up and in His strength be strong.

3. Here among us now
   Christ the Light
   Kindles brighter flames
   In our trembling hearts.
   Living Word, our lamp, come guide our feet
   As we walk as one in light and peace till
   Justice and truth shine like the sun.

4. Like a city bright
   So let us blaze;
   Lights in every street
   Turning night to day.
   And the darkness shall not overcome
   Till the fullness of Christ's kingdom comes,
   Dawning to God's eternal day.

79. Dear Lord and Father of mankind

Ex 16:14;
1 Kings 19:11–12

Capo 3 (C)
REPTON

Charles Hubert Hastings Parry (1848-1918)

1. Dear Lord and Fa - ther of man-kind, for - give our fool - ish

ways; re - clothe us in our right-ful mind; in

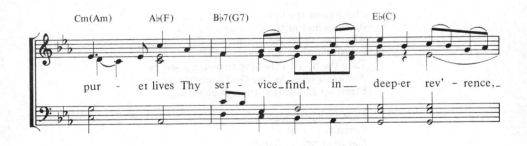

pur - er lives Thy ser - vice find, in __ deep-er rev' - rence, __

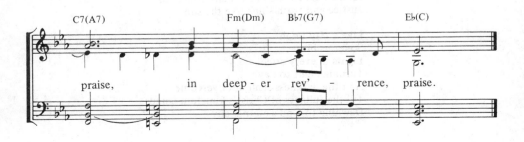

praise, in deep - er rev' - rence, praise.

2. In simple trust like theirs who heard,
   Beside the Syrian sea,
   The gracious calling of the Lord,
   Let us, like them, without a word
   Rise up and follow Thee,
   Rise up and follow Thee.

3. O sabbath rest by Galilee!
   O calm of hills above,
   Where Jesus knelt to share with Thee
   The silence of eternity,
   Interpreted by love,
   Interpreted by love.

4. With that deep hush subduing all
   Our words and works that drown
   The tender whisper of Thy call,
   As noiseless let Thy blessing fall
   As fell Thy manna down,
   As fell Thy manna down.

5. Drop Thy still dews of quietness,
   Till all our strivings cease;
   Take from our souls the strain and stress,
   And let our ordered lives confess
   The beauty of Thy peace,
   The beauty of Thy peace.

6. Breathe through the heats of our desire
   Thy coolness and Thy balm;
   Let sense be dumb, let flesh retire;
   Speak through the earthquake, wind and fire,
   O still small voice of calm,
   O still small voice of calm!

John Greenleaf Whittier (1807-92)

*Now to the King eternal, immortal,
invisible, the only God, be honour and
glory for ever and ever. Amen.*

1 TIMOTHY 1:17

80. Do something new, Lord

Mt 26:39, 42; Mk 14:36;
Lk 22:42

Chris Bowater

With feeling

Do some-thing new, Lord, in my heart, make a start; do some-thing new, Lord, do some-thing new.

(Fine)

I o-pen up my heart, as much as can be known;

I o-pen up my will to con-form to Yours a-lone.

2. I lay before Your feet
   All my hopes and my desires;
   Unreservedly submit
   To what Your spirit may require.

3. I only want to live
   For Your pleasure now;
   I long to please You, Father —
   Will You show me how?

81. Draw me closer

Mt 9:20; Mk 5:27; Lk 8:44; Jn 9:6

Stuart Devane/Glenn Gore

82.
El-Shaddai

Gen 17:1; 22:13; Ex 14:21; Ps 7:17

Capo 5(C)

John Thompson/Michael Card

El - Sha- ddai, ___ El - Sha-ddai, ___ El - El- yon ___ na A - don- ai, ___

___ age to age ___ You're still the same ___ by the pow-

- er of ___ the Name. ___ El - Sha - ddai, ___ El - Sha - ddai, ___

___ Er - kam - ka - na A - don - ai, _____ we will praise ___

and lift You high, __ El - Sha - ddai. __

1. Through Your love __ and through the ram __ You saved the son __

of A - bra - ham, __ through the pow - er of __ Your hand, __

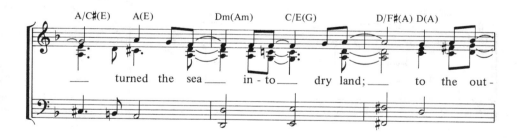

turned the sea __ in - to __ dry land; __ to the out -

cast on __ her knees, __ You were the God __ who real - ly sees, __

2. Through the years You made it clear
   That the time of Christ was near,
   Though the people could not see
   What Messiah ought to be;
   Though Your word contained the plan,
   They just could not understand
   Your most awesone work was done
   Through the frailty of Your Son.

83.

Emmanuel

Is 7:14; Mt 1:23

Bob McGee

Em-man - u - el, _____ Em-man - u - el, _____

_ we call Your name, _____ Em-man - u - el. _____

_ God with us, _____ re -vealed in us, _____

_ we call Your name, _____ Em-man - u - el. _____

84.

Enter in

Heb 10:19; Rev 1:5

Carol Mundy

Capo 3 (D)

With feeling, not too slow

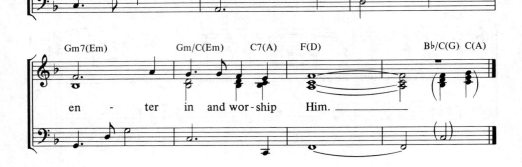

Enter in to His great love, kneel ___ before His throne; for His blood has washed a - way your sin, so enter in and wor - ship Him. ___

85. Eternal God

Heb 10:19–20; Eph 1:20

David Fellingham

Joyfully with strength

E-ter-nal God, we come to You, we come be-fore Your throne; we ent-er by a new and liv-ing way, with con-fid-ence we come. We declare Your faithfulness, Your promises are true; we will now draw near to wor-ship You.

86.

Exalted, You are exalted

Eph 1:20; Phil 2:9–10

Dave Bilbrough

Ex - alt - ed, You are ex - alt - ed, Lord of hea - ven and the earth. Ex - alt - ed, You are ex - alt - ed, Ru - ler of the u - ni - verse. For at the

Who may ascend the hill of the Lord?
Who may stand in his holy place?
He who has clean hands and a pure heart.

PSALM 24:3–4

87.
Exalt the Lord our God

Ps 99:5

Rick Ridings

Ex - alt the Lord our God, _____ ex - alt the Lord our God, _____ and wor - ship at His foot - stool, wor - ship at His foot - stool; ho - ly is He, ho - ly is He. _____

88. Facing a task unfinished

Mt 28:19; Heb 12:1

Capo 2 (C)
AURELIA
Moderate

Samuel Sebastian Wesley (1810-76)

1. Fac - ing a task un - fin - ish'd, that drives us to our
knees, a need that, un - dim - in - ish'd, re -
bukes our sloth - ful ease, we who re - joice to
know Thee, re - new be - fore Thy throne the
sol - emn pledge we owe Thee, to go and make Thee known.

2. Where other lords beside Thee
Hold their unhindered sway,
Where forces that defied Thee
Defy Thee still today;
With none to heed their crying
For life, and love, and light,
Unnumbered souls are dying,
And pass into the night.

3. We bear the torch that flaming
Fell from the hands of those
Who gave their lives proclaiming
That Jesus died and rose.
Ours is the same commission,
The same glad message ours,
Fired by the same ambition,
To Thee we yield our powers.

4. O Father who sustained them,
O Spirit who inspired,
Saviour, whose love constrained them
To toil with zeal untired,
From cowardice defend us,
From lethargy awake!
Forth on Thine errands send us
To labour for Thy sake.

Frank Houghton (1894-1972)

89.
Faithful One

Ps 18:2

Brian Doerksen

With feeling

Faith - ful One so un - chang - ing, ___ Age - less One You're my rock ___ of _ peace. ___ Lord of all I de - pend on You, I call out to You a - gain and _ a - gain. I call out to You

90. Father

Rom 8:15; Gal 4:6

Danny Daniels

Tenderly

Fa - ther, I can call You
Fa - ther, how I love You
Fa - ther, I will serve You,

Fa - ther, for I am Your child
Fa - ther, I will sing Your praise
Fa - ther, I will seek Your face

to - day, to -
to - day, to -
to - day, to -

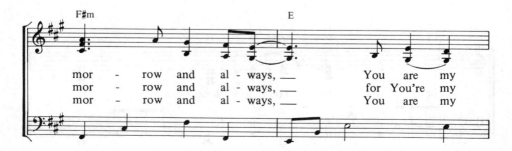

mor - row and al - ways, You are my
mor - row and al - ways, for You're my
mor - row and al - ways, You are my

——— □ ▢ □ ———

*The Son is the radiance of God's glory
and the exact representation of his
being, sustaining all things by his
powerful word.*

HEBREWS 1:3

——— □ ▢ □ ———

91.

Father God

Capo 3(D)

Jack W. Hayford

Fa-ther God, I give all thanks and praise to Thee,____ Fa-ther God, my hands I hum-bly raise to Thee;____ for Your migh-ty pow'r and love a-maz-es me, a-maz-es me and I stand in awe and wor-ship, Fa-ther God.____

92.

Father God I wonder

(I will sing Your praises)

Rom 8:15; Gal 4:5–6; Eph 1:5

Ian Smale

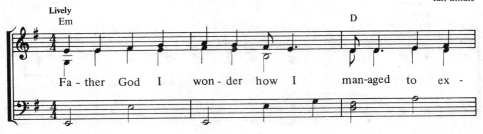

Fa-ther God I won-der how I man-aged to ex-

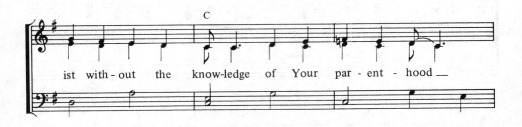

ist with-out the know-ledge of Your par-ent-hood

and Your lov-ing care. But now I am Your

son I am a-dopt-ed in Your fam-i-ly and

93. Father God we worship You

Jn 4:23

Graham Kendrick

1. Father God, we worship You, make us part of all You do. As You move among us now we worship You.

2. Jesus King, we worship You,
   Help us listen now to You.
   As You move among us now
   We worship You.

3. Spirit pure, we worship You,
   With Your fire our zeal renew.
   As You move among us now
   We worship You.

94.

Father, here I am
(Let forgiveness flow)

Danny Daniels

Father, here I am again, in need
In my heart and in my mind, in word

of mer-cy, hurt from sin,
and deed I've been so blind, } so by the blood and

Je-sus' love, let for-give-ness flow.

To me, from me, so my heart will know;

ful-ly and sweet-ly, let for-give-ness flow.

95.

Father in heaven
(We will crown Him)

Capo 3 (Am)

Is 53:11–12; Phil 2:7;
Rev 5:13; 19:12

Dave Bilbrough

1. Fa- ther in hea-ven, our voi-ces we raise, re-ceive our de-vo-tion, re-ceive now our praise; as we sing of the glo-ry — of all that You've done, the great-est love sto-ry that's ev-er been sung. And we will crown You Lord of all, yes, we will crown You Lord of

all ... for You have won the vic-to-ry, Yes we will crown You Lord of ___ all. ___ all. ___ 3. We will all. ___

2. Father in heaven,
   Our lives are Your own;
   We've been caught by a vision
   Of Jesus alone,
   Who came as a servant
   To free us from sin,
   Father in heaven,
   Our worship we bring:

3. We will sing 'Hallelujah',
   We will sing to the King,
   To our Mighty Deliverer
   Our Hallelujahs will ring.
   Yes, our praise is resounding
   To the Lamb on the throne,
   He alone is exalted
   Through the love He has shown.

96. Father in heaven how we love You
(Blessèd be the Lord God Almighty)

Ps 22:3;
145:4;
Rev 1:8; 4:8

Bob Fitts

Fa-ther in hea-ven how we love You, — we lift Your name in al' the earth. — May Your king-dom be est-ab-lish'd in our prai-ses — as Your peo-ple de-clare Your migh-ty works. — Bless-èd be the Lord God Al-migh-ty, — who was and is and is to come, — bless-èd be the Lord God Al-migh-ty, — who reigns for e-ver-more. —

97.

Father, I place into Your hands

Ps 31:5; Lk 23:46;
Jn 5:19

Capo 1 (E)

Jenny Hewer

Gently

1. Fa-ther, I place in - to Your hands the things I can - not do.

Fa-ther, I place in - to Your hands—the things that I've been through.

Fa-ther, I place in - to Your hands the way that I should go, For I

know I al - ways can trust You.

2. Father, I place into Your hands
My friends and family.
Father, I place into Your hands
The things that trouble me.
Father, I place into Your hands
The person I would be,
For I know I always can trust You.

3. Father, we love to see Your face,
We love to hear Your voice,
Father, we love to sing Your praise
And in Your name rejoice,
Father, we love to walk with You
And in Your presence rest,
For we know we always can trust You.

4. Father, I want to be with You
And do the things You do.
Father, I want to speak the words
That You are speaking too.
Father, I want to love the ones
That You will draw to You,
For I know that I am one with You.

98.
Father make us one

Ps 133:1, 3; Jn 17:21

Capo 1 (G)

Rick Ridings

2. Behold how pleasant and how good it is
For brethren to dwell in unity,
For there the Lord commands the blessing,
Life for evermore.

99.

Father, we adore You

Rom 12:1

Capo 3(D)

Terrye Coelho

2. Jesus, we adore You. . . *(etc)*.

3. Spirit, we adore You. . . *(etc)*.

100.

Father, we adore You
(Fountain of life)

Ps 36:8–9

Philip Lawson-Johnston

Gently

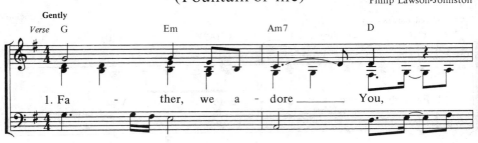

1. Fa - ther, we a - dore You,

we are Your child-ren ga-thered here; to

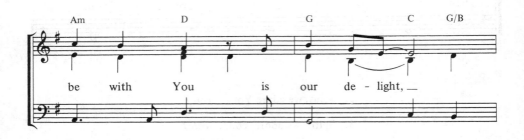

be with You is our de - light,

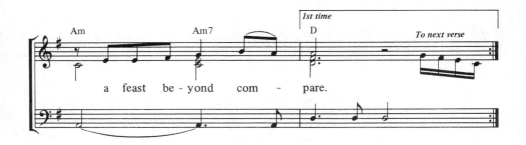

a feast be - yond com - pare.

2. Father, in Your presence
   There is such freedom to enjoy.
   We find in You a lasting peace
   That nothing can destroy.

101. Father, we adore You, You've drawn us

(All the earth shall worship)

Ex 15:11; Ps 40:2; 69:2, 14;
Mt 3:11; Lk 3:16; Jn 6:44;
1 Jn 4:19

With strength

Carl Tuttle

1. Fa-ther,__ we a - dore __ You, You've drawn us to this place. We bow down be - fore __ You, hum-bly on our face.

Chorus

All the earth shall wor - ship at the throne of the King. Of His great and awe - some power,

2. Jesus we love You,
   Because You first loved us,
   You reached out and healed us
   With Your mighty touch.

3. Spirit we need You,
   To lift us from this mire,
   Consume and empower us
   With Your holy fire.

—— □ ▢ □ ——

Heaven is my throne
   and the earth is my footstool.
Where is the house you will build for
   me?
   Where will my resting place be?
Has not my hand made all these things,
   and so they came into being?

ISAIAH 66:1–2

—— □ ▢ □ ——

102.

Father, we love You

Jn 12:28

Donna Adkins

Worshipfully

1. Fa - ther, we love You, we wor - ship and a - dore You,

Glo - ri - fy Your name in all the earth.

Glo - ri - fy Your name, Glo - ri - fy Your name,

Glo - ri - fy Your name in all the earth.

2. Jesus, we love You . . . *(etc.)*

3. Spirit, we love You . . . *(etc.)*

103.

Father, You are my portion
(My delight)

Ps 73:25–26; 119:57;
Lam 3:24; Mt 6:21;
Lk 12:34

Andy Park

1. Fa - ther, You are my

por - tion in this ___ life, ___

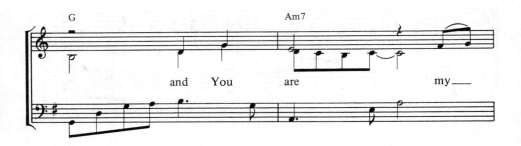

and You are my ___

hope and my de - light, ___

2. Jesus, You are my treasure in this life,
   And You are so pure and so kind,
   And I love You, yes, I love You,
   Lord, I love You, my delight.

104.

Father Your love is precious
(Your love overwhelms me)

Capo 3 (D)

Everett Perry

Worshipfully

Father __ Your love __ is pre-cious __ be-yond all loves, Father __ Your

love ov-er-whelms me. ____ Father __ Your love overwhelms

me. ____ So I lift up __ my hands, an expression of my love, and I

give You __ my heart in joyful o-be-di-ence. Father __ Your love __ is

pre-cious __ be-yond all loves, Father __ Your love overwhelms me. ____

——————————— □ ▢ □ ———————————

*May the God of peace, who through the
blood of the eternal covenant brought
back from the dead our Lord Jesus,
that great Shepherd of the sheep,
equip you with everything good for
doing his will, and may he work in us
what is pleasing to him, through Jesus
Christ, to whom be glory for ever and
ever. Amen.*

HEBREWS 13:20–21

——————————— □ ▢ □ ———————————

105.

Fear not

Is 43:1–2

Phil Pringle

Steady rock rhythm

Fear _ not, for I am with _ you, fear _

not, for I am with _ you, fear _

not, for I am with _ you, says the Lord. _____

1st time *2nd time*

Fear _ _ I have re - deemed you, I've

106. Fear not, rejoice and be glad

Joel 2:21–24, 29;
Mt 5:14; 24:32;
Mk 13:28; Lk 21:29–30;
Acts 2:17; 1 Cor 12:13;
Rev 14:15

Priscilla Wright Porter

With breadth

Fear not, re - joice and be glad, the

Lord hath done a great thing; hath

poured out His Spi - rit on all man - kind, ___ on

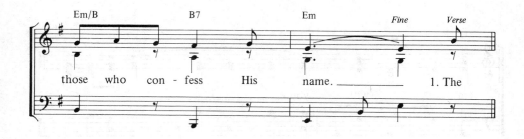

those who con - fess His name. _____ 1. The

fig tree is bud - ding, the vine bear - eth fruit, the wheat fields are gold-en with grain. ___ Thrust in the si - ckle, the har-vest is ripe, the Lord ___ has gi - ven us rain. ___

2. Ye shall eat in plenty and be satisfied,
   The mountains will drip with sweet wine.
   My children shall drink of the fountain of life,
   My children will know they are mine.

3. My people shall know that I am the Lord,
   Their shame I have taken away.
   My Spirit will lead them together again,
   My Spirit will show them the way.

4. My children shall dwell in a Body of love,
   A light to the world they will be.
   Life shall come forth from the Father above,
   My Body will set mankind free.

Fight the good fight

Deut 33:27; Is 40:31; 1 Cor 9:24–25;
1 Tim 1:18; 6:12; Heb 12:1–3

DUKE STREET

John Hatton (d. 1793)

Triumphantly

1. Fight the good fight with all thy might,
Christ is thy strength, and Christ thy right;
lay hold on life, and it shall be thy joy and crown e-ter-nal-ly.

2. Run the straight race through God's good grace,
Lift up thine eyes and seek His face;
Life with its way before thee lies,
Christ is the path, and Christ the prize.

3. Cast care aside, lean on thy Guide;
His boundless mercy will provide;
Lean, and the trusting soul shall prove
Christ is its life, and Christ its love.

4. Faint not, nor fear, His arms are near,
He changeth not, and thou art dear;
Only believe, and thou shalt see
That Christ is all in all to thee.

John Samuel Bewley Monsell (1811-75)

108. Fill Thou my life, O Lord my God *Heb 13:15*

ST FULBERT

Smoothly

Henry John Gauntlett (1805-76)

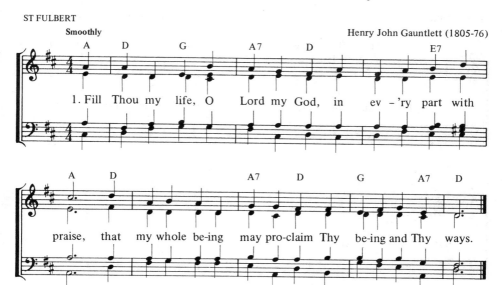

1. Fill Thou my life, O Lord my God, in ev-'ry part with praise, that my whole be-ing may pro-claim Thy be-ing and Thy ways.

2. Not for the lip of praise alone
   Nor e'en the praising heart,
   I ask, but for a life made up
   Of praise in every part:

3. Praise in the common things of life,
   Its goings out and in;
   Praise in each duty and each deed,
   However small and mean.

4. Fill every part of me with praise;
   Let all my being speak
   Of Thee and of Thy love, O Lord,
   Poor though I be and weak.

5. So shall Thou, gracious Lord, from me
   Receive the glory due;
   And so shall I begin on earth
   The song for ever new.

6. So shall no part of day or night
   From sacredness be free;
   But all my life, in every step,
   Be fellowship with Thee.

Horatius Bonar (1808-89)

109.

For all the saints

Rev 2:10; 7:9; 14:13

SINE NOMINE

R. Vaughan Williams (1872-1958)

With strength

1. For all the saints, who from their la-bours rest, who Thee ___ by faith be-fore the world con - fessed, Thy name, O ___ Je - sus, be for - ev - er ___ blest. Hal - le - lu - jah! Hal - le - lu - jah!

2. Thou wast their Rock, their fortress, and their might;
   Thou, Lord, their Captain in the well fought fight;
   Thou in the darkness drear their one true light.
   Hallelujah!

3. O may Thy soldiers, faithful, true and bold,
   Fight as the saints who nobly fought of old,
   And win, with them, the victor's crown of gold!
   Hallelujah!

4. O blest communion, fellowship divine!
   We feebly struggle, they in glory shine;
   Yet all are one in Thee, for all are Thine.
   Hallelujah!

5. And when the strife is fierce, the warfare long,
   Steals on the ear the distant triumph song,
   And hearts are brave again, and arms are strong.
   Hallelujah!

6. The golden evening brightens in the west;
   Soon, soon to faithful warriors cometh rest;
   Sweet is the calm of paradise the blest.
   Hallelujah!

7. But lo! there breaks a yet more glorious day;
   The saints triumphant rise in bright array;
   The King of glory passes on His way.
   Hallelujah!

8. From earth's wide bounds, from ocean's farthest coast,
   Through gates of pearl streams in the countless host,
   Singing to Father, Son and Holy Ghost.
   Hallelujah!

W.W. How (1823-97)

110. For His name is exalted

Ps 57:5, 11; 108:5;
Rev 1:8; 4:8–9

Dale Garratt

Worshipfully

For His name is ex - alt - ed, ____ His

glory above hea - ven and earth. ____ Holy is the Lord God Al-

1st time

migh - ty, who was and who is and who is to come.

2nd time

sitteth on the throne and who lives for ev - er - more. __

111. For I'm building a people of power

Is 43:21;
Eph 2:21–22

Dave Richards

For I'm build-ing a peo-ple of pow-er___ And I'm mak-ing a peo-ple of praise, That will move thro' this land by My Spi-rit,___ And will glo-ri-fy My prec-ious Name. Build Your Church, Lord, Make us strong, Lord, Join our hearts, Lord, through Your Son. Make us one, Lord, in Your Bo-dy, In the King-dom of Your Son.___

112.
For the beauty of the earth

Capo 2 (G)

ENGLAND'S LANE

Heb 13:15

English melody
adapted and harmonised by Geoffrey Shaw (1879-1943)

1. For the beauty of the earth, for the beauty of the skies, for the love which from our birth over and around us lies: Father, unto Thee we raise this our sacrifice of praise.

2. For the beauty of each hour
Of the day and of the night,
Hill and vale, and tree and flower,
Sun and moon, and stars of light:
Father, unto Thee we raise
This our sacrifice of praise.

3. For the joy of human love,
Brother, sister, parent, child,
Friends on earth, and friends above;
For all gentle thoughts and mild:
Father, unto Thee we raise
This our sacrifice of praise.

4. For each perfect gift of Thine
To our race so freely given,
Graces, human and divine,
Flowers of earth, and buds of heaven:
Father, unto Thee we raise
This our sacrifice of praise.

Folliott S. Pierpoint (1835-1917) alt.

To him who is able to keep you from falling and to present you before his glorious presence without fault and with great joy—to the only God our Saviour be glory, majesty, power and authority, through Jesus Christ our Lord, before all ages, now and evermore! Amen.

JUDE 24–25

113.

For the Lord is marching on

Josh 5:14; Ps 68:7

Capo 4(Am)

Bonnie Low

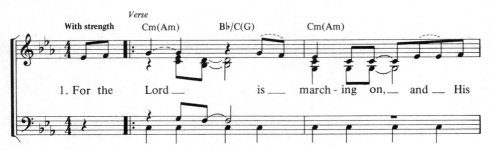

1. For the Lord — is — march-ing on, — and — His

ar - my is — ev - er strong, and His glo - ry shall be

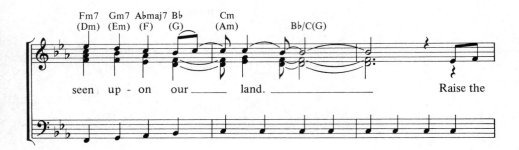

seen up - on our — land. — Raise the

an - them, sing the vic-tor's song, praise the Lord — for the

2. We are marching in Messiah's band,
   The keys of victory in His mighty hand;
   Let us march on to take our promised land!
   For the Lord is marching on,
   And His army is ever strong,
   And His glory shall be seen upon our land.

114.

For this purpose

Rom 6:9; 1 Pet 2:24; 1 Jn 3:8;
Rev 12:10–11

Capo 2(C)

Flowing
Intro.

Graham Kendrick

1. For this pur - pose Christ was re - veal'd to de - stroy all the works of the Ev - il One. Christ in us has ov - er - come, — so with glad-ness we sing — and wel-come His king- dom in.

Over sin He has con-quer'd, Hal-le-lu-jah, He has con-quer'd. Ov-er
death vic-tor-ious, Hal-le-lu-jah, vic-tor-ious. Ov-er
sick-ness He has tri-umph'd, Hal-le-lu-jah, He has tri-umph'd.
Je-sus reigns __ ov-er all!

2. In the name of Jesus we stand,
    By the power of His blood
    We now claim this ground.
    Satan has no authority here,
    Powers of darkness must flee,
    For Christ has the victory.

115.

For Thou O Lord art high
(I exalt Thee)

Ps 97:9

Capo 5 (C)

Pete Sanchez Jnr

Worshipfully with strength

Ps 97:9

116.

For unto us a child is born

Is 9:6

Author unknown
Arr. Margaret Evans

For unto us a child is born, unto us a Son is given. And the government shall be upon His shoulder, and His name shall be called Wonderful Counsellor, the Mighty God, the Everlasting Father, and the Prince of Peace is He.

117.

For we see Jesus

Heb 2:9; Rev 5:13

Capo 4 (C)

Sue Hutchinson

With majesty

For we see Je - sus_____ en - throned on high, Clothed in His right - eous-ness_____ we wor - ship Him. Glo - ry and hon - our we give____ un - to You, We see You in Your ho - li-ness and bow be-fore Your throne. You are the Lord,____ Your Name en-dures for ev - er, ____ Je - sus the Name high ov - er all.

118. For Your wonderful deeds

Capo 3 (G)

David J. Hadden

2. For Your bountiful grace we give You thanks, Lord,
   For the peace and the joy You bestow on the people You love.
   We honour You, we honour You,
   For Your bountiful grace we honour You.

119. From all that dwell below the skies

Ps 113:3;
Phil 2:11

LASST UNS ERFREUEN
Jubilant
Verse

Geistliche Kirchengesang
Cologne (1623)

1. From all that dwell be - low the skies let
the Cre - a - tor's praise a - rise: Al - le -
lu - ia! Al - le - lu - ia! Let
the Re - deem - er's name be sung through
ev - 'ry land, by ev - 'ry tongue: Al - le -

Chorus

Arranged by Ralph Vaughan Williams
from the English Hymnal by permission of Oxford University Press.

lu - ia! Al - le - lu - ia! Al - le - lu - ia! Al - le -

lu - ia! Al - le - lu - ia!

2. Eternal are Thy mercies, Lord;
Eternal truth attends Thy word:
Alleluia! Alleluia!
Thy praise shall sound from shore to shore,
Till suns shall rise and set no more.

3. Your lofty themes, ye mortals, bring
In songs of praise divinely sing:
Alleluia! Alleluia!
The great salvation loud proclaim,
And shout for joy the Saviour's name.

4. In every land begin the song;
To every land the strains belong.
Alleluia! Alleluia!
In cheerful sounds all voices raise,
And fill the world with loudest praise.

Isaac Watts (1674-1748)

120.

From heaven You came
(The Servant King)

Is 53:11; Mt 20:28; 26:39;
Mk 10:45; 14:36; Lk 22:42;
Jn 20:27; Rom 12:1;
Eph 6:7; Phil 2:7

Capo 3(C)

Graham Kendrick

1. From heav'n You came, help-less babe, en-ter'd our world, Your glo-ry veil'd; not to be served but to serve, and give Your life that we might live. This is our God, the Ser-vant

2. There in the garden
   Of tears,
   My heavy load
   He chose to bear;
   His heart with sorrow
   Was torn,
   'Yet not my will
   But Yours,' He said.

3. Come see His hands
   And His feet,
   The scars that speak
   Of sacrifice,
   Hands that flung stars
   Into space
   To cruel nails
   Surrendered.

4. So let us learn
   How to serve,
   And in our lives
   Enthrone Him;
   Each other's needs
   To prefer,
   For it is Christ
   We're serving.

— □ ☐ □ —

Hallelujah!
For our Lord God Almighty
reigns.
Let us rejoice and be glad
and give him glory!

REVELATION 19:6–7

— □ ☐ □ —

121.
From the rising of the sun

Ps 113:1–3

Capo 3 (C)

Paul S. Deming

122.

From the sun's rising

Ps 113:1–3; Mt 9:37–38; 28:18–20; Lk 10:2

Capo 2 (C)

Graham Kendrick

Steadily

Verse

From the sun's ri-sing, un-to the sun's set-ting, Je-sus our Lord shall be

great in the earth; and all earth's king-doms shall be His dom-in-ion,

all of cre-a-tion shall sing of His worth. ____

Chorus

Let ev-ery heart,_ ev-ery voice,_ ev-ery tongue join with spi - rits a-

blaze; one in His love, we will cir-cle the world_with the song _ of His

2. To every tongue, tribe
   And nation He sends us,
   To make disciples
   To teach and baptise.
   For all authority
   To Him is given;
   Now as His witnesses
   We shall arise.

3. Come let us join with
   The church from all nations,
   Cross every border,
   Throw wide every door;
   Workers with Him
   As He gathers His harvest,
   Till earth's far corners
   Our Saviour adore.

123.
Give me life, Holy Spirit

Eph 5:18

Capo 3(D)

Danny Daniels

Give me life, — Ho - ly — Spi - rit,
guide my steps in Your — sight; — help me
al - ways give You plea - sure, — keep me
walk - ing — in Your — light. —
Give me life, — Ho - ly — Spi - rit,

124.

Give thanks

Joel 3:10; 2 Cor 8:9; 12:10;
Jas 2:5; Rev 2:9

Henry Smith

Capo 3 (D)

Flowing

Give thanks with a grate-ful heart. Give thanks to the

Ho - ly One. Give thanks be-cause He's gi-ven Je - sus

Christ, His Son. Give Son. And

now Let the weak say 'I am strong', let the

125.

Give thanks to the Lord

Ps 105:1–3

Kevin Gould

Capo 3 (D)

———— □ ☐ □ ————

God is spirit, and his worshippers
must worship in spirit and in truth.

JOHN 4:24

———— □ ☐ □ ————

126. Glorious Father

Jn 12:28; Rev 22:20

Danny Reed

Worshipfully

Glo - ri - ous Fa - ther, we ex - alt __ You, ____

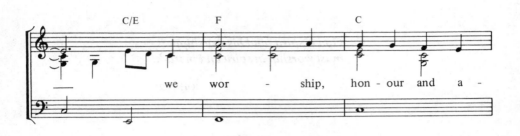

__ we wor - ship, hon - our and a -

- dore __ You. ____ We de - light __ to

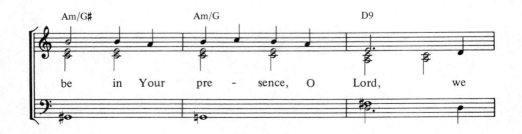

be in Your pre - sence, O Lord, we

127. Glorious things of thee are spoken

Ex 13:21;
16:15; 17:6;
Ps 87:2–3; Rev 21:2

Capo 3(C)

AUSTRIA

Franz Joseph Haydn (1732-1809)

Triumphantly

1. Glo - rious things of thee are spo - ken, Zi - on, cit - y
of our God! He whose word can-not be bro-ken, form'd thee for His
own a - bode. On the Rock of A - ges foun - ded,
what can shake thy sure re- pose? With sal - va - tion's
walls sur - round - ed, thou may'st smile at all thy foes.

2. See! The streams of living waters,
   Springing from eternal love,
   Well supply thy sons and daughters,
   And all fear of want remove;
   Who can faint, whilst such a river
   Ever flows their thirst to assuage?
   Grace which, like the Lord, the Giver,
   Never fails from age to age.

3. Round each habitation hovering,
   See the cloud and fire appear!
   For a glory and a covering,
   Showing that the Lord is near.
   He who gives them daily manna,
   He who listens when they cry:
   Let Him hear the loud hosanna
   Rising to His throne on high.

4. Saviour, if of Zion's city
   I, through grace, a member am,
   Let the world deride or pity,
   I will glory in Thy name.
   Fading is the worldlings pleasure,
   All his boasted pomp and show,
   Solid joys and lasting treasure
   None but Zion's children know.

John Newton (1725-1807)

128.

Glory

Rev 5:13

Danny Daniels

Bright, joyful feel

Glo - ry, glo-ry in the high-est; glo-ry,—

to the Al - might - y; glo-ry to the Lamb of God,— and

glo-ry to the liv - ing Word; — glo - ry

to the Lamb!

1st time

129. God forgave my sin

(Freely, freely)

Mt 10:8; 28:19; Jn 3:3; 17:20

Carol Owens

Capo 3(C)

1. God for-gave my sin in Je - sus' name, I've been born a - gain in Je - sus' name; and in Je - sus' name I come to you to share His love as He told me to.

2. All power is given in Jesus' name,
   In earth and heaven in Jesus' name;
   And in Jesus' name I come to you
   To share His power as He told me to.

130.

God has exalted Him

Phil 2:9–11

Austin Martin

God has ex-alt-ed Him to the high-est place, gi - ven Him the name _____ that is a-bove ev - 'ry name. _____ And ev -'ry knee shall bow and ev - 'ry tongue con - fess _____ that Je-sus Christ is Lord to the glo - ry of God the Fa - ther. _____

131. God has spoken to His people

Mt 9:16–17;
Mk 2:21–22;
Lk 5:36–37; Acts 13:26; Heb 1:1

Brightly

Stuart Baugh

1. God has spo - ken to His peo - ple, through His pro - phets long a-
go, of the days __ in which we're liv-ing, and the things __ His church should

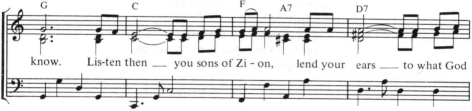

know. Lis-ten then __ you sons of Zi - on, lend your ears __ to what God

says, then res - pond __ in full o - be-di-ence, gladly walk in all His ways.

2. These are times of great refreshing
Coming from the throne in heaven,
Times of building and of shaking,
When God rids His church of leaven.
Not a patching up of wineskins,
Or of garments that are old,
But a glorious restoration,
Just exactly as foretold.

3. Reign on, O God victorious,
Fulfil Your promises.
Seed of Abraham remember
You will see all nations blessed.
Powers of darkness, we remind you
Of Christ's victory on the cross.
Hear the truth we are declaring,
Jesus won and you have lost.

I will proclaim the name of the
    Lord.
  Oh, praise the greatness of our
    God!
He is the Rock, his works are
    perfect,
  and all his ways are just.
A faithful God who does no wrong,
  upright and just is he.

DEUTERONOMY 32:3–4

132.

God is good

Ps 100:5

Graham Kendrick

133.   God is here, God is present

Ps 63:4

Ian Smale

134. God is our Father

Ps 47:1; 149:3; 150:4;
Rom 8:15; Gal 4:6

Alex Simons & Freda Kimmey

God is our Fa - ther, — for He has made us His own, —

made Je - sus our bro - ther, — and hand in hand we'll

grow to - geth-er as one. Sing praise to the Lord —

— with the tambourine, sing praise to the Lord —

God is working His purpose out

Hab 2:14;
Jn 5:19;
1 Cor 3:6; Eph 1:11

Capo 5(C)

BENSON

Millicent Douglas Kingham (1866-1927)

1. God is work-ing His pur-pose out, as year suc-ceeds to year; God is work-ing His pur-pose out, and the time is draw-ing near; near-er and near-er draws the time, the time that shall sure-ly be, when the earth shall be fill'd with the glo-ry of God, as the wa-ters co-ver the sea.

2. From utmost East to utmost West,
   Where'er man's foot hath trod,
   By the mouth of many messengers
   Goes forth the voice of God;
   Give ear to Me, ye continents,
   Ye isles, give ear to Me,
   That the earth may be filled
   With the glory of God,
   As the waters cover the sea.

3. March we forth in the strength of God
   With the banner of Christ unfurled,
   That the light of the glorious gospel of truth
   May shine throughout the world:
   Fight we the fight with sorrow and sin,
   To set their captives free,
   That the earth may be filled
   With the glory of God,
   As the waters cover the sea.

4. All we can do is nothing worth,
   Unless God blesses the deed;
   Vainly we hope for the harvest-tide
   Till God gives life to the seed;
   Yet nearer and nearer draws the time,
   The time that shall surely be,
   When the earth shall be filled
   With the glory of God,
   As the waters cover the sea.

Arthur Campbell Ainger (1841-1919)

136.

God of all comfort
(To seek Your face)

Ps 27:8; 105:4; Jn 6:44

John Wimber

2. Because You have called us,
   We're gathered in this place,
   Oh, we have come to seek You,
   We have come to seek Your face.

———————— □ ☐ □ ————————

There is now no condemnation for those who are in Christ Jesus, because through Christ Jesus the law of the Spirit of life set me free from the law of sin and death.

ROMANS 8:1–2

———————— □ ☐ □ ————————

137.

God of glory

Is 61:1; Lk 4:18

Capo 2 (C)

David Fellingham

Brightly with strength and feeling

God of glo - ry, we ex-alt Your name,

You who reign _____ in maj-est - y. _____ We

lift our hearts to You _____ and we will wor - ship, praise and

mag-ni-fy Your ho - ly name. _____ In power res-

138.

God of grace
(I stand complete in You)

Eph 2:8

Chris Bowater

God of grace, — I turn my face to
Striv - ings and — all an - guished dreams in

You, I can - not hide; my
rags lie at my feet, and

na - ked - ness, — my shame, my guilt, — are
on - ly grace — pro - vides the way — for

all be - fore Your eyes.
me to stand com - plete. And Your

139. God of grace and God of glory

Eph 6:10

RHUDDLAN

Welsh Traditional Melody

Steadily

1. God of grace and God of glo - ry, on Thy peo-ple pour Thy pow'r;

crown Thine an-cient Chur-ch's sto - ry; bring her bud to glo - rious flower.

Grant us wis - dom, grant us cour - age, for the fac-ing of this hour.

2. Lo! the hosts of evil round us
   Scorn Thy Christ, assail His ways!
   Fears and doubts too long have bound us;
   Free our hearts to work and praise.
   Grant us wisdom,
   Grant us courage,
   For the living of these days.

3. Heal Thy children's warring madness;
   Bend our pride to Thy control;
   Shame our wanton, selfish gladness,
   Rich in things and poor in soul.
   Grant us wisdom,
   Grant us courage,
   Lest we miss Thy kingdom's goal.

4. Set our feet on lofty places;
   Gird our lives that they may be
   Armoured with all Christlike graces
   In the fight to set men free.
   Grant us wisdom,
   Grant us courage,
   That we fail not man nor Thee.

5. Save us from weak resignation
   To the evils we deplore;
   Let the search for Thy salvation
   Be our glory evermore.
   Grant us wisdom,
   Grant us courage,
   Serving Thee whom we adore.

H.E. Fosdick (1878-1969)

140.
Good Christian men, rejoice

Lk 2:7; Jn 10:9;
1 Cor 15:55

Capo 3 (D)

German Carol Melody, 14th cent.

IN DULCI JUBILO

1. Good Christ-ian men, re - joice ___ with heart and soul and voice; ___ give ye heed to what we say, Je - sus Christ is born to-day; ox and ass be - fore Him bow, and He is in the man-ger now. Christ is born to - day; ___ Christ is born to - day! ___

2. Good Christian men, rejoice
With heart and soul and voice;
Now ye hear of endless bliss,
Jesus Christ was born for this:
He hath opened heaven's door
And man is blessed forever more.
Christ was born for this;
Christ was born for this!

3. Good Christian men, rejoice
With heart and soul and voice;
Now ye need not fear the grave,
Jesus Christ was born to save;
Calls you one and calls you all
To gain His everlasting hall.
Christ was born to save;
Christ was born to save!

John Mason Neale (1818-66) altd.

141.
Great and marvellous

Rev 15:3–4

Bob Pitcher

Flowing

Great and marvellous are Thy works, O Lord God the Almighty,

Righteous and true are Thy ways, O Thou King of the nation.

Who will not fear, O Lord, And glorify Thy name? For

Thou alone art holy and all the nations will come before Thee and

worship, worship, worship before Thee, And

worship, worship, worship before Thee.

142. Great and marvellous are Thy works

(King of saints)

Rev 15:3–4

Kevin Prosch

With strength

Great and mar - vel - lous are ___ Thy works, ___

Lord God ___ Al - might - y; ___

just and true ___ are Thy ways O Lord ___ for

You are the King ___ of ___ saints. ___

Who shall not ___ fear ___ Thee, who shall not ___ glo - ri-fy Thy

name, O _ Lord?_____ For on - ly Thou art ho - ly. ___

___ All the na - tions shall come and wor-ship be - fore _ Thee, __

for Thy judge - ments are made man - i - fest.

For Thy judge - ments

are made man - i - fest. __

143. Great and wonderful

Rev 15:3-4

Stuart Dauermann

With pace

Great and wonderful __ are Thy wondrous deeds, __ O Lord God the Al -

migh - ty. __ Just and true __ are __ all Thy ways, O Lord, __

King of the a-ges art Thou. __ Who shall not fear and glo-ri-fy

Thy __ name, O Lord? For Thou a - lone art ho - ly,

Thou a - lone. All the nations shall come and worship Thee,_

for Thy glo - ry shall be re - veal - èd. Hal - le - lu - jah,_ Hal - le - lu - jah,_

Hal - le - lu - jah, A - men. Lai-lai-lai - lai - lai, lai-lai-lai-

lai - lai-lai,_ lai-lai-lai - lai - lai, lai-lai-lai - lai - lai-lai, _ lai-lai-lai-

lai - lai, lai-lai-lai - lai - lai - lai,_ lai-lai-lai - lai - lai,- lai lai-lai-lai - lai.

—— □ ▢ □ ——

O Lord, our Lord,
  how majestic is your name in all
    the earth!
You have set your glory
  above the heavens.

PSALM 8:1

—— □ ▢ □ ——

144.

Great is the Lord

Ps 48:1–2; Eph 4:4–5

Author unknown
Arr. Margaret Evans

Joyfully with swing

Great is the Lord and great-ly to be praisèd in the ci-ty of our God, In the moun-tain of His ho-li-ness. Beau-ti-ful for sit-u - a -tion,_ the joy of the whole earth is Mount Zion on the sides of the north, the ci -ty of the great King, _ is Mount Zion on the sides of the north the ci -ty of the great King. One bo-dy,_ one Spi - rit,_ one faith, one Lord, one peo - ple,_ one na - tion,_ praise ye the Lord.

145.Great is the Lord and most worthy of praise

Ps 48:1–2

Steve McEwan

Great _____ is the Lord and most wor-thy of praise, the
ci-ty of our God, the ho-ly place, the joy of the __ whole earth.
_____ Great _____ is the
Lord in, whom we have the vict-or-y, _____ He aids us a-gainst the en-em-
-y, we bow down on __ our knees. _____

146.   Great is the Lord and mighty in power

Ps 147:5, 11, 13–15, 20

Capo 3 (Am)

Dale Garratt

Great is the Lord and might-y in pow-er, His und-er-stand-ing has no lim-it. The Lord delights in those who fear Him, who put their hope in His unfailing love. He strengthens the bars of your gates, He grants you peace in your borders, He re-veals His word to His peo-ple, He has done this for no other na-tion. Great is the Lord and might-y in pow-er, His under-stand-ing has no lim-it. Ex-tol the Lord, O Je-rus-a-lem, praise your God, O people of Zi - on.

———————— □ ▢ □ ————————

I urge you, brothers, in view of God's mercy, to offer your bodies as living sacrifices, holy and pleasing to God— which is your spiritual worship.

ROMANS 21:1

———————— □ ▢ □ ————————

147.

Great is Thy faithfulness

Gen 8:22; Ps 89:1;
Lam 3:22–23; Mal 3:6

RUNYAN

William M. Runyan (1870-1957)

Morn - ing by morn - ing new mer - cies I see;
all I have need - ed Thy hand hath pro - vi - ded,
great is Thy faith - ful - ness, Lord, un - to me!

2. Summer and winter, and springtime and harvest,
   Sun, moon and stars in their courses above,
   Join with all nature in manifold witness
   To Thy great faithfulness, mercy and love.

3. Pardon for sin and a peace that endureth,
   Thine own dear presence to cheer and to guide;
   Strength for today and bright hope for tomorrow,
   Blessings all mine, with ten thousand beside!

Thomas O. Chisholm (1866-1960)

148. Guide me, O Thou great Jehovah

Ex 13:22;
16:15;
Josh 3:17; Ps 24:8; Jn 6:35, 58

CWM RHONDDA
Boldly

John Hughes (1873-1932)

1. Guide me, O Thou great __ Je - hov - ah,
pil - grim through this bar - ren land; I am weak, but
Thou __ art __ migh - ty, hold me with Thy __ power-ful hand:
Bread of hea - ven, Bread of hea - ven, feed me now and e - ver -
more, feed me now __ and __ e - ver - more.

(e - ver - more)

2. Open Thou the crystal fountain
   Whence the healing stream doth flow;
   Let the fiery, cloudy pillar
   Lead me all my journey through:
   Strong Deliverer, strong Deliverer,
   Be Thou still my strength and shield,
   Be Thou still my strength and shield.

3. When I tread the verge of Jordan
   Bid my anxious fears subside;
   Death of death, and hell's destruction,
   Land me safe on Canaan's side:
   Songs of praises, songs of praises,
   I will ever give to Thee,
   I will ever give to Thee.

William Williams (1717-91)
Tr. Peter Williams (1727-96)

149. Hail, Thou once despisèd Jesus

Is 53:3–4;
2 Cor 5:19; Eph 1:7;
Heb 7:25; Rev 5:12

LUX EOI

Arthur Seymour Sullivan (1842-1900)

1. Hail, Thou once de - spi - sèd Je - sus, hail, Thou Ga - li -

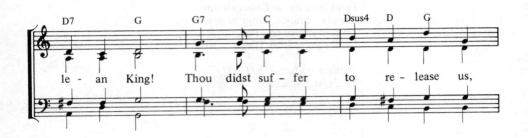

le - an King! Thou didst suf - fer to re - lease us,

Thou didst free sal - va - tion bring. Hail, Thou ag - on -

iz - ing Sa - viour, bear - er of our sin and shame,

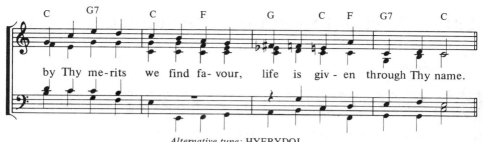

by Thy me-rits   we find fa-vour,   life   is   giv-en   through Thy name.

Alternative tune: HYFRYDOL

2. Paschal Lamb, by God appointed,
   All our sins on Thee were laid.
   With almighty love anointed
   Thou hast full atonement made.
   All Thy people are forgiven
   Through the virtue of Thy blood:
   Opened is the gate of heaven,
   Man is reconciled to God.

3. Jesus, hail! enthroned in glory,
   There for ever to abide;
   All the heavenly hosts adore Thee,
   Seated at Thy Father's side:
   There for sinners Thou art pleading,
   There Thou dost our place prepare,
   Ever for us interceding,
   Till in glory we appear.

4. Worship, honour, power and blessing
   Thou art worthy to receive:
   Loudest praises, without ceasing,
   Right it is for us to give;
   Come, O mighty Holy Spirit,
   As our hearts and hands we raise,
   Help us sing our Saviour's merits,
   Help us sing Immanuel's praise.

John Bakewell (1721-1819)

150. Hail to the Lord's Anointed   *Ps 72; Is 9:7; Lk 1:32*

CRÜGER

Johann Crüger (1598-1662)

Majestically

1. Hail to the Lord's A - noint - ed, great Da - vid's great- er

Son! Hail in the time ap - point - ed, His

reign on earth be - gun! He comes to break op -

pres - sion, to set the cap - tive free, to

take a - way trans - gres - sion, and rule in e - qui - ty.

2. He comes, with succour speedy,
   To those who suffer wrong;
   To help the poor and needy,
   And bid the weak be strong;
   To give them songs for sighing,
   Their darkness turn to light,
   Whose souls, condemned and dying,
   Were precious in His sight.

3. He shall come down like showers
   Upon the fruitful earth;
   Love, joy, and hope, like flowers,
   Spring in His path to birth;
   Before Him, on the mountains,
   Shall peace, the herald, go;
   And righteousness, in fountains,
   From hill to valley flow.

4. Kings shall fall down before Him,
   And gold and incense bring;
   All nations shall adore Him,
   His praise all people sing;
   To Him shall prayer unceasing
   And daily vows ascend,
   His kingdom still increasing,
   A kingdom without end.

5. O'er every foe victorious,
   He on His throne shall rest;
   From age to age more glorious,
   All-blessing and all-blessed.
   The tide of time shall never
   His covenant remove;
   His name shall stand for ever,
   His changeless name of Love.

James Montgomery (1771-1854)

151. Hallelujah, for the Lord our God

Rev 19:6–7

(Hallelujah . . . our God reigns)

Dale Garratt

Triumphantly

Lyrics:
Hal - le - lu - jah, ___ for the Lord our God the Al - might - y ___ reigns. ___

Hal - le - reigns. ___ Let us re - joice ___

and be glad ___ and

———————— □ ▢ □ ————————

God has ascended amid shouts of
joy,
the Lord amid the sounding of
trumpets.
Sing praises to God, sing praises;
sing praises to our King, sing
praises.
For God is the King of all the earth;
sing to him a psalm of praise.

PSALM 47:5–7

———————— □ ▢ □ ————————

152.

Hallelujah my Father

Is 53:5; Rom 5:10

Tim Cullen

Worshipfully

Hal-le-lu -jah my_ Fa - ther_ for -giving us Your Son;

send-ing Him _ in - to _the world_to be gi -ven up for men.

Know - ing _ we would bruise Him _ and smite Him from_the earth. Halle-

lu - jah my_ Fa - ther, _ in His death _ is my birth; _ Halle-

lu - jah my_ Fa - ther, _ in His life _ is my life.

153. Hallelujah! sing to Jesus

Ps 45:6; Mt 28:20;
Jn 6:35, 58; 14:18;
Acts 1:9; Heb 1:8; 7:25;
Rev 5:9

Capo 5 (C)
HALLELUJAH

Samuel Sebastian Wesley (1810-76)

Majestically

1. Hal - le - lu - jah! sing to Je - sus; His the scep - tre, His the throne; Hal - le - lu - jah! His the tri - umph, His the vic - to - ry a - lone. Hark, the songs of ho - ly Zi - on thun - der like a migh - ty flood: 'Je - sus out of ev - 'ry_ na - tion hath re-deem'd us by His blood.'

Alternative tune: HYFRYDOL

2. Hallelujah! not as orphans
   Are we left in sorrow now;
   Hallelujah! He is near us,
   Faith believes, nor questions how.
   Though the clouds from sight received Him
   When the forty days were o'er,
   Shall our hearts forget His promise,
   'I am with you evermore'?

3. Hallelujah! Bread of heaven,
   Thou on earth our food, our stay;
   Hallelujah! here the sinful
   Flee to Thee from day to day.
   Intercessor, Friend of sinners,
   Earth's Redeemer, plead for me
   Where the songs of all the sinless
   Sweep across the crystal sea.

4. Hallelujah! sing to Jesus;
   His the sceptre, His the throne;
   Hallelujah! His the triumph,
   His the victory alone.
   Hark, the songs of holy Zion
   Thunder like a mighty flood:
   'Jesus out of every nation
   Hath redeemed us by His blood.'

William Chatterton Dix (1837-98)

154. Hark the glad sound

Is 61:1; Lk 4:18

BRISTOL

Ravenscroft's Psalter, 1621

1. Hark the glad sound! The Saviour comes, the
Saviour promised long; let ev - 'ry heart pre -
pare a throne, and ev - 'ry voice a song.

2. He comes the prisoners to release,
   In Satan's bondage held;
   The gates of brass before Him burst,
   The iron fetters yield.

3. He comes the broken heart to bind,
   The bleeding soul to cure,
   And with the treasures of His grace
   To enrich the humble poor.

4. Our glad hosannas, Prince of Peace,
   Thy welcome shall proclaim;
   And heaven's eternal arches ring
   With Thy belovèd name.

   Philip Doddridge (1702-51) altd.

———————— □ ☐ □ ————————

*I have been crucified with Christ and
I no longer live, but Christ lives in
me. The life I live in the body, I
live by faith in the Son of God, who
loved me and gave himself for me.*

GALATIANS 2:20

———————— □ ☐ □ ————————

155.   Hark! the herald-angels sing

Is 7:14; 9:6; Mal 4:2;
Lk 2:13–14; Jn 3:3;
Phil 2:7

Capo 3 (D)

MENDELSSOHN

F. Mendelssohn-Bartholdy (1809-47)
arranged W.H. Cummings (1831-1915)

1. Hark the he - rald an - gels sing ____
'Glo - ry to the new-born King! Peace on earth, and
mer - cy mild, ___ God and sin - ners re - con-ciled!'
Joy - ful, all ye na - tions rise, ___ join the tri - umph
of the skies, ___ with the an - ge - lic host pro - claim,

'Christ is___ born in Beth - le - hem.' Hark! the he - rald
an - gels sing 'Glo - ry ___ to the new - born King!'

2. Christ, by highest heaven adored,
   Christ, the everlasting Lord,
   Late in time behold Him come,
   Offspring of a virgin's womb.
   Veiled in flesh the Godhead see!
   Hail the incarnate Deity!
   Pleased as man with man to dwell,
   Jesus, our Immanuel,
   Hark! the herald angels sing:
   'Glory to the new-born King.'

3. Hail the heaven-born Prince of Peace!
   Hail, the Sun of righteousness!
   Light and life to all He brings,
   Risen with healing in His wings,
   Mild, He lays His glory by;
   Born that man no more may die;
   Born to raise the sons of earth;
   Born to give them second birth,
   Hark! the herald angels sing:
   'Glory to the new-born King.'

   Charles Wesley (1707-88) altd.

156.   Have Thine own way, Lord

Ps 51:7; 139:23;
Jer 18:6; Mt 8:3;
Mk 1:41; Lk 5:13; Rom 9:21;
2 Cor 3:18; Eph 5:18

Capo 3(D)
THINE OWN WAY, LORD!
Prayerfully

George C. Stebbins (1846-1945)

1. Have Thine own way, Lord, have Thine own
way; _____ Thou art the Pot - ter,
I am the clay. _____ Mould me and make
me, af - ter Thy will, _____ while I am
wait - ing yield - ed and still. _____

2. Have Thine own way, Lord,
   Have Thine own way;
   Search me and try me,
   Master today.
   Whiter than snow, Lord,
   Wash me just now,
   As in Thy presence
   Humbly I bow.

3. Have Thine own way, Lord,
   Have Thine own way;
   Wounded and weary,
   Help me, I pray.
   Power, all power,
   Surely is Thine;
   Touch me and heal me,
   Saviour divine.

4. Have Thine own way, Lord,
   Have Thine own way;
   Hold o'er my being
   Absolute sway.
   Fill with Thy Spirit
   Till all shall see
   Christ only, always,
   Living in me.

   A.A. Pollard (1862-1934)

157.

Healing grace

Is 53:5; 1 Pet 2:24

With a gentle 'country feel'

Dave Bilbrough

Chorus

Heal-ing grace, heal-ing grace, show me more of Your heal-ing grace. Fill my life a-new as I wor-ship You, for Your heal-ing grace to me. 1. My eyes have been o-pened and now I can see the love of the Fa-ther giv-en to me.

2. My Saviour, Deliverer,
   The reason I sing,
   To You I surrender,
   For You are my King.

158. Hear, O Lord, our cry
(Revive us again)

Ps 85:6

With strength

Graham Kendrick

1. Hear, O Lord, our cry: re-vive us, re-vive us a-gain.
For the sake of Your glo - ry, — re-vive us, — re-vive us a - gain. —
Lord, — hear our cry. —
Lord, — hear our cry. —

2. Hear, O Lord, our cry,
Revive us, revive us again.
For the sake of the children
Revive us, revive us again.
Lord, hear our cry.
Lord, hear our cry.

159.

Hear, O Shepherd
(Awaken Your power)

Ps 85:4; Jn 10:11, 14

David Fellingham

With feeling

Hear, O Shep-herd of Your peo - ple, let Your face shine and we will be saved. Shine forth, O God, in this pa - gan dark - ness. A - wak-en Your power, and come to re - store.

2. Let Your power fall upon us,
   Give strength unto the sons of Your right hand.
   We now hear the call to seek You,
   Awaken Your power, and come to restore.

———— □ ▢ □ ————

*The Lord is good and his love endures
for ever;
his faithfulness continues through
all generations.*

PSALM 100:5

———— □ ▢ □ ————

160. Heavenly Father, I appreciate You

Jn 14:16, 26;
15:26

author unknown
arranged Margaret Evans

2. Son of God, what a wonder You are,
   Son of God, what a wonder You are.
   You cleansed my soul from sin,
   You set the Holy Ghost within,
   Son of God, what a wonder You are.

3. Holy Ghost, what a comfort You are,
   Holy Ghost, what a comfort You are.
   You lead us, You guide us,
   You live right inside us,
   Holy Ghost, what a comfort You are.

161.

He came to earth
(King of kings)

Is 53:12; Mt 20:28; Mk 10:45;
1 Tim 6:15; Rev 17:14; 19:16

John Pantry

1. He came to earth, not to be served, but gave His life to be a ran - som for ma - ny; the Son of God, the Son of man, He shared our pain and

2. And so I stand, a broken soul,
   To see the pain that I have brought to Jesus;
   And yet each heart will be consoled,
   To be made new, the joy of all believers.

3. And from now on, through all my days,
   I vow to live each moment here for Jesus;
   Not looking back, but giving praise
   For all my Lord has done for this believer.

162.
He gave me beauty
(Beauty for ashes)

Is 61:3

Capo 3 (D)

Robert Whitney Manzano

He gave me beau-ty for ashes, — the oil of joy for mourning, — the gar-ment of praise for the spi-rit of heav-i-ness. That we might be trees of right-eous-ness, — the plant-ing of the Lord, that He might be glor-i-fied. _____

163.

He holds the key

Jn 8:12; 14:6; Rev 1:18

Joan Parsons

2. He is the Rock ever standing,
No man could break Him down.
He is the Truth everlasting:

3. He is a Light in the darkness,
All men shall see His face.
He breaks all chains to redeem us:

4. All power to Him who is mighty,
All praise to Him who is God.
All glory now and for ever:

164.

He is exalted

Eph 1:20; Phil 2:9

Twila Paris

He is ex-alt-ed, the King is ex-alt-ed on high, I will praise Him.

He is ex-alt-ed, for-ev-er ex-alt-ed and I will praise His name. He is the Lord, for-ev-er His truth shall reign. Heav-en and earth re-joice in His ho-ly name. He is ex-alt-ed, the King is ex-alt-ed on high.

165.

He is Lord

Phil 2:10–11

Author unknown

He is Lord, He is Lord, He is ri-sen from the dead and He is Lord. Ev-'ry

knee shall bow, ev-'ry tongue con-fess that Je-sus Christ is Lord.

166.
He is our peace

Eph 2:14; 1 Pet 5:7

Kandela Groves

Capo 4(C)

Tenderly

He is our peace, who has bro-ken down ev-ery wall;

He is our peace, ____ He is our peace.

1st time

2nd time

peace. ____ Cast all your cares on Him, ____ for He cares for

you; ____ He is our peace, ____ He is our

1st time / *2nd time* / *Last time*

peace. ____ Cast all your peace. ____

─────────── □ ▢ □ ───────────

*God raised us up with Christ and
seated us with him in the heavenly
realms in Christ Jesus, in order that
in the coming ages he might show the
incomparable riches of his grace
expressed in his kindness to us in
Christ Jesus.*

EPHESIANS 2:6–7

─────────── □ ▢ □ ───────────

167.

Here I am

Josh 24:15; Is 6:8; Mt 5:13–14; 9:37;
Lk 10:2; Jn 4:35

Capo 4 (C)

Chris Bowater

Thoughtfully

Here I am, whol-ly a-vail - a - ble. As for me, I will serve the Lord. (1. The) Lord. fields are white un - to

har - vest _____ but O, the lab'-rers are so

few, so Lord I give my-self to help the

D.C. al Fine

reap - ing, to ga-ther pre-cious souls un-to You.

2. The time is right in the nation
   For works of power and authority;
   God's looking for a people who are willing
   To be counted in His glorious victory.

3. As salt are we ready to savour,
   In darkness are.we ready to be light,
   God's seeking out a very special people
   To manifest His truth and His might.

168.

Here is love

Rom 5:5; 1 Tim 2:5

Capo 1 (G)

William Rees
Robert Lowry 1826-99

Dim Ond Iesu

1. Here is love vast as the o - cean, lov-ing-kind-ness as the flood, when the
Prince of life, our ran - som shed for us His pre-cious blood. Who His
love will not re-mem-ber?_ Who can cease to sing His praise? He can
ne - ver be for - got - ten_through - out heaven's e - ter - nal days.

2. On the Mount of Crucifixion
   Fountains opened deep and wide;
   Through the floodgates of God's mercy
   Flowed a vast and gracious tide.
   Grace and love, like mighty rivers,
   Poured incessant from above,
   And heaven's peace and perfect justice
   Kissed a guilty world in love.

169.

Here we are
(Family song)

Rom 8:15; Gal 4:6

Capo 4(C)

Steve Hampton

Here we are, — {gath-er'd / sing-ing} to-geth-er as a fam-i-ly; — bound as one, lift-ing up _ our voi-ces to the King of kings. {We cry: / We sing:} 'Ab-ba, Fa-ther, {wor-thy / ho-ly} is your name. Ab-ba, Fa-ther, {wor-thy / ho-ly} is Your _ name.'

170.

He shall reign

1 Tim 6:15; Rev 17:14; 19:16

John Watson/Stuart Townend

Capo 2 (D)

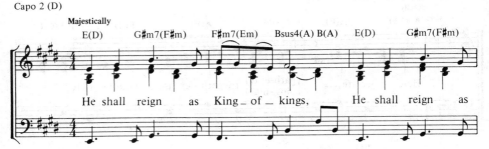

He shall reign as King of kings, He shall reign as

Lord of lords; Messiah God, the living Word, hal-

le - lu - jah, hal - le - lu - jah, let earth de-clare Him

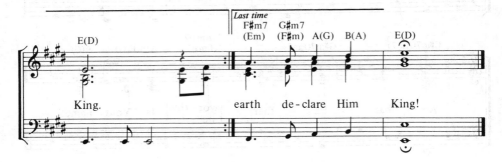

King. earth de-clare Him King!

———— □ ☐ □ ————

Sing to the Lord a new song;
   sing to the Lord, all the earth.
Sing to the Lord, praise his name;
   proclaim his salvation day after
      day.
Declare his glory among the nations,
   his marvellous deeds among all
      peoples.

PSALM 96:1–3

———— □ ☐ □ ————

171.

He that is in us

Phil 2:9; 1 Jn 4:4; Rev 17:14

Capo 2 (C)

Graham Kendrick

2. All the powers of death and hell and sin
Lie crushed beneath His feet.
Jesus owns the Name above all names,
Crowned with honour and majesty.

172.
He walked where I walk
(God with us)

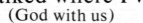

Is 7:14; Mt 1:23; Heb 4:15

Graham Kendrick

Quite quick, with a steady rhythm

(3 times)

Csus2 C Csus2   C   Csus2 C Csus2   C

Csus2 C Csus2   C   G

Verse C   Csus2   C   Csus2   C

(Leader)
1. { He walked where I ___ walk,   (All) (He walked where I ___ walk.)
   { He knows my frail - ty,   (He knows my frail - ty.)

F/C   C   Am

(Leader)
He stood where I ___ stand, (All) (He stood where I ___ stand,)
shared my hu - ma - ni - ty,   (shared my hu - ma - ni - ty,)

C   Csus2   C   Csus2   C

(Leader)
He felt what I ___ feel, (All) (He felt what I ___ feel,)
tempt - ed in ev - 'ry way,   (tempt - ed in ev - 'ry way,)

(Leader) He un-der-stands. (All) (He un-der-stands.)
yet with-out sin. (Yet with-out sin.)

Chorus

(All) God ___ with us, ___ so close to us, ___
___ God ___ with us, ___ Im-man-u-el! ___

To next verse D.C.

(Leader)   (All)
2. One of a hated race,   (echo)
   Stung by the prejudice,   (echo)
   Suff'ring injustice,   (echo)
   Yet He forgives.   (echo)
   Wept for my wasted years,   (echo)
   Paid for my wickedness,   (echo)
   He died in my place,   (echo)
   That I might live.   (echo)

173.

He was pierced
(Like a lamb)

Is 53:5–8

Maggi Dawn

1. He was pierced for our trans - gres-sions, ____ and bruised for our in-i - qui - ties; and to bring us peace He was pun - ished, ____ and by His stripes we are healed.

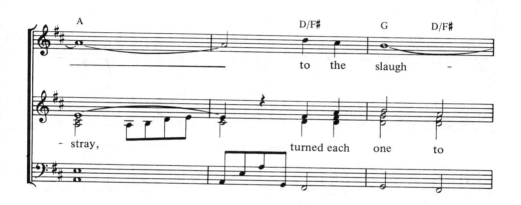

2. He was led like a lamb to the slaughter,
   Although He was innocent of crime;
   And cut off from the land of the living,
   He paid for the guilt that was mine.

174.
He who would valiant be

Heb 11:13; 1 Pet 2:11

Capo 1 (D)
MONKS GATE

English Traditional Melody
arranged by Ralph Vaughan Williams (1872-1958)

1. He ___ who would va - li -ant be 'gainst all di - sas - ter, ___ let ___ him in con - stan - cy fol - low the Mas - ter. ___ There's no dis - cour - age - ment shall make him once re - lent his first a - vowed in - tent to be a pil - grim.

2. Who so beset him round
   With dismal stories,
   Do but themselves confound —
   His strength the more is.
   No foes shall stay his might,
   Though he with giants fight;
   He will make good his right
   To be a pilgrim.

3. Since, Lord, Thou dost defend
   Us with Thy Spirit,
   We know we at the end
   Shall life inherit.
   Then fancies flee away!
   I'll fear not what men say,
   I'll labour night and day
   To be a pilgrim.

John Bunyan (1628-88) and others

175.

Higher, higher

Jn 3:14; 1 Pet 5:7

Capo 3 (D)

Author unknown
Arr. Stuart Townend

176.

His name is higher

Is 9:6; Phil 2:9

author unknown
arranged Margaret Evans

His name is high - er ___ than an-y oth - er, ___ His name is Je - sus, ___ His name is Lord. ___ His name is Won - der-ful, ___ His name is Coun - sell- or, ___ His name is Prince of Peace, ___ the might-y God. ___ His name is high - er ___ than an-y oth - er ___ His name is Je - sus, ___ His name is Lord. ___

177.
His name is Wonderful

Is 9:6; Jn 10:11

Capo 3 (D)

Audrey Meir

———— □ ☐ □ ————

God exalted him to the highest place
and gave him the name that is
above every name,
that at the name of Jesus every knee
should bow,
in heaven and on earth and under
the earth,
and every tongue confess that Jesus
Christ is Lord,
to the glory of God the Father.

PHILIPPIANS 2:9–11

———— □ ☐ □ ————

178.

His voice is the sea
(Jesus is Lord)

Jn 10:11, 14; Phil 2:10–11;
Rev 1:14–16

Bill Anderson

Capo 3 (D)

With breadth

1. His voice is the sea and the sound-ing of the trum-pets; and the call-ing of the Shep-herd is so sweet. His face is the sun, bright-er than the morn-ing; and all cre-a-tion bows down at His feet.

Chorus

Je - sus is Lord, and all the earth a -

2. His mouth is a sword
   That rules o'er the nations,
   And His sword will draw His children to His side.
   His eyes are a fire
   That burns throughout the kingdom,
   And the burning purifies the Master's bride.

179.

Hold me Lord

Eph 5:18

Danny Daniels

Al – le – lu – ia, _____ sing-ing

Al – le – lu – ia, _____ sing-ing Al – le – lu –

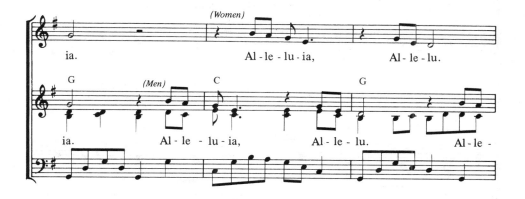

ia.   *(Women)* Al - le -lu - ia,   Al - le - lu.

ia.   *(Men)* Al - le -lu - ia,   Al - le - lu.   Al - le –

Al - le -lu -ia,   *1st time* Al - le -lu.   *2nd time* Al - le -lu.

lu – ia,   Al - le -lu.   – lu.

180.

Holiness unto the Lord

Ex 28:36; 39:30

Danny Daniels

Quite slow, with strength

Ho - li - ness, un - to the Lord,

un - to the King.

Ho - li - ness, un - to Your

name I will sing.

Ho - li -ness___ un - to Je - sus,

ho - li -ness _ un - to You, _ Lord. _____

Ho - li - ness _ un - to Je - sus,

ho - li -ness _ un -to You, Lord. ___

2. I love You,
   I love Your ways, I love Your name.
   I love You,
   And all my days I'll proclaim:

181.

Holy, holy, holy
(Isaiah 6)

Is 6:3

Andy Park

Slowly

Verse G   D   C

Ho - ly, ho - ly, ho - ly

Am   Am/G   3   D/F#   D

is the Lord God __ Al - might - y.

G   D   C

Ho - ly, ho - ly, ho - ly

Am   Fmaj7   3   D/F#   D   C

is the Lord God __ Al - might - y. All the

Chorus
G   Fmaj7   Em7   G/D   D   C

an - gels cry out ho - ly; all the

an - gels ex - alt Your ___ name, cry - ing ho - ly, ho - ly, ho - ly, ho - ly is the Lord. ___

2. Holy, holy, holy is the Lord God Almighty.
    Holy, holy, holy is the Lord God Almighty.
    All Your people cry out holy;
    All Your people exalt Your name,
    Crying holy, holy, holy,
    Holy is the Lord.

3. Glory, glory, glory to the Lord God Almighty.
    Glory, glory, glory to the Lord God Almighty.
    The whole earth is filled with Your glory;
    The whole earth will exalt Your name,
    Crying holy, holy, holy,
    Holy is the Lord.

182. Holy, holy, holy is the Lord

Rev 4:8

Author unknown
Arr. Margaret Evans

1. Ho - ly, ho - ly, ho - ly is the Lord, ho - ly is the Lord God Al - migh - ty. - ty, who was and is and is — to come. Ho - ly, ho - ly, ho - ly is the Lord.

2. Worthy, worthy, worthy is . . . (*etc*).

3. Jesus, Jesus, Jesus is . . . (*etc*).

4. Glory, glory, glory to . . . (*etc*).

Sing to the Lord a new song;
* sing to the Lord, all the earth.*
Sing to the Lord, praise his name;
* proclaim his salvation day after*
*   day.*
Declare his glory among the nations,
* his marvellous deeds among all*
*   peoples.*

PSALM 96:1–3

183. Holy, holy, holy, Lord God Almighty!

Capo 2 (C)
NICAEA

(First tune)

Is 6:2–3; Rev 4:4, 6, 8, 10

John Bacchus Dykes (1823-76)

With strength

1. Ho - ly, ho - ly, ho - ly, Lord God Al - migh - ty! Ear - ly in the morn - ing our song shall rise to Thee: ho - ly, ho - ly, ho - ly, mer - ci - ful and migh - ty, God in three Per - sons, bless - èd Tri - ni - ty!

2. Holy, holy, holy! all the saints adore Thee,
   Casting down their golden crowns
   Around the glassy sea;
   Cherubim and seraphim falling down before Thee,
   Who were, and are, and evermore shall be.

3. Holy, holy, holy! though the darkness hide Thee,
   Though the eye of sinful man
   Thy glory may not see;
   Only Thou art holy, there is none beside Thee
   Perfect in power, in love and purity.

4. Holy, holy, holy, Lord God Almighty!
   All Thy works shall praise Thy name,
   In earth, and sky, and sea;
   Holy, holy, holy, merciful and mighty,
   God in three Persons, blessèd Trinity!

   Reginald Heber (1783-1826)

Holy, holy, holy, Lord God Almighty!
(Second tune)

TERSANCTUS

Triumphantly

Gordon Frederick James Hartless (1913-)

1. Ho - ly, ho - ly, ho - ly, Lord God Al - migh - ty! Ear - ly in the morn - ing our song shall rise to Thee: ho - ly, ho - ly, ho - ly, mer - ci - ful and migh - ty, God in three Per - sons, bless - èd Tri - ni - ty! ty!

To repeat

Last time

2. Holy, holy, holy! all the saints adore Thee,
   Casting down their golden crowns
   Around the glassy sea;
   Cherubim and seraphim falling down before Thee,
   Who were, and are, and evermore shall be.

3. Holy, holy, holy! though the darkness hide Thee,
   Though the eye of sinful man
   Thy glory may not see;
   Only Thou art holy, there is none beside Thee
   Perfect in power, in love and purity.

4. Holy, holy, holy, Lord God Almighty!
   All Thy works shall praise Thy name,
   In earth, and sky, and sea;
   Holy, holy, holy, merciful and mighty,
   God in three Persons, blessèd Trinity!

Reginald Heber (1783-1826)

184.

Holy, holy, holy, Lord

Is 6:3

Capo 3 (D)

Music: Peter Scholtes

185.

Holy is the Lord

186.
Holy One

Capo 3 (D)

Chris Bowater

Ho - ly One, _ Ho - ly One, _ bless - ed be _ the Ho - ly One, _ Al - migh - ty e - ver liv - ing God, _____ I wor - ship on - ly You. You, Ho - ly One. _____

187. Holy Spirit, lead me to my Father

Ps 91:1–2;
Jn 14:16, 20

Alun Leppitt

Ho-ly Spi-rit, lead me to my Fa-ther, to bow be-fore Him, and wor-ship at His throne, _____ for He's my re-fuge, my strength and de-liv-er-er, I will dwell _ in the sha-dow of Al-might-y _ God. _____

188. Holy Spirit, we welcome You

Jn 14:17; Acts 2:2–3

Chris Bowater

With expression

1. Ho - ly Spi - rit, __ we wel-come You. __

Ho - ly Spi - rit, __ we

wel - come You. __ Move a - mong

__ us __ with ho - ly fire, __

as we lay a - side __ all earth - ly de - sires, __

hands　　reach out, ＿　　　and our hearts　a - spire. ＿　　　Ho - ly

Spi - rit, ＿＿＿＿　　　Ho - ly Spi - rit, ＿＿＿＿　　　Ho - ly

Spi - rit, ＿＿＿＿　　we wel-come You. ＿＿＿＿

2. Holy Spirit, we welcome You.
    Holy Spirit, we welcome You.
    Let the breeze of Your presence blow,
    That Your children here might truly know
    How to move in the Spirit's flow.
    Holy Spirit, Holy Spirit,
    Holy Spirit, we welcome You.

3. Holy Spirit, we welcome You.
    Holy Spirit, we welcome You.
    Please accomplish in me today
    Some new work of loving grace, I pray;
    Unreservedly have Your way.
    Holy Spirit, Holy Spirit,
    Holy Spirit, we welcome You.

189.

Hosanna

Mt 21:9, 15; Mk 11:9–10; Lk 19:38; Jn 12:13

Carl Tuttle

1. Ho -san - na, Ho - san - na, Ho - san - na in the high - est! Ho - san - na, Ho - san - na, Ho - san -na in the high - est!
2. Glo - ry, glo - ry, glo - ry to the King of kings! Glo - ry, glo - ry, glo -ry to the King of kings!

Lord, we lift up Your name, with hearts full of praise; be ex - alt-ed, O — Lord, my God! Ho - san-na in the high - est! Glo-ry to the King of kings!

190.

How I love You
(You are the One)

Jn 14:6

Keith & Melody Green

1. I was so lost
   But You showed the way,
   'Cause You are the Way.
   I was so lost
   But You showed the way to me!

2. I was lied to
   But You told the truth,
   'Cause You are the Truth.
   I was lied to
   But You showed the truth to me!

3. I was dying
   But You gave me life,
   'Cause You are the Life.
   I was dying
   And You gave Your life for me!

   How I love You,
   You are the One,
   You are the One.
   How I love You,
   You are the One,
   God's risen Son.
   You are the One for me!

4. Hallelujah!
   You are the One,
   You are the One.
   Hallelujah!
   You are the One for me!

191. How lovely is Thy dwelling place

Ps 84:1–2, 10–11

Author unknown
Arr. Stuart Townend

With feeling

How love-ly is Thy dwell-ing place, O Lord of hosts. My soul longs and yearns _ for Your courts, _____ and my heart and flesh sing for joy to the liv-ing God. _____ One day in Your pre-sence is far bet-ter to me than gold, or to

192. How lovely on the mountains
(Our God reigns)

Is 52:7–10

Leonard E. Smith Jnr.

Capo 1 (A)

Triumphantly with pace

1. How love-ly on the moun-tains are the feet of Him
Who brings good news, _____ good news,
Pro-claim-ing peace, an-nounc-ing news of hap-pi-ness, _____
[orig. version] An-nounc-ing peace, pro-claim-ing news of hap-pi-ness,
Our God reigns _____ Our God reigns. _____
[orig. version] Saying to Zi-on: Your God reigns.
Our God reigns _____ Our God reigns _____
[orig. version] Your God reigns Your God reigns

Eb(D)   F(E)   Bb(A)

Our God reigns _____ Our God reigns. _____

[orig. version] Your God reigns Your God reigns.

Popular Version.

2.   You watchmen lift your voices joyfully as one,
     Shout for your King, your King.
     See eye to eye the Lord restoring Zion:
     Your God reigns, your God reigns!

3.   Waste places of Jerusalem break forth with joy,
     We are redeemed, redeemed.
     The Lord has saved and comforted His people:
     Your God reigns, your God reigns!

4.   Ends of the earth, see the salvation of your God,
     Jesus is Lord, is Lord.
     Before the nations He has bared His holy arm:
     Your God reigns, your God reigns!

Original Version.

2.   He had no stately form, He had no majesty,
     That we should be — drawn to Him.
     He was despised and we took no account of Him,
     Yet now He reigns — with the Most High.
          Chorus: Now He reigns   *(three times)*
                    With the Most High!

3.   It was our sin and guilt that bruised and wounded Him,
     It was our sin — that brought Him down.
     When we like sheep had gone astray, our Shepherd came
     And on His shoulders — bore our shame.
          Chorus: On His shoulders *(three times)*
                    He bore our shame.

4.   Meek as a lamb that's led out to the slaughterhouse,
     Dumb as a sheep — before its shearer,
     His life ran down upon the ground like pouring rain,
     That we might be — born again.
          Chorus: That we might be *(three times)*
                    Born again.

5.   Out from the tomb He came with grace and majesty,
     He is alive — He is alive.
     God loves us so — see here His hands, His feet, His side,
     Yes, we know — He is alive.
          Chorus: He is alive! *(four times)*

6.   How lovely on the mountains are the feet of Him
     Who brings good news, good news,
     Announcing peace, proclaiming news of happiness:
     Our God reigns, our God reigns.
          Chorus: Our God reigns! *(four times)*

193.

How precious, O Lord

Ps 36:7–9

Capo 3 (C)

Phil Rogers

Brightly

How pre - cious, O Lord, is Your un - fail - ing

love; we find re - fuge in the shadow — of Your

wings. _____ We feast, Lord Je - sus, — on the a -

bund - ance of Your house and drink from Your

194. How sweet the name of Jesus sounds

Ex 16:15; Is 65:19; Joel 2:32; Jn 6:58;
Acts 4:12; Rom 10:13; Heb 12:2

ST PETER

Gently

Alexander Robert Reinagle (1799-1877)

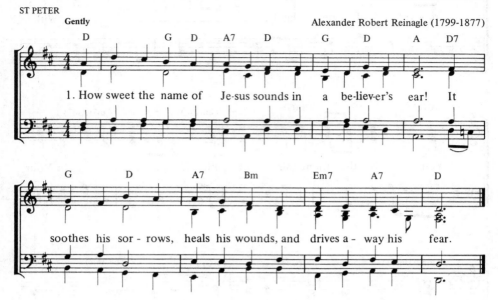

1. How sweet the name of Je-sus sounds in a be-liev-er's ear! It
soothes his sor - rows, heals his wounds, and drives a - way his fear.

2. It makes the wounded spirit whole,
   And calms the troubled breast;
   'Tis manna to the hungry soul,
   And to the weary, rest.

3. Dear name, the rock on which I build,
   My shield and hiding place,
   My never-failing treasury, filled
   With boundless stores of grace!

4. Jesus! My Shepherd, Saviour, Friend,
   My Prophet, Priest and King,
   My Lord, my Life, my Way, my End,
   Accept the praise I bring.

5. Weak is the effort of my heart,
   And cold my warmest thought;
   But when I see Thee as Thou art,
   I'll praise Thee as I ought.

6. Till then I would Thy love proclaim
   With every fleeting breath;
   And may the music of Thy name
   Refresh my soul in death.

John Newton (1725-1807)

195.
How You bless our lives

196.

I am a lighthouse

Mt 5:14; 25:4

Graham Kendrick

Capo 4(C)

I am a light-house, a shi-ning and bright-house out in the waves of a stor-my sea. The oil of the Spi - rit keeps my lamp burn - ing; Je -sus, my Lord, is the light in me. And when peo-ple see _ the good things that I do, _ they'll give prai-ses to God _ who has

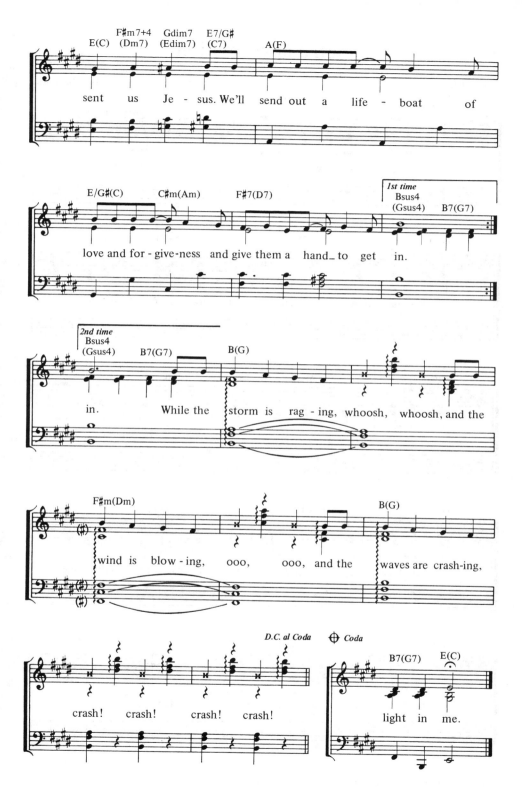

197.

I am a new creation

Rom 5:2; 8:1;
2 Cor 5:17; 1 Pet 1:8

Dave Bilbrough

Capo 3 (C)

With drive

I am — a new — cre-a-tion, no more — in con-dem - na - tion, here in — the grace — of God — I stand.

My heart — is ov-er flow - ing, my love — just keeps — on grow - ing,

here in — the grace — of God — I stand. —

198.

I am a wounded soldier
(Wounded soldier)

Is 53:5; Eph 6:11; 1 Pet 2:24

Danny Daniels

I am a woun-ded sol-dier but I will not leave the fight be-cause the Great Phy-si-cian is heal-in' me. So I'm stand-in' in the bat - tle, __ in the arm- our of His light, __ be cause His migh-ty pow-er is real __ in' __ me. __ I am __

199.
I am not ashamed

Rom 8:31; Phil 2:10; 2 Tim 1:12

Capo 3 (D)

John Pantry

I am not a-shamed to be-long _____ to Je-sus;
I am not a-fraid _____ to stand my ground, _____ for there is no high-er cause _____ than work-ing for the King. _____ To Him I lift my praise, for I am not a-shamed. _____

Verse

1. Whom then shall I fear? ___ What shall daunt my spi - rit?
Sure and _ stead-fast, an-chored firm to the ___ cross,
stand - ing with my bro - thers, serv - ing God and oth - ers.
Though the _ world may rid - i - cule, I'll still say:

2. At the King's returning,
   Every soul will know Him,
   All creation shall bow down to His name;
   Brothers all, together
   Serving Him forever,
   He who gave His life for me, I will praise:

   (Last Chorus)
   We are not ashamed to belong to Jesus,
   We are not afraid to stand our ground,
   For there is no higher cause
   Than working for the King.
   To Him we lift our praise,
   For we are not ashamed.

200.

I am the bread of life

Mt 16:16; Mk 8:29; Lk 9:20;
Jn 6:35, 44, 51, 53; 11:25, 27

Capo 3 (G)

S. Suzanne Toolan

Triumphantly

1. I am the bread of life, _____ he who comes to Me shall not ___

hun-ger, he who be-lieves in Me shall not thirst.

No one can come to Me ___ un - less the __ Fa - ther

draw him, and I will raise _____ him up, and I will

raise _____ him up,   and I will   raise _____ him

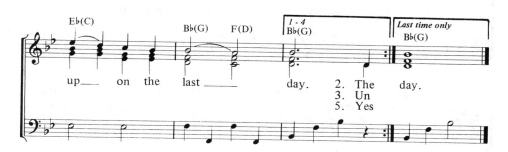

up __ on   the   last _____   day.   2. The   day.
                                           3. Un
                                           5. Yes

2. The bread that I will give
    Is My flesh for the life of the world,
    And he who eats of this bread,
    He shall live for ever,
    He shall live for ever.

3. Unless you eat
    Of the flesh of the Son of man
    And drink of His blood,
    And drink of His blood,
    You shall not have life within you.

4. I am the resurrection,
    I am the life,
    He who believes in Me,
    Even if he die,
    He shall live for ever.

5. Yes Lord we believe
    That You are the Christ,
    The Son of God
    Who has come
    Into the world.

201. I am the God that healeth thee

Ex 15:26

Capo 4(C)

Don Moen

1. I am the God that heal - eth thee, I am the Lord, your heal - er. I sent My word and healed your di - sease, I am the Lord, your heal - er.

2. You are the God that healeth me,
   You are the Lord, my healer.
   You sent Your word and healed my disease,
   You are the Lord my healer.

202. I am trusting Thee, Lord Jesus

Is 30:21; Jn 14:1; Heb 10:22

BULLINGER
Flowing

Ethelbert William Bullinger (1837-1913)

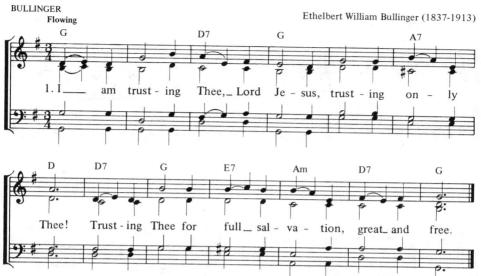

1. I____ am trust-ing Thee,_ Lord Je-sus, trust-ing on-ly Thee! Trust-ing Thee for full_ sal-va-tion, great_ and free.

2. I am trusting Thee for pardon,
   At Thy feet I bow;
   For Thy grace and tender mercy,
   Trusting now.

3. I am trusting Thee for cleansing
   In the crimson flood;
   Trusting Thee to make me holy,
   By Thy blood.

4. I am trusting Thee for power,
   Thine can never fail;
   Words which Thou Thyself shalt give me
   Must prevail.

5. I am trusting Thee to guide me,
   Thou alone shalt lead;
   Every day and hour supplying
   All my need.

6. I am trusting Thee, Lord Jesus;
   Never let me fall;
   I am trusting Thee for ever,
   And for all.

Frances Ridley Havergal (1836-79)

203.

I believe in Jesus

Mt 16:16; 18:20; Jn 14:1

With conviction

Marc Nelson

I ____ be-lieve in { Je - sus; *(v.1)* / You, ____ Lord; }

I be-lieve { He is / You are } the Son of God.

I be-lieve { He / You } died and rose a-gain, ____

I be-lieve { He / You } paid for us all.

(Women — not 1st time) I be-lieve that You're here, _ stand-ing in our

(Men) And I be-lieve { He's } { You're } here now, _ stand-ing in our

midst. With the pow - er to

midst. Here with the pow - er to heal _ now, _

To repeat *Last time only*

heal, _ and the grace to for - give. - give.

and the grace to for - give. - give.

204. I can almost see
(Spirit of God)

Eph 5:18

Peter & Hanneke Jacobs

I can al - most _ see Your _
ho - li - ness, as I look a -
round this place, _____ with my
hands stretched _ out to re -
ceive Your _ love, I can

205.

I cannot tell

Is 61:1; Lk 2:7; 4:18; Jn 10:11, 14;
1 Jn 4:14; Rev 11:15

LONDONDERRY AIR
With feeling

Traditional Irish melody
Arranged by John Barnard (1949 -)

1. I can-not tell why He, whom an-gels wor - ship,_ should set His love up-on the sons of men,_ or why, as Shep-herd, He should seek the wan - d'rers,_ to bring them back, they know not how or when._ But this I know, that He was born of Ma - ry,_ when Beth-l'hem's man - ger was His on-ly home,_ and that He liv'd at Naz-ar-eth and

la - bour'd,__ and so the Sa-viour, Sa-viour of the world, is come.__

2. I cannot tell how silently He suffered,
   As with His peace He graced this place of tears,
   Or how His heart upon the cross was broken,
   The crown of pain to three-and-thirty years.
   But this I know, He heals the broken-hearted,
   And stays our sin, and calms our lurking fear,
   And lifts the burden from the heavy-laden,
   For yet the Saviour, Saviour of the world, is here.

3. I cannot tell how He will win the nations,
   How He will claim His earthly heritage,
   How satisfy the needs and aspirations
   Of East and West, of sinner and of sage
   But this I know, all flesh shall see His glory,
   And He shall reap the harvest He has sown,
   And some glad day His sun shall shine in splendour,
   When He the Saviour, Saviour of the world, is known.

4. I cannot tell how all the lands shall worship,
   When, at His bidding, every storm is stilled,
   Or who can say how great the jubilation
   When all the hearts of men with love are filled.
   But this I know, the skies will thrill with rapture,
   And myriad, myriad human voices sing,
   And earth to heaven, and heaven to earth, will answer:
   'At last the Saviour, Saviour of the world, is King!'

William Young Fullerton (1857-1932)

206. I delight greatly in the Lord

Is 61:10

Capo 5 (C)

Chris Bowater

With swing

I de-light greatly in the Lord, my soul re-joices in my God. __ I delight greatly in the Lord, my soul re-joices in my God. For He has clothed me with garments of sal-va-tion and arrayed me in a robe of righteousness; He has clothed me with garments of sal-va-tion and a-rrayed me in a robe of righteousness.

*God was pleased to have all his
fulness dwell in him, and through him
to reconcile to himself all things,
whether things on earth or things in
heaven, by making peace through his
blood, shed on the cross.*

COLOSSIANS 1:19–20

207. I exalt You

Ex 15:11; Rev 15:3

Cecily Feldman

I ex-alt You, just and true are all Your ways. I ex-alt You, and glo-ri-fy Your name. I ex-alt You, just and true are all Your ways. I ex-alt You, and glo-ri-fy Your name. For You are re-splend-ent in Your ma-je-sty, there is no o-ther god be-

208.

If I were a butterfly
(The butterfly song)

Rom 8:17; Gal 4:7

Brian Howard

1. If I were a but-ter-fly,— I'd thank You, Lord, for giv-ing me wings. And if I were a ro-bin in a tree, I'd thank You, Lord, that I could sing. And if I were a fish in the sea,— I'd wig-gle my tail — and I'd gig-gle with glee; but I just thank You, Fa-ther, for mak-ing me me. ____

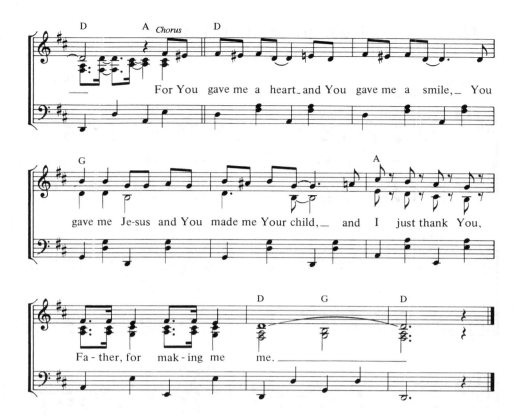

For You gave me a heart_ and You gave me a smile,_ You gave me Je-sus and You made me Your child,_ and I just thank You, Fa-ther, for mak-ing me me._____

2. If I were an elephant,
   I'd thank You, Lord, by raising my trunk.
   And if I were a kangaroo,
   You know I'd hop right up to You.
   And if I were an octopus,
   I'd thank You, Lord, for my fine looks;
   But I just thank You, Father, for making me me.

3. If I were a wiggly worm,
   I'd thank You, Lord, that I could squirm.
   And if I were a billy goat,
   I'd thank You, Lord, for my strong throat.
   And if I were a fuzzy wuzzy bear,
   I'd thank You, Lord, for my fuzzy wuzzy hair;
   But I just thank You, Father, for making me me.

209.
I get so excited, Lord
(I'm forgiven)

Eph 1:7

Capo 2 (G)

Mick Ray

1. I get so ex-cit-ed, Lord, ev-'ry time I re-a-lize ____ I'm for-gi-ven, ____ I'm for-gi-ven,

Je-sus Lord, You've done it all, You've paid the price. ____ I'm for-gi-ven, ____ I'm for-gi-ven.

Chorus

Hal-le-lu-jah, Lord, my heart just fills with praise, ____

2. Living in Your presence, Lord, is life itself.
I'm forgiven, I'm forgiven.
With the past behind, grace for today
and a hope to come.
I'm forgiven, I'm forgiven.

210.
I give You all the honour
(I worship You)

Is 61:1; Lk 4:18

Carl Tuttle

1. I give You all the hon-our and praise that's due Your name, for You are the King of Glo-ry, the Cre-a-tor of all things. And I wor-ship You, I give my life to You, I fall down on my

2. As Your Spirit moves upon me now
   You meet my deepest need,
   And I lift my hands up to Your throne,
   Your mercy, I've received.

3. You have broken chains that bound me,
   You've set this captive free,
   I will lift my voice to praise Your name
   For all eternity.

211.

I give You now
(Go)

Mt 28:19
Amy Rose

Capo 3 (D)

I give you now all I have, I

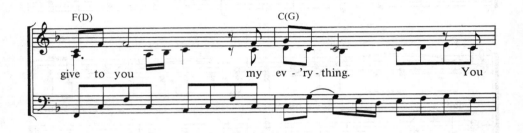

give to you my ev - 'ry - thing. You

have the pow'r in - side of you to

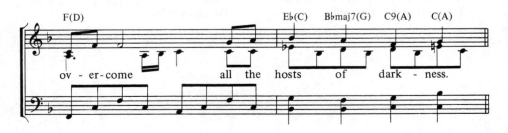

ov - er - come all the hosts of dark - ness.

212.

I have a destiny

Jn 15:16; Rom 8:29; Eph 1:11;
Phil 1:6

Mark Altrogge
Dedicated to Larry Tomczak

Verse

1. Long be-fore __ the a - ges You pre - des-tin'd me __ to walk in all __ the works __ You have pre- par'd for me. __ You've giv-en me __ a part to play in his - to - ry __ to help pre - pare __ a bride __ for e - ter - ni - ty. _____

2. I did not choose You but You have chosen me
    And appointed me for bearing fruit abundantly.
    I know You will complete the work begun in me,
    By the power of Your Spirit working mightily.

213.

I have found

Rom 12:1

Marc Nelson

1. I have found such joy in my sal - va - tion __

since I gave my heart to You.

I have found __ the rea - son __ I'm liv - ing, __

so in love, so near to

2. Oh my Lord, my life I'm giving,
   A living sacrifice to You.
   Oh my Lord, the reason I'm living
   Is to serve and worship You.

214.   I have made a covenant

Ps 89:1–8, 15, 20, 26, 28–29

Karen Barrie

Steadily

Verse

1. I have made a cov-e-nant _ with _ My cho-sen, _ giv-en My ser-vant My word. _ I have made Your name _ to last _ for ev-er, built to out-last _ all time. _

Chorus

I will cel-e-brate Your love for ev-er, Yah-weh, age on age _

2. Yahweh, that assembly of those who love You
   Applaud Your marvellous word.
   Who in the skies can compare with Yahweh?
   Who can rival Him?

3. Happy the people who learn to acclaim You,
   They rejoice in Your light.
   You are our glory and You are our courage,
   Our hope belongs to You.

4. I have revealed My chosen servant
   And He can rely on Me,
   Given Him My love to last for ever,
   He shall rise in My name.

5. He will call to Me, 'My Father, my God!'
   For I make Him My firstborn Son.
   I cannot take back My given promise,
   I've called Him to shine like the sun.

215.
I heard the voice of Jesus say

Mt 11:28; Jn 7:37; 8:12; Rev 21:23

Capo 3 (Em)
VOX DELECTI

John Bacchus Dykes (1823-76)

1. I heard the voice of Je - sus say: 'Come un - to Me and rest; lay down, thou wear - y one, lay down thy head up - on My breast.' I came to Je - sus as I was wear - y and worn and sad, I found in Him a rest - ing place, and He has made me glad.

2.   I heard the voice of Jesus say:
    'Behold, I freely give
    The living water, thirsty one,
    Stoop down and drink and live.'
    I came to Jesus, and I drank
    Of that life-giving stream;
    My thirst was quenched, my soul revived,
    And now I live in Him.

3.   I heard the voice of Jesus say:
    'I am this dark world's Light;
    Look unto Me, thy morn shall rise,
    And all thy day be bright.'
    I looked to Jesus, and I found
    In Him my Star, my Sun;
    And in that light of life I'll walk,
    Till travelling days are done.

Horatius Bonar (1808-89)

216.

I hear the sound of rustling

Ps 45:1; Ezek 33:2; 37:7

Ronnie Wilson

1. I hear the sound of rust-ling in the leaves of the trees, The Spi-rit of the Lord has come down on the earth. The Church that seemed in slum-ber has now ris-en from its knees And dry bones are res-pond-ing with the fruits of new birth. Oh this is now a time for dec-la-ra-tion, _____ The

word will go to all men ev-'ry - where, _____ The Church is here for heal-ing of the
na-tions, _____ Be - hold the day of Je-sus draw-ing near. _____ My
tongue will be the pen of a rea - dy wri-ter, _____ And what the Fa-ther gives to me I'll
sing, _____ I on - ly want to be His breath, _____
_____ I on - ly want to glo - ri - fy the King. _____

2. And all around the world the body waits expectantly,
The promise of the Father is now ready to fall.
The watchmen on the tower all exhort us to prepare
And the church responds — a people who will answer the call.
And this is not a phase which is passing,
It's the start of an age that is to come.
And where is the wise man and the scoffer?
Before the face of Jesus they are dumb.

3. A body now prepared by God and ready for war,
The prompting of the Spirit is our word of command.
We rise, a mighty army, at the bidding of the Lord,
The devils see and fear, for their time is at hand.
And children of the Lord hear our commission
That we should love and serve our God as one.
The Spirit won't be hindered by division
In the perfect work that Jesus has begun.

217.　I hear the sound of the army of the Lord

Josh 6:20

Dave Moody

With pace

I hear the sound __ of the ar-my of the Lord, __

I hear the sound __ of the ar-my of the Lord. __ It's the

sound of praise, it's the sound of __ war, __ the

ar-my of the Lord, __ the ar-my of the Lord, __ the army of the Lord __

__ is march-ing on. __

218.
I just want to praise You

Capo 5(C)

Arthur Tannous

219.

I just want to praise You
(Lord, I lift You high)

Eph 5:20; 1 Thess 5:18

Dave Bilbrough

Capo 2 (D)

220. I know not why God's wondrous grace

Jn 3:8; 16:8; Rom 8:28; Eph 2:8;
1 Thess 4:17; 2 Tim 1:12

I KNOW WHOM I HAVE BELIEVÈD

James McGranahan (1840-1907)

1. I know not why God's won-drous grace to me hath been made known; nor why un-wor-thy as I am He claim'd me for His own. But I know whom I have be-liev-ed; and am per-sua-ded that He is a-ble to keep that which I've com-mit-ted un-to Him a-gainst that day.

2. I know not how this saving faith
   To me He did impart;
   Or how believing in His word
   Wrought peace within my heart.

3. I know not how the Spirit moves,
   Convincing men of sin;
   Revealing Jesus through the Word,
   Creating faith in Him.

4. I know not what of good or ill
   May be reserved for me,
   Of weary ways or golden days
   Before His face I see.

5. I know not when my Lord may come;
   I know not how, nor where;
   If I shall pass the vale of death,
   Or meet Him in the air.

   D. W. Whittle (1840-1901)

———————— □ ▢ □ ————————

*The Lord is good and his love endures
for ever;
his faithfulness continues through
all generations.*

PSALM 100:5

———————— □ ▢ □ ————————

221.

I lift my eyes up

(Psalm 121)

Ps 121:1–2

Brian Doerksen

222.

I lift my hands
(Most of all)

Ps 63:4

Eddie Espinosa

1. I lift my hands, I raise my voice, I give my heart to You my Lord and I re-joice. There are man-y, man-y rea-sons why I do the things I do, O but most of all, I

2. I lift my hands,
    I raise my voice,
    I give my life to You my Lord,
    And I rejoice.
    There are many, many reasons why I do the things I do,
    O but most of all, I love You,
    Most of all I love You,
    Jesus, most of all I love You because You're You.

3. I lift my hands,
    I raise my voice,
    I give my love to You my Lord,
    And I rejoice.
    There are many, many reasons why I love You like I do,
    O but most of all, I love You,
    Most of all I love You,
    Jesus, most of all I love You because You're You.

223.
I lift my hands
(I will serve no foreign god)

Ex 3:14; 20:3; Deut 5:7; Ps 63:4

Capo 2(D)

Gently flowing

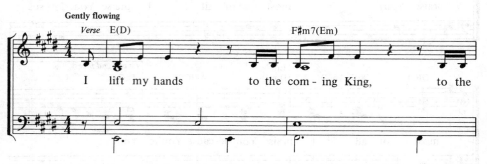

I lift my hands to the com - ing King, to the

great 'I AM', to You I sing, for

You're the One who reigns with - in my

heart. And I will serve no

224. I lift my voice

Mt 5:14; Gal 2:20

Dave Bilbrough

I lift my voice to praise Your name that through my life I might proclaim the praises of the one who reigns: Jesus, my Lord. Like a mighty flame that burns so bright, I am a

225.

I live

Rom 5:10

Rich Cook

Majestically

I live, I live be - cause He is ri - sen, I live, I live with pow'r ov-er sin. I live, I live be - cause He is ri-sen, I live, I live to wor - ship Him. Thank You Je - sus, thank You Je - sus, be - cause You're a - live, be - cause You're a - live, be -cause You're a - live I live.

226.
I love You, Lord

Capo 3 (D)

Laurie Klein

With feeling

I love You, Lord,___ and I lift my voice___ — to wor - ship You, O my soul re - joice. Take joy, my King,___ — in ___ what You hear,___ {may it / let me} be a sweet, sweet___ sound in Your ear.___

227.
I love You my Lord

Rom 1:17; 5:17; 8:2; 10:9;
16:20; 1 Jn 1:7

David Fellingham

Capo 1 (G)

I love You my Lord for giv-ing to me ___ Your great ___ sal-va-tion, set-ting me free from sin and death and the king-dom of Sa-tan's de-struc-tion. There's pow'r in the blood to cleanse all my sin, ___ I know I'm for-gi-ven. I'm reigning in

life. I'm liv-ing by faith, I'm now un-it-ed with

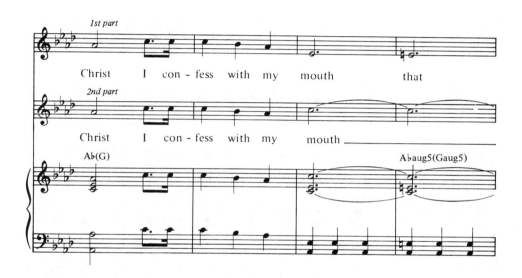

1st part

Christ I con-fess with my mouth that

2nd part

Christ I con-fess with my mouth ___

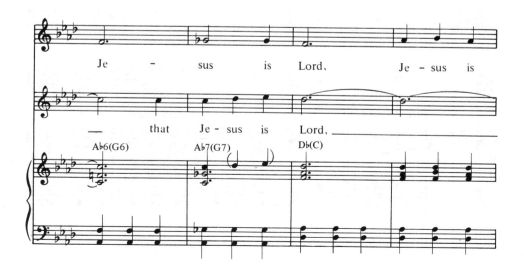

Je - sus is Lord, Je - sus is

___ that Je - sus is Lord, ___

228. I love you with the love of the Lord

1 Jn 4:11

James M. Gilbert

Flowing

I — love you with the love — of the Lord, ___
— yes I love you with the love — of the Lord. ___
— I can see in you the glo-ry of my
King, and I love you with the love — of the Lord. ___

229.

I'm accepted

Rom 8:1

Capo 4(C)

Rob Hayward

Worshipfully

I'm ac-cept-ed, I'm for-giv-en, I am fa-ther'd by the true and liv-ing God.

I'm ac-cept - ed, no con-demn-a - tion, I am lov'd by the true and liv-ing God. There's no guilt or fear as I draw near to the Sa-viour and Cre-a-tor of the world. There is joy and peace as I re-lease my wor-ship to You,__ O Lord.

─────── □ ▢ □ ───────

Fight the good fight of the faith.
Take hold of the eternal life to which
you were called when you made your
good confession in the presence of
many witnesses.

1 TIMOTHY 6:12

─────── □ ▢ □ ───────

230.

I'm gonna thank the Lord

Dave Bilbrough

1. I'm gon-na thank the Lord — He set me free, —
I'm gon-na thank the Lord — He set me free, _____ for my Sav-
iour He re-deemed me, for my Sav - iour res-cued me. — Yes,
I'm gon-na thank the Lord — He set me free. —

2. I'm gonna clap my hands and stamp my feet. . . *(etc)*.

3. I'm gonna sing and shout aloud for joy. . . *(etc)*.

4. I'm gonna raise my hands in victory. . . *(etc)*.

231.   I'm in love with You

Rom 8:16; Gal 4:5

Danny Daniels

232.
Immanuel

Is 7:14; 9:6; 53:3, 5, 7; Mt 1:23; 11:19; Lk 7:34

With feeling

Chorus

Graham Kendrick

Im-man-u-el, __ God is with __ us, __

Im-man-u-el, __ He is here.

Im-man-u-el, __ He is a-mong __ us,

Im-man-u-el, __ His king-dom is here.

Verse

1. Won-der-ful Coun-sell-or, they laughed at his

2. He was despised and rejected,
    A man of sorrows acquainted with grief.
    From Him we turned and hid our faces;
    He was despised, Him we did not esteem.

3. But He was wounded for our transgressions,
    He was bruised for our iniquities.
    On Him was the punishment that made us whole,
    And by His stripes we are healed.

4. He was oppressed, He was afflicted,
    And yet He opened not His mouth.
    Like a lamb that is led to the slaughter,
    Like a sheep before his shearers He did not speak.

Suggested order: Chorus, v.1, v.2, chorus, v.3, v.4, chorus.

233.

Immanuel, O Immanuel

Is 7:14; 53:5;
Mt 1:23; Heb 4:15

Graham Kendrick

— □ ▢ □ —

God has ascended amid shouts of
*   joy,*
* the Lord amid the sounding of*
*   trumpets.*
Sing praises to God, sing praises;
* sing praises to our King, sing*
*   praises.*
For God is the King of all the earth;
* sing to him a psalm of praise.*

PSALM 47:5–7

— □ ▢ □ —

234.   ·Immortal, invisible

Is 40:6–8; Dan 7:9;
1 Tim 1:17; 6:16

ST DENIO

Welsh hymn melody

With strength

1. Im - mor - tal, in - vis - i - ble,___ God on - ly

wise, in light in ac - cess - i - ble ___

hid from our eyes, most bless - èd, most

glor - ious the An - cient of Days, Al - migh - ty, vic -

tor - ious Thy ___ great name we praise.

2. Unresting, unhasting, and silent as light,
   Nor wanting, nor wasting, Thou rulest in might;
   Thy justice like mountains high soaring above
   Thy clouds which are fountains of goodness and love.

3. To all life Thou givest, to both great and small;
   In all life Thou livest, the true life of all;
   We blossom and flourish as leaves on the tree,
   And wither and perish; but naught changeth Thee.

4. Great Father of glory, pure Father of light,
   Thine angels adore Thee, all veiling their sight;
   All laud we would render: O help us to see
   'Tis only the splendour of light hideth Thee.

5. Immortal, invisible, God only wise,
   In light inaccessible hid from our eyes,
   Most blessèd, most glorious, the Ancient of Days,
   Almighty, victorious, Thy great name we praise.

Walter Chalmers Smith (1824-1908)

235.

I'm not alone

Mt 28:20

Diane Davis

I'm not a-lone for my Fa-ther is with me,
with me wher-ev - er I ____ go. ___
Speak-ing words of faith, of cour-age and of love, He's
with me, He loves me wher - ev - er I go.

1. Wak-ing in __ the morn - ing, __ get-ting read-y for school,

2. And when I find myself in a mess,
   I can trust in Him,
   Call on His name and watch Him move,
   He's with me, He loves me, wherever I go.

3. All of my life, everywhere that I go,
   I will walk with Him,
   Praising Him and blessing His name,
   He's with me, He loves me, wherever I go.

236.

I'm special

Jn 3:16; 15:15

Capo 2(C)

Graham Kendrick

With feeling

I'm spe-cial be-cause God has lov'd me, for He gave the best thing that He had to save me; His own Son Je-sus, cru - ci-fied to take the blame, for all the bad things I have done.

237.

In heavenly armour
(The battle belongs to the Lord)

1 Sam 17:47; Eph 6:11

Jamie Owens-Collins

With strength

Verse

1. In heaven-ly ar-mour we'll en-ter the land, — the bat-tle be-longs — to the Lord.

No wea-pon that's fash-ion'd a-gainst us will stand, — the bat-tle be-longs — to the Lord.

Chorus

And we sing glo-ry, hon-our,

power and strength to the Lord. ___ We sing glo - ry, hon - our, pow-er and strength to the Lord.

2. When the Power of Darkness
   comes in like a flood,
   The battle belongs to the Lord.
   He'll raise up a standard,
   the power of His blood,
   The battle belongs to the Lord.

3. When your enemy presses in hard,
   do not fear,
   The battle belongs to the Lord.
   Take courage my friend, your
   redemption is near,
   The battle belongs to the Lord.

238.

In heavenly love abiding

Ps 23:1–3

Capo 2(C)

PENLAN

David Jenkins (1849-1915)

1. In heav'n-ly love a - bid-ing, _____ no change my heart shall fear; _____ and safe is such con - fid - ing, _____ for no - thing chang - es here: _____ the storm may roar with - out me, _____ my heart may low be laid; _____

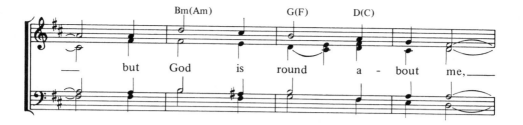

but God is round a - bout me,

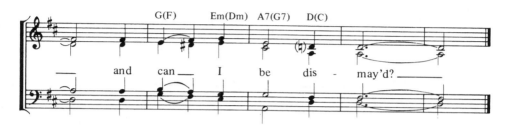

and can I be dis - may'd?

2. Wherever He may guide me,
   No want shall turn me back;
   My Shepherd is beside me,
   And nothing can I lack:
   His wisdom ever waketh,
   His sight is never dim;
   He knows the way He taketh,
   And I will walk with Him.

3. Green pastures are before me,
   Which yet I have not seen;
   Bright skies will soon be o'er me,
   Where darkest clouds have been;
   My hope I cannot measure,
   My path to life is free;
   My Saviour has my treasure,
   And He will walk with me.

   Anna Laetitia Waring (1820-1910)

───────── □ ▢ □ ─────────

But we see Jesus, who was made a
little lower than the angels, now
crowned with glory and honour because
he suffered death, so that by the
grace of God he might taste death for
everyone.

HEBREWS 2:9

───────── □ ▢ □ ─────────

239. In Him we live and move

Ps 100:1–2; Acts 17:28

Randy Speir

With energy

In Him we live and move and have our being, ___ in Him we live and move and have our being. ___ being. ___

Make a joy _ ful noise, sing un-to _ the Lord, tell Him of _ your love, dance be-fore Him. Make a joy-ful noise, sing un-to _ the Lord, tell Him of _ your love: Hal-le-lu - jah! In Him we

240.

In majesty He comes
(We shall rise)

Mt 21:7; Mk 11:7; Lk 19:35–36;
Jn 12:14; 1 Thess 4:17; 1 Tim 6:15;
Rev 17:14; 19:12–13, 16

David Fellingham

With strength

In ma - jes - ty He comes, ____

the Lamb who once was slain; ____

____ rid-ing in ma - jes - ty, faith-ful and true, _

eyes a - blaze, _ crowns on His head, _ robe dipped in

blood from His suff -'ring, He is the Word of God,

241. In moments like these

David Graham

In mo - ments like these, _____ I sing out a

song, I sing out a love song to

Je - sus. In mo - ments like

these, _____ I lift up my hands, I

242.

In my life, Lord
(Lord, be glorified)

Bob Kilpatrick

Capo 3 (C)

1. In my life, Lord, be glo-ri-fied, — be glo-ri-fied. — In my life, Lord,

be glo - ri-fied _ to-day. _

Last time only

2. In Your church, Lord,
    Be glorified, be glorified.
    In Your church, Lord,
    Be glorified today.

243.

In the bleak midwinter

Lk 2:7; Rev 20:11

Capo 3 (D)

Gustav Holst (1874-1934)

CRANHAM

1. In the bleak mid - win - ter, frost - y wind made moan; earth stood hard as ir - on, wa - ter like a stone. Snow had fall - en, snow on snow, snow __ on __ snow; in the bleak mid - win - ter, long __ a - go.

2.
Our God, heaven cannot hold Him,
Nor earth sustain,
Heaven and earth shall flee away
When He comes to reign.
In the bleak midwinter
A stable place sufficed
The Lord God Almighty,
Jesus Christ.

3.
Angels and archangels
May have gathered there,
Cherubim and seraphim
Thronged the air.
But His mother only,
In her maiden bliss,
Worshipped the Belovèd
With a kiss.

4.
What can I give Him,
Poor as I am?
If I were a shepherd,
I would bring a lamb.
If I were a wise man,
I would do my part;
Yet what can I give Him? —
Give my heart.

Christina Rossetti (1830-94)

— □ ▢ □ —

Let the name of the Lord be praised
both now and for evermore.
From the rising of the sun to the
place where it sets
the name of the Lord is to be
praised.

PSALM 113:2–3

— □ ▢ □ —

244.
In the presence of Your people
(Celebration song)

Ps 22:3, 22

Brent Chambers

2.   Lai, lai, lai-lai-lai-lai-lai-lai. . . (*etc*).

245.

In the tomb so cold
(Christ is risen!)

Mt 27:60; 28:6; Mk 15:46; 16:6;
Lk 23:53; 24:6; Jn 19:42; 21:14

Graham Kendrick

Triumphantly

1. In the tomb so cold they laid ___ Him, death its vic-tim claim'd. Pow'rs of hell, they

could not hold _ Him; back to life He came!

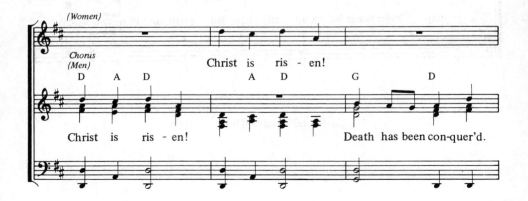

(Women)

Chorus
(Men)

Christ is ris - en!

Christ is ris - en! Death has been con-quer'd.

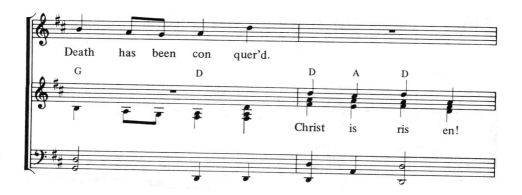

Death has been con quer'd.

Christ is ris en!

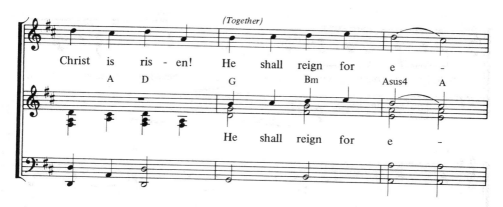

(Together)

Christ is ris - en! He shall reign for e -

He shall reign for e -

Last time

ver.

2. Hell had spent its fury on Him,
    Left Him crucified.
    Yet, by blood, He boldly conquered,
    Sin and death defied.

3. Now the fear of death is broken,
    Love has won the crown.
    Pris'ners of the darkness listen,
    Walls are tumbling down.

4. Raised from death to heaven ascending,
    Love's exalted King.
    Let His song of joy, unending,
    Through the nations ring!

(Chorus twice to end.)

246.

In through the veil

Ps 141:2; Heb 6:19; Rev 8:3

Bruce Clewett

In through the veil now we en-ter, bold-ly ap-proach-ing Your throne, bear-ing a sac-ri-fice of fra-grance sweet; the fruit of some seeds You have sown. From our lips we of-fer these prais-es, may You be bless'd as we sing. Lord we a-dore You, like in-cense be-fore You our

247.

In Thy presence

Ps 16:8–9, 11

Mike Kerry

In Thy presence there's full-ness of joy, full-ness of joy, full-ness of joy.

At Thy right hand are pleasures for ev-er, pleasures for ev-er-more. more.

I keep the Lord be - fore me, I shall not be moved. My heart is glad and my

soul re -joi-ces; I shall dwell in safe - ty. And in Thy presence there's

248.

I receive Your love

Rom 5:5

Paul Armstrong

2. I confess Your love,
   I confess Your love,
   From my heart I confess Your love, O Lord.
   I confess Your love
   By Your Spirit within me,
   I confess, I confess Your love.

249.

I see the Lord

Is 6:1, 3

author unknown
arranged Margaret Evans

With warmth

I see the Lord, — I see the Lord, — He is high and lift-ed up and His train fills the tem-ple, — He is high and lift-ed up — and His train fills the tem-ple. — The an-gels cry, Ho-ly, — the an-gels cry, Ho-ly, — the an-gels cry, Ho-ly is the Lord. —

250.

Isn't He beautiful?

Ps 27:4; Is 9:6

John Wimber

Capo 2 (G)

Worshipfully

2. Yes, You are beautiful . . .

251.   It came upon the midnight clear

NOEL

Capo 3 (D)

English Traditional Melody
arranged by Caradog Roberts (1878-1935)

Lk 2:14

1. It _ came up - on the _ mid - night clear, that glo - rious song _ of old, from _ an - gels bend - ing near the earth to _ touch their harps of gold: "Peace on the earth, good - will to men from heav'n's all gra - cious King!" The world in sol - emn _ still - ness lay, to _ hear _ the an - gels sing.

2. Still through the cloven skies they come,
   With peaceful wings unfurled,
   And still their heavenly music floats
   O'er all the weary world:
   Above its sad and lowly plains
   They bend on hovering wing,
   And ever o'er its Babel sounds
   The blessèd angels sing.

3. Yet with the woes of sin and strife
   The world has suffered long,
   Beneath the angel-strain have rolled
   Two thousand years of wrong;
   And man, at war with man, hears not
   The love-song which they bring:
   O hush the noise, ye men of strife,
   And hear the angels sing.

4. For lo! the days are hastening on,
   By prophet bards foretold,
   When with the ever-circling years
   Comes round the age of gold;
   When peace shall over all the earth
   Its ancient splendours fling,
   And all the world send back the song
   Which now the angels sing.

E.H. Sears (1810-76)

252. It is a thing most wonderful

Is 53:3; 1 Tim 1:15

BROOKFIELD

English Traditional Melody

Smoothly

1. It is a thing most won - der - ful, al - most too

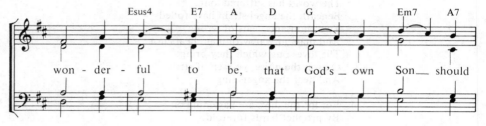

won - der - ful to be, that God's _ own Son _ should

come _ from heav'n and die to save a child _ like me.

2. And yet I know that it is true;
   He came to this poor world below,
   And wept, and toiled, and mourned, and died,
   Only because He loved us so.

3. I cannot tell how He could love
   A child so weak and full of sin;
   His love must be most wonderful,
   If He could die my love to win.

4. It is most wonderful, to know
   His love for me so free and sure;
   But 'tis more wonderful to see
   My love for Him so faint and poor.

5. And yet I want to love Thee, Lord;
   O light the flame within my heart
   And I will love Thee more and more,
   Until I see Thee as Thou art.

W.W. How (1823-97)

253.

It is good for me

Ps 73:25–26

Tim Blomdahl

Joyfully with pace

It is good for me to draw near un - to God;— Lord I
put my trust in Thee, ———— that I may de-clare_ all Thy
works, O my God,_Lord I put my trust in Thee. __ My flesh and my heart_they
fail_me, ———— but God is the strength_of my life. You are my portion both
now and ever-more,_ there is none that I de-sire but Thee.

254.   It is no longer I that liveth

Gal 2:20

Sally Ellis

Joyfully

It is no long-er I that liv-eth — but Christ that liv-eth in me, It is no long-er I that liv-eth — but Christ that liv-eth in me. He lives, He lives, Je-sus is a-live in me. It is no long-er I that liv-eth — but Christ that liv-eth in me.

2. The life that I live in the body
   I live by faith in the Son.   } (x2)
   He loves, He loves,
   Jesus gave Himself for me.
   The life that I live in the body
   I live by faith in the Son.

255.
It's a happy day

Capo 3 (D)

Brightly

Gary Pfeiffer

2. It's a grumpy day, and I can't stand the weather.
   It's a grumpy day, living it for myself.
   It's a grumpy day, and things aren't gonna get better,
   Living each day with my Bible up on my shelf.

3. *As verse 1.*

256.

It's the presence of Your Spirit, Lord, we need

Jn 14:16

Len Magee

Prayerfully

1. It's the pre - sence of Your Spi - rit, Lord, we need, _____

it's the pre - sence of Your Spi - rit, Lord, we need. _____

So help us, Lord, _ to wor - ship

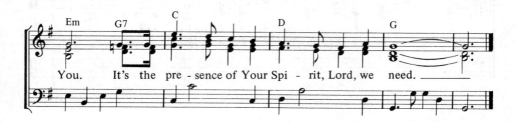

You. It's the pre - sence of Your Spi - rit, Lord, we need. _____

2. It's the presence of Your Spirit, Lord, we love . . . *etc.*

3. For the moving of Your Spirit, Lord, we pray . . . *etc.*

257.

It's Your blood

Ps 51:7; 1 Jn 1:7

Capo 3(G)

Michael Christ

Steadily

It's Your blood that clean - ses me, it's Your blood that gives me life, it's Your blood that took my place in re - deem - ing sac - ri - fice, and wash-es me whi - ter than the snow, than the snow. My Je - sus, God's pre-cious sac - ri - fice.

— □ ▢ □ —

Is any one of you in trouble? He should pray. Is anyone happy? Let him sing songs of praise.

JAMES 5:13

— □ ▢ □ —

258.

I wanna sing

Dave Renehan

With pace and strength

1. I ____ wanna sing, ___ wanna sing, ___
I ____ wanna sing, ___ wanna sing ___ for Jesus, for Je - sus, for Je sus. Oh I ___
___ wanna sing ____ for ___ Him.

2. I wanna clap... *etc.*

3. I wanna dance... *etc.*

4. I wanna praise... *etc.*

5. I wanna work... *etc.*

6. I wanna love... *etc.*

7. I wanna live... *etc.*

259. I want to be a history maker
(History makers)

Mt 6:10; Lk 11:2;
Rom 7:4; Eph 1:4;
5:18

Graham Kendrick

1. I want to be a his-to-ry ma-ker, (I want to be a his-to-ry ma-ker)

I want to be a world shaker, (I want to be a world shaker)

to be a pen on his-to-ry's pa-ges, (to be a pen on his-to-ry's pa-ges)

faith-ful to the end of the a-ges. (faith-ful to the end of the a-ges)

I want to see Your king-dom come,

2. I believe I was called and chosen (*echo*)
   Long before the world's creation, (*echo*)
   Called to be a holy person, (*echo*)
   Called to bear good fruit for heaven. (*echo*)

3. We want to be the generation (*echo*)
   Taking the news to every nation, (*echo*)
   Filled with the Spirit without measure, (*echo*)
   Working for a heavenly treasure. (*echo*)

260. I want to serve the purpose of God

(In my generation)

I Cor 3:12

Mark Altrogge

1. I want to serve the pur-pose of God in my gen-er-at-ion. I want to serve the pur-pose of God while I am a-live. I want to give my life for some-thing that-'ll last for-ev - er, — oh, I de-light, I de-light to do Your will.

2. I want to build with silver and gold in my generation.
   I want to build with silver and gold while I am alive . . . (etc.)

3. I want to see the kingdom of God . . . (etc.)

4. I want to see the Lord come again . . . (etc.)

261.   I want to walk with Jesus Christ

Mt 4:19; 8:22; 9:9; 16:24; 19:21; Mk 2:14;
8:34; 10:21; Lk 5:27; 9:23, 59; 18:22;
Jn 1:43; 10:27; 12:26; 21:19

Words: C. Simmonds
Music: Swiss folk melody

1. I___ want to__ walk__ with Je - sus Christ all the days I
   Fol-low Him, fol-low Him, yield Your life to Him, He has con - quered

live of this life on earth; to give to Him ___ com -
death, He is King of kings; ac - cept the joy that He

plete con - trol of bo - dy and__ of soul. _____
brings to those who yield their lives to Him. _____

2. I want to learn to speak to Him,
   To pray to Him, confess my sin;
   To open my life and let Him in,
   For joy will then be mine:

3. I want to learn to speak of Him,
   My life must show that He lives in me;
   My deeds, my thoughts, my words must speak
   All of His love for me:

4. I want to learn to read His word,
   For this is how I know the way
   To live my life as pleases Him,
   In holiness and joy:

5. O Holy Spirit of the Lord,
   Enter now into this heart of mine;
   Take full control of my selfish will,
   And make me wholly Thine:

262. I was made to praise You

Eph 5:20; 1 Thess 5:18

Chris Christensen

1. I ____ was made to praise _ You, I ____ was made to glo-ri-fy Your ___ name, in ev-'ry cir-cum-stance to find a chance to thank You. __ I was made to love __ You, I ____ was made to wor-ship at Your feet, and to o-bey You, Lord, I was made for You.

2. I will always praise You,
   I will always glorify Your name,
   In every circumstance
   I'll find a chance to thank You.
   I will always love You,
   I will always worship at Your feet,
   And I'll obey You, Lord,
   I was made for You.

263.
I was once in darkness

Lk 15:4; 1 Thess 4:17

Joan Parsons

Two-part round
Happily

I was once in dark-ness, Now my eyes can see, I was lost but Je-sus sought and found me. O what love He off-ers, O what peace He gives, I will sing for ev-er-more, He lives.

Hal-le-lu-jah Je-sus! Hal-le-lu-jah Lord! Hal-le-lu-jah Fa-ther, I am shield-ed by His word. I will live for ev-er, I will nev-er die, I will rise up to meet Him in the sky.

—— □ ▢ □ ——

The Lord will roar from Zion
and thunder from Jerusalem;
the earth and the sky will
tremble.
But the Lord will be a refuge for
his people,
a stronghold for the people of
Israel.

JOEL 3:16

—— □ ▢ □ ——

264.

I will build My church

Mt 16:18

Graham Kendrick

265.

I will call

Ps 18:3

Capo 2(C)

Steadily (men and women in canon)

Victor Rubbo

prais'd. So shall I be —

sav'd, so shall I be —

sav'd from my en - e - mies.

I will en - e - mies.

———————— □ ▢ □ ————————

Do not be afraid. I am the First and the Last. I am the Living One; I was dead, and behold I am alive for ever and ever!

REVELATION 1:17–18

———————— □ ▢ □ ————————

266. I will call upon the Lord

Ps 18:3, 46

Michael O'Shields

Brightly

(Ladies) I will call. . .

(Men) I will call up-on the Lord, who is wor thy to be

(Ladies) Who is worthy. . .   *(Ladies)* So shall I. . .   *(Together)*

praised. So shall I be saved from mine en-e-mies. The

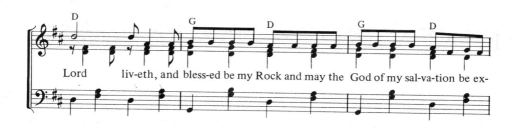

Lord liv-eth, and bless-ed be my Rock and may the God of my sal-va-tion be ex-

alt - ed. The Lord liv-eth, and bless-ed be my Rock and may the

God of my sal - va - tion be ex - alt - ed.

267.

I will change your name

Rev 3:12

D. J. Butler

268.

I will enter His gates

Ps 92:4; 100:4

Leona von Brethorst

Capo 3 (C)

With pace and swing

I will en-ter His gates with thanks-giv-ing in my heart, I will en-ter His courts with praise, I will say this is the day that the Lord has made, I will re-joice for He has made me glad. He has made me glad, He has made me glad, I will re-joice for He has made me glad. _____ He has made me glad, He has made me glad, I will re-joice for He has made me glad.

———— □ ▢ □ ————

Peace I leave with you; my peace I give you. I do not give to you as the world gives. Do not let your hearts be troubled and do not be afraid.

JOHN 14:27

———— □ ▢ □ ————

269.   I will give thanks to Thee

Ps 57:9–11; Heb 7:26

Capo 3 (G)

Brent Chambers

With steady strength

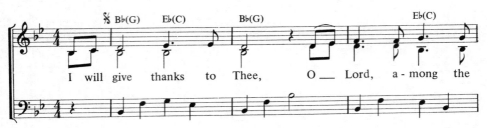

I will give thanks to Thee, O Lord, a-mong the

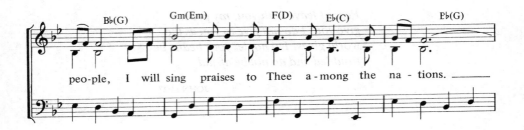

peo-ple, I will sing praises to Thee a-mong the na - tions.

For Thy stead - fast love is great, is great to the

hea-vens, and Thy faith-fulness, Thy faith-fulness to the clouds.

270.

I will give You praise

Ex 15:11; Is 9:6; Mt 28:20

Tommy Walker

Capo 2(C)

With strength

I will give You praise, I will sing Your song, — I will

bless Your ho - ly name; — for there is

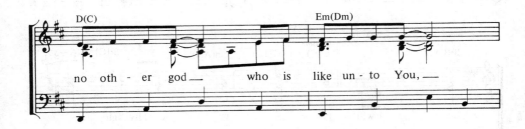

no oth - er god — who is like un - to You, —

You're the on - ly way. — On - ly You —

271.

I will magnify

Ps 34:3

Capo 3(G)

Scott Palazzo

With strength

I will mag-ni-fy Thy name a-bove all the earth; I will mag-ni-fy Thy name a-bove all the earth.

earth. I will sing un-to Thee __ the prai-ses in my heart; I will sing un-to Thee ____ the prai-ses in __ my heart. __

272.
I will praise You all my life
(O faithful God)

Mark Altrogge

With strength

I will praise You all my life; I will sing to You with my whole _ heart. I will trust in You, my hope and my help, _ my Ma-ker and my faith-ful _ God. O faith-ful God, O faith-ful God, _ You lift me up and You up-hold my cause; You give me life, You dry my eyes, _ You're al-ways near, You're a faith-ful God.

273.   I will rejoice in You and be glad

Song 1:4

Author unknown
Arr. Margaret Evans

I will re - joice _____ in You and be glad, _

I will ex - tol _ Your love more than wine. _

Draw me af - ter You and let us run to - geth - er,

I will re - joice _____ in You and be glad. _

— □ ▢ □ —

Praise him with the sounding of the
*   trumpet,*
*   praise him with the harp and*
*   lyre,*
praise him with tambourine and
*   dancing,*
*   praise him with the strings and*
*   flute,*
praise him with the clash of
*   cymbals.*

PSALM 150:3–5

— □ ▢ □ —

274. I will rejoice, I will rejoice

Ps 23:5-6

David Fellingham

Capo 3 (Em)

275.   I will rise and bless You, Lord

Ps 119:62;
145:4; Rom 8:39

Capo 5 (C)

Diane Fung

Joyfully

I will rise and bless You, Lord, _ lift my hands _ and

shout Your praise. _ I will tell of the mar - vel-lous things You have done _ and de-

clare Your faith - ful - ness. I will rise and

bless You, Lord, _ lift You high _ and dance for joy. _ Oh _

nothing can sep-ar - ate me _ from Your wonderful, won-der-ful love.

276.   I will seek Your face, O Lord

Ps 27:8

Capo 3(D)

Noel & Tricia Richards

Verse

1. Lord, how awe-some is Your pre-sence. ___ Who can stand in Your Light? ___ Those who by Your grace and mer-cy ___ are made ho-ly in ___ Your sight. ___

D.C. al Fine

2. I will dwell in Your presence
   All the days of my life;
   There to gaze upon Your glory,
   And to worship only You.

277.

I will sing of the mercies

Ps 89:1

J.H. Fillmore

For you did not receive a spirit that
makes you a slave again to fear, but
you received the Spirit of sonship.
And by him we cry, 'Abba, Father.'

ROMANS 8:15

278.

I will sing the wondrous story

Ps 23:2; Jn 15:4, 11; 16:24; Rev 4:6

Capo 5 (C)
HYFRYDOL

Rowland Hugh Prichard (1811-87)

1. I will sing ___ the won - drous sto - ry
of the Christ who died ___ for me,
how He left ___ His home in glo - ry
for the cross on Cal - va - ry.
I was lost ___ but Je - sus found ___ me,

found the sheep__ that went __ a - stray;

threw __ His lov - ing arms __ a - round _____ me,

drew me back ___ in - to His way.

2. I was bruised but Jesus healed me,
Faint was I from many a fall;
Sight was gone, and fears possessed me,
But He freed me from them all.
Days of darkness still come o'er me;
Sorrow's paths I often tread,
But the Saviour still is with me,
By His hand I'm safely led.

3. He will keep me till the river
Rolls its waters at my feet,
Then He'll bear me safely over,
All my joys in Him complete.
Yes, I'll sing the wondrous story
Of the Christ who died for me;
Sing it with the saints in glory,
Gathered by the crystal sea.

Francis Harold Rawley (1854-1952)

279.

I will sing unto the Lord

Ps 104:33–35

Donya Brockway

Easy waltz feel

I will sing un-to the Lord as long as I live,

I will sing praise to my God while I have my be-ing,_____

_____ My me - di - ta - tion of Him

shall __ be sweet, I will be glad I will be glad in the

Lord. _____ Bless thou the Lord, O my soul,

Praise ye the Lord. _____ Bless thou the Lord, O my

soul, Praise ye the Lord. _____ Bless thou the Lord,

O my soul, praise ye the Lord. _____ Bless thou the

Lord, O my soul, praise ye the Lord. _____

280.

I will speak out

Ps 82: 3–4; Is 61:1; Lk 4:18

Capo 2 (D)

D. Bankhead/R. Goudie
S. Rinaldi/S. Bassett

With strength

1. I will speak out for
those who have no voi - ces,
I will stand up for the
rights of all the op - pressed;
I will speak truth and jus - tice, I'll de -

2. I will speak out for those who have no choices,
   I will cry out for those who live without love;
   I will show God's compassion
   To the crushed and broken in spirit,
   I will lift up the weak in Jesus' name.

281. I will worship You, Lord

Deut 6:5; Mt 22:37;
Mk 12:30; Lk 10:27

Daniel Gardner

I will wor-ship You, Lord, with all of my might, I will

praise You with __ a __ psalm. I will

wor - ship You, Lord, with all of my might, I will

praise You all __ day __ long. For

282. I worship You, Almighty God

Ex 15:11; Is 9:6;
Jer 23:6; 33:16

Sondra Corbett

283.
Jehovah Jireh, God will provide
(Hebrew names for God)

Gen 22:14;
Ex 15:26; 17:15;
Lev 19:2; Judg 6:24; Ps 23:1;
Jer 23:6; 33:16; Ezek 48:35

Ian Smale

284.   Jehovah Jireh, my Provider

Gen 22:14; Ps 91:11;
2 Cor 12:9; Phil 4:19

Merla Watson

Je - ho - vah Ji - reh, my Pro - vi - der, His

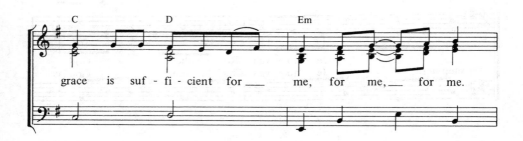

grace is suf - fi - cient for __ me, for me, __ for me.

Je - ho - vah Ji - reh, my Pro - vi - der, His

grace is suff - fi - cient for __ me. My

285. Jesus Christ is risen today

Mt 28:6; Mk 16:6; Lk 24:6; Jn 21:14; Heb 12:2

EASTER HYMN

Melody from *Lyra Davidica* (1708)

Joyfully

1. Je-sus Christ is ris'n to-day;__ Ha - le - lu - jah!
Our tri-umph-ant ho - ly day;__ Ha - le - lu - jah!
Who did once up - on the cross; Ha - le - lu - jah!
Suf-fer__ to re - deem our loss; Ha - le - lu - jah!

2. Hymns of praise then let us sing; Hallelujah!
   Unto Christ our heavenly King; Hallelujah!
   Who endured the cross and grave; Hallelujah!
   Sinners to redeem and save: Hallelujah!

3. But the pains, which He endured; Hallelujah!
   Our salvation have procured; Hallelujah!
   Now in heaven above He's King; Hallelujah!
   Where the angels ever sing: Hallelujah!

Lyra Davidica (1708)

― □ ▢ □ ―

*Who may ascend the hill of the
Lord?
Who may stand in his holy place?
He who has clean hands and a pure
heart.*

PSALM 24:3–4

― □ ▢ □ ―

286.

Jesus has sat down

Ps 110:1; Is 9:6–7; 61:1; Lk 4:18;
Phil 2:9–11; Heb 1:3, 13;
1 Pet 2:9; Rev 11:15

Capo 5 (C)

Triumphantly

Verse

Jonathan Wallis

1. Je-sus has sat down at God's right hand, _____
He is reign-ing now on Dav-id's throne. _____
God has placed all things be-neath His feet, _____ His
en-e-mies will be His footstool. _____ For the gov-ern-ment is
now up-on His shoul-der, _____ for the gov-ern-ment is

now up-on His shoul-der, _____ and of the in-crease of His

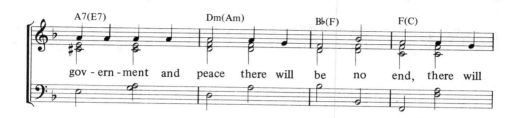

gov-ern-ment and peace there will be no end, there will

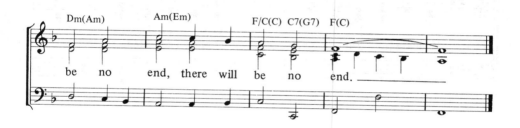

be no end, there will be no end.

2. God has now exalted Him on high,
   Given Him a name above all names.
   Every knee will bow and tongue confess
   That Jesus Christ is Lord.

3. Jesus is now living in His church,
   Men who have been purchased by His blood.
   They will serve their God, a royal priesthood,
   And they will reign on earth.

4. Sound the trumpets, good news to the poor,
   Captives will go free, the blind will see,
   The kingdom of this world will soon become
   The kingdom of our God.

287.

Jesus, how lovely You are

Mt 11:29; 25:6; Jn 3:29;
Rev 22:17

Dave Bolton

Capo 2 (D)

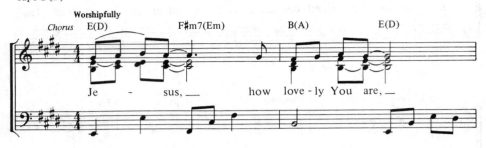

Je - sus, — how love - ly You are, —

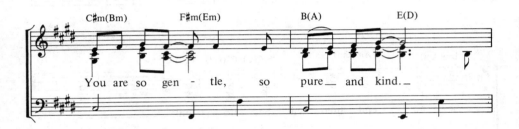

You are so gen - tle, so pure — and kind. —

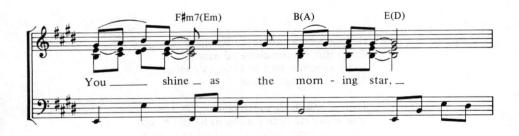

You — shine — as the morn - ing star, —

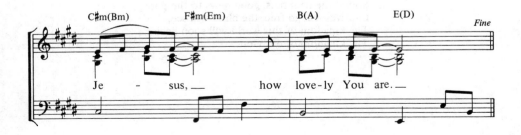

Je - sus, — how love - ly You are. —

2. Hallelujah, Jesus died and rose again;
   Hallelujah, Jesus forgave all my sin.

3. Hallelujah, Jesus is meek and lowly;
   Hallelujah, Jesus is pure and holy.

4. Hallelujah, Jesus is the Bridegroom;
   Hallelujah, Jesus will take His bride soon.

288.
Jesus, I love You
(Alleluia)

Jude Del Hierro

Je - sus, I love ____ You; I bow down be - fore _ You. Prai - ses and wor - ship ____ to our ____ King.

289.
Capo 5 (C)

Jesus is King

Eph 1:20; 5:18; Heb 4:14; 7:25

Wendy Churchill

Joyfully

1. Je - sus is King and I will ex - tol Him,
give Him the glo - ry and hon - our His name.
He reigns on high, en - throned in the hea - vens,
Word of the Fa - ther, ex - alt - ed for us.

2. We have a hope that is steadfast and certain,
   Gone through the curtain and touching the throne.
   We have a Priest who is there interceding,
   Pouring His grace on our lives day by day.

3. We come to Him, our Priest and Apostle,
   Clothed in His glory and bearing His name,
   Laying our lives with gladness before Him;
   Filled with His Spirit we worship the King.

4. O holy One, our hearts do adore You;
   Thrilled with Your goodness we give You our praise.
   Angels in light with worship surround Him,
   Jesus, our Saviour, for ever the same.

290.

Jesus is Lord!

Jn 1:3; Phil 2:11; 1 Tim 2:6

David Mansell

Capo 1 (G)

With majesty

1. Je - sus is Lord! Cre - a - tion's voice pro - claims it, For by His power each tree and flower was planned and made. Je - sus is Lord! the un - i-verse de -clares it, Sun, moon and stars in hea - ven cry

Chorus

'Je - sus is Lord!' Je - sus is Lord! Je - sus is Lord! Praise Him with Ha-lle - lu - jahs for Je - sus is Lord!

2. Jesus is Lord! yet from His throne eternal
In flesh He came to die in pain
On Calv'ry's tree.
Jesus is Lord! from Him all life proceeding,
Yet gave His life a ransom
Thus setting us free.

3. Jesus is Lord! o'er sin the mighty conqueror,
From death He rose, and all His foes
Shall own His Name.
Jesus is Lord! God sent His Holy Spirit
To show by works of power
That Jesus is Lord.

291.

Jesus is Lord of all

Mt 28:18; Rom 16:20;
Eph 2:6; Rev 21:2

Marilyn Baker

Majestically

1. Je - sus is Lord of all, — Sa - tan is un - der His feet, — Je - sus is reign-ing on high — and all pow'r is giv - en to Him in heav'n and earth. Him.

1st time / *Last time*

2. We are joined to Him,
Satan is under our feet,
We are seated on high
And all authority is given
To us through Him.

3. One day we'll be like Him,
Perfect in every way,
Chosen to be His bride,
Ruling and reigning with Him
For evermore.

292. Jesus, I worship You

1 Tim 6:15; Rev 17:14; 19:16

Capo 5(C)

Chris Bowater

293.

Jesus, Jesus
(Holy and anointed One)

Ps 119:103, 105; Jn 7:38–39; Eph 1:20

John Barnett

With feeling

Je - sus, Je - sus,

{ ho - ly and an-oint-ed One, — }
{ ris - en and ex - alt - ed One, — } Je - sus.

1st and last times Fine

2nd time
sus. Your name is like hon - ey on my lips, — Your Spi-rit like wa-

- ter to — my soul. — Your word is a lamp — un-to — my — feet. —

Je - sus, I love — You, — I love — You. *D.C. al Fine*

294.

Jesus, Jesus, Jesus

Capo 3 (G)

Chris Bowater

295.

Jesus, King of kings

Mt 6:10; Lk 11:2; Phil 2:9;
1 Tim 6:15; Rev 17:14; 19:16

Chris Rolinson

Worshipfully (slow 4)

1. Je - sus, King of kings, we

wor - ship and a - dore You. Je - sus,

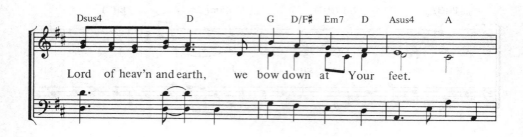

Lord of heav'n and earth, we bow down at Your feet.

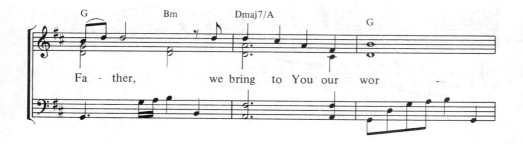

Fa - ther, we bring to You our wor -

ship, Your sov-'reign will be done, on

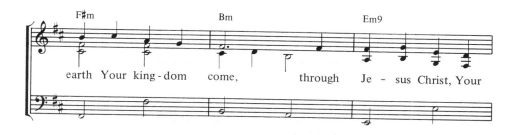

earth Your king-dom come, through Je - sus Christ, Your

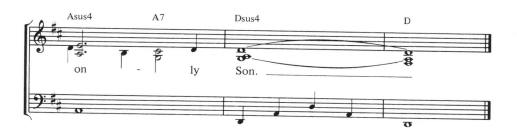

on - ly Son.

2. Jesus, Sovereign Lord,
   We worship and adore You.
   Jesus, Name above all names,
   We bow down at Your feet.
   Father, we offer You our worship,
   Your sovereign will be done,
   On earth Your Kingdom come,
   Through Jesus Christ, Your only Son.

3. Jesus, Light of the world,
   We worship and adore You.
   Jesus, Lord Emmanuel,
   We bow down at Your feet.
   Father, for Your delight we worship,
   Your sovereign will be done,
   On earth Your Kingdom come,
   Through Jesus Christ, Your only Son.

—— □ ▢ □ ——

*Love does not delight in evil but
rejoices with the truth.*

1 CORINTHIANS 13:6

—— □ ▢ □ ——

296.

Jesus lives

Rom 8:38–39; 1 Cor 15:55

Capo 3 (G)

ST. ALBINUS

Henry John Gauntlett (1805-76)

1. Je - sus lives! thy ter - rors now can, O death, no more ap -
pal us; Je - sus lives! by this we know, thou, O
grave, canst not en - thral us. Hal - le - lu - jah!

2. Jesus lives! henceforth is death
But the gate of life immortal;
This shall calm our trembling breath,
When we pass its gloomy portal.
Hallelujah!

3. Jesus lives! for us He died;
Then, alone to Jesus living,
Pure in heart may we abide,
Glory to our Saviour giving.
Hallelujah!

4. Jesus lives! our hearts know well,
Nought from us His love shall sever;
Life, nor death, nor powers of hell,
Tear us from His keeping ever.
Hallelujah!

5. Jesus lives! to Him the throne
Over all the world is given:
May we go where He is gone,
Rest and reign with Him in heaven.
Hallelujah!

Christian F. Gellert (1715-69)
tr. Frances Elizabeth Cox (1812-97)

297.
Jesus, lover of my soul

Ps 36:7–9; 46:2; 57:1;
Mt 8:26; Jn 1:17; Rev 22:1

ABERYSTWYTH
Majestically

Joseph Parry (1841-1903)

1. Je - sus, __ lov - er of my soul, let me to Thy bo - som fly, while the __ near - er wa - ters roll, while the __ temp - est still is high; hide me, O my Sa - viour, __ hide, till the storm of life is __ past; safe in - to the ha - ven guide, O re - ceive __ my soul at last.

2. Other refuge have I none,
   Hangs my helpless soul on Thee;
   Leave, ah, leave me not alone,
   Still support and comfort me.
   All my trust on Thee is stayed,
   All my help from Thee I bring;
   Cover my defenceless head
   With the shadow of Thy wing.

3. Thou, O Christ, art all I want;
   More than all in Thee I find;
   Raise the fallen, cheer the faint,
   Heal the sick, and lead the blind.
   Just and holy is Thy name,
   I am all unrighteousness;
   False and full of sin I am,
   Thou art full of truth and grace.

4. Plenteous grace with Thee is found,
   Grace to cover all my sin;
   Let the healing streams abound,
   Make and keep me pure within.
   Thou of life the fountain art;
   Freely let me take of Thee;
   Spring Thou up within my heart,
   Rise to all eternity.

Charles Wesley (1707-88)

298.

Jesus, Name above all names

Is 7:14; Acts 4:12;
Phil 2:9

Naida Hearn

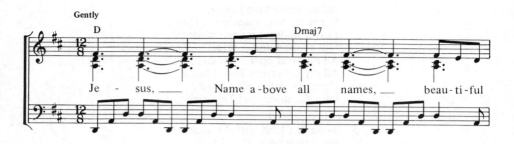

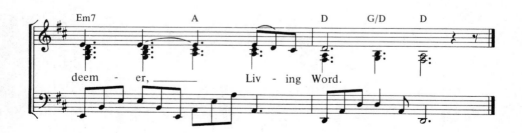

299.

Jesus put this song into our hearts

Ps 30:11; Eph 2:14

Capo 5 (Am)

Graham Kendrick

'Hebrew' style, getting faster

1. Je - sus put this song in - to our hearts, _____

Je -sus put this song in-to our hearts, _____ it's a song of joy no one can

take a -way, _____ Je-sus put this song _____ in-to our

hearts. _____

2. Jesus taught us how to live in harmony,
   Jesus taught us how to live in harmony,
   Different faces, different races, He made us one,
   Jesus taught us how to live in harmony.

3. Jesus taught us how to be a family,
   Jesus taught us how to be a family,
   Loving one another with the love that He gives,
   Jesus taught us how to be a family.

4. Jesus turned our sorrow into dancing,
   Jesus turned our sorrow into dancing,
   Changed our tears of sadness into rivers of joy,
   Jesus turned our sorrow into a dance.

5. *Instrumental.*

300.

Jesus, send more labourers

Is 6:8; Mt 9:37; Lk 10:2; Jn 4:35

Chris Rolinson

1. Je - sus, send more la - bour - ers, for, Lord, we see the need; the land is rea - dy for har - vest, the fields are ripe in - deed.

Oh Lord, but start with me, Je - sus be - gin with me. Who will go for

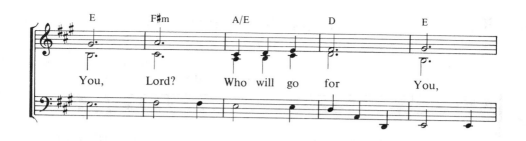

You, Lord? Who will go for You,

Lord? Here _ I am, Lord, _____ send

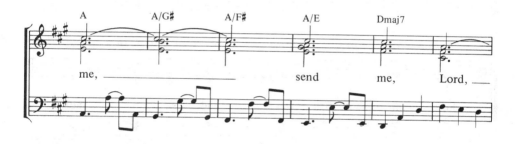

me, _____ send me, Lord, ___

___ send me. _____

Last time

2. Lord, we love our country,
   Countless lives to be won;
   Jesus bring revival,
   That through us Your will be done.

3. Lord, we sense Your moving,
   Touching our lives with power;
   We are ready to serve You,
   To go this day, this hour.

301.

Jesus shall reign
(First tune)

Ps 72:5–12

Capo 3(D)
RIMINGTON

Francis Duckworth (1862-1941)

1. Je - sus shall reign wher - e'er the sun doth his suc - ces - sive jour - neys run; His king-dom stretch from shore___ to___ shore, till moons shall wax and wane no more.

2. For Him shall endless prayer be made,
   And praises throng to crown His head;
   His name like sweet perfume shall rise
   With every morning sacrifice.

3. People and realms of every tongue
   Dwell on His love with sweetest song,
   And infant voices shall proclaim
   Their early blessing on His name.

4. Blessings abound where'er He reigns;
   The prisoner leaps to lose his chains;
   The weary find eternal rest,
   And all the sons of want are blessed.

5. Let every creature rise and bring
   Peculiar honours to our King;
   Angels descend with songs again,
   And earth repeat the loud Amen!

Isaac Watts (1674-1748)

Jesus shall reign
(Second tune)

TRURO

Triumphantly

Psalmodia Evangelica (1789)

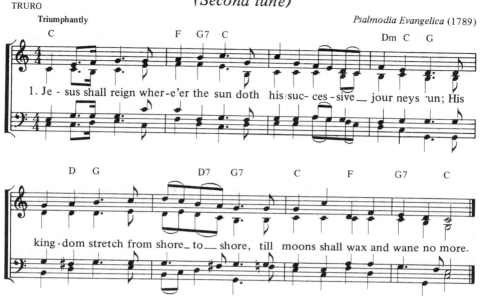

1. Je - sus shall reign wher-e'er the sun doth his suc- ces -sive jour neys un; His
king -dom stretch from shore to shore, till moons shall wax and wane no more.

2. For Him shall endless prayer be made,
And praises throng to crown His head;
His name like sweet perfume shall rise
With every morning sacrifice.

3. People and realms of every tongue
Dwell on His love with sweetest song,
And infant voices shall proclaim
Their early blessing on His name.

4. Blessings abound where'er He reigns;
The prisoner leaps to lose his chains;
The weary find eternal rest,
And all the sons of want are blessed.

5. Let every creature rise and bring
Peculiar honours to our King;
Angels descend with songs again,
And earth repeat the loud Amen!

Isaac Watts (1674-1748)

302. Jesus shall take the highest honour

Phil 2:9–11; Rev 5:13

Chris Bowater

———— □ ▢ □ ————

Praise the Lord, O my soul;
all my inmost being, praise his
holy name.
Praise the Lord, O my soul,
and forget not all his benefits.

PSALM 103:1–2

———— □ ▢ □ ————

303.

Jesus, stand among us

Mt 18:20; 26:26; Mk 14:22;
Lk 22:19; 1 Cor 11:23–24;
Eph 2:13; 4:15–16

Capo 3 (C)

Graham Kendrick

2. So to You we're gathering
Out of each and every land,
Christ the love between us
At the joining of our hands;
O, Jesus, we love You . . . (etc.)

(Optional verse for communion)

3. Jesus stand among us
At the breaking of the bread,
Join us as one body
As we worship You, our Head.
O, Jesus, we love You . . . (etc.)

304. Jesus, stand among us in Thy risen power

(First tune)

Mt 18:20; 24:42; 25:13; Lk 12:40; Jn 20:22

NORTH COATES

Timothy Richard Matthews (1826-1910).

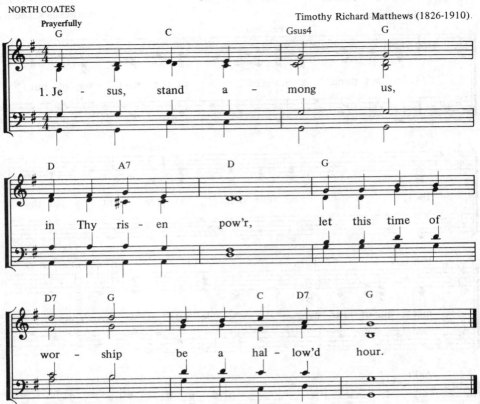

Prayerfully

1. Je - sus, stand a - mong us, in Thy ris - en pow'r, let this time of wor - ship be a hal - low'd hour.

Alternative tune: CASWALL

2. Breathe Thy Holy Spirit
   Into every heart,
   Bid the fears and sorrows
   From each soul depart.

3. Thus with quickened footsteps
   We'll pursue our way,
   Watching for the dawning
   Of eternal day.

William Pennefather (1816-73)

Jesus, stand among us in Thy risen power

(Second tune)

Capo 2 (C)
QUIETUDE

Harold Green (1871-1931)

2. Breathe Thy Holy Spirit
    Into every heart,
    Bid the fears and sorrows
    From each soul depart.

3. Thus with quickened footsteps
    We'll pursue our way,
    Watching for the dawning
    Of eternal day.

    William Pennefather (1816-73)

305. Jesus take me as I am

Rom 8:3

Dave Bryant

Capo 4 (C)

Tenderly

Je - sus take me as I am,

I can come no oth-er way.

Take me deep-er in to You,

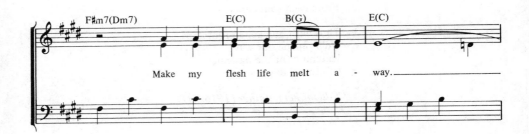

Make my flesh life melt a - way.

F#m(Dm) B(G)

Make me like a prec-ious

E(C) E7(C7) F#m(Dm)

stone, Crys-tal

E(C) C#m7(Am7) B7(G)

clear and fine-ly honed.

E(C) Emaj7(Cmaj7) C#m(Am)

Life of Je-sus shin-ing through,

F#m7(Dm7) E(C) B(G) E(C)

Giv-ing glo-ry back to You.

306.
Jesus the Name above all names
(Emmanuel)

Is 7:14;
Acts 4:12;
Phil 2:9

Capo 3 (D)

Hilary Davies

Gentle, but rhythmic

Je-sus, the Name a-bove all names, for-ev-er-more the same, and lift-ing up our hands we ex-alt You; come a-mong us once-a-gain and glo-ri-fy Your name, so

307.
Jesus! the name high over all

Gen 3:15; Ps 34:8;
Is 61:1; Mt 28:18;
Lk 4:18; Jn 1:29; 1 Cor 1:30;
Phil 2:9; Jas 2:19

LYDIA

Thomas Phillips (1735-1807)

Triumphantly

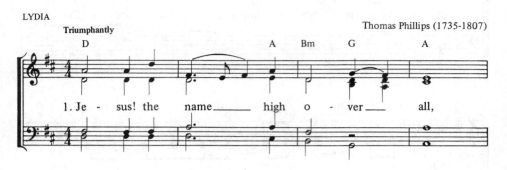

1. Je - sus! the name___ high o - ver___ all,

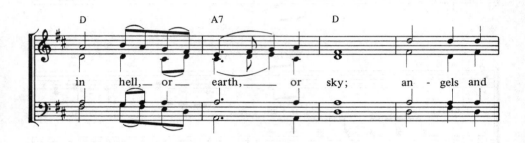

in hell,___ or___ earth,___ or sky; an - gels and

men be - fore it fall,___ and de - vils fear and

fly,___ and de - vils___ fear___ and___ fly.

2. Jesus! the name to sinners dear,
   The name to sinners given;
   It scatters all their guilty fear,
   It turns their hell to heaven,
   It turns their hell to heaven.

3. Jesus! the prisoners' fetters breaks,
   And bruises Satan's head;
   Power into strengthless souls it speaks,
   And life into the dead,
   And life into the dead.

4. O that the world might taste and see
   The riches of His grace!
   The arms of love that compass me
   Would all mankind embrace,
   Would all mankind embrace.

5. His only righteousness I show,
   His saving grace proclaim;
   'Tis all my business here below
   To cry: 'Behold the Lamb!'
   To cry: 'Behold the Lamb!'

6. Happy if with my latest breath
   I might but gasp His name;
   Preach Him to all, and cry in death:
   'Behold, behold the Lamb!'
   'Behold, behold the Lamb!'

Charles Wesley (1707-88)

308. Jesus, the very thought of Thee

Ps 27:8;
Mt 5:4–5; Heb 12:2

ST AGNES
Smoothly

John Bacchus Dykes (1823-76)

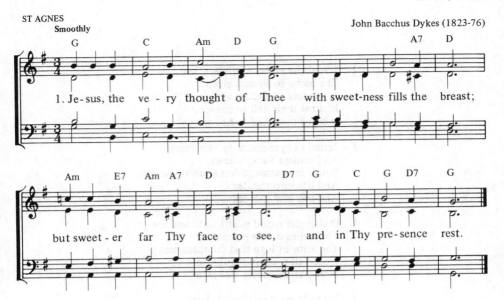

1. Je-sus, the ve - ry thought of Thee with sweet-ness fills the breast;

but sweet - er far Thy face to see, and in Thy pre-sence rest.

2. Nor voice can sing, nor heart can frame,
   Nor can the memory find
   A sweeter sound than Thy blessed name,
   O Saviour of mankind!

3. O hope of every contrite heart,
   O joy of all the meek,
   To those who fall how kind Thou art,
   How good to those who seek!

4. But what to those who find? Ah, this
   Nor tongue nor pen can show:
   The love of Jesus, what it is
   None but His loved ones know.

5. Jesus, Thy mercies are untold
   Through each returning day;
   Thy love exceeds a thousandfold
   Whatever we can say.

6. Jesus, our only joy be Thou,
   As Thou our prize wilt be;
   Jesus, be Thou our glory now,
   And through eternity.

   Bernard of Clairvaux (1091-1153)
   Tr. Edward Caswall (1814-78)

Praise be to the God and Father of our Lord Jesus Christ, who has blessed us in the heavenly realms with every spiritual blessing in Christ.

EPHESIANS 1:3

309.   Jesus, we celebrate Your victory

Rom 5:10; 8:15;
Gal 5:1; Heb 4:16;
1 Jn 4:18

John Gibson

Jesus, we celebrate Your victory; Jesus, we re-vel in Your love. Jesus, we rejoice, You've set us free; Jesus, Your death has brought us life.

To continue

Last time to Coda

1. It was for free-dom____ that Christ has set us free,_____ no
long-er to____ be sub - ject____ to a yoke of sla - ve - ry;____
____ so we're re - joic - ing_____
in God's vic - to - ry,____ our hearts re - spon-ding to His
love._____ life._____

D.S. al Coda   ⊕ *CODA*

2. His Spirit in us releases us from fear,
   The way to Him is open, with boldness we draw near.
   And in His presence our problems disappear;
   Our hearts responding to His love.

310.

Jesus, we enthrone You

Ps 22:3; Mt 18:20

Capo 2 (G)

Paul Kyle

With reverence

Lord Je - sus,— we en - throne You,—

ALTERNATIVE

Je - sus — we en -

we pro - claim You our King, —

Stand - ing here — in the midst of us —

— we raise You up — with our

311. Jesus, You are changing me

Jer 18:6; Rom 9:21

Marilyn Baker

Capo 3 (C)

Je - sus, You are chang-ing me, by Your Spi - rit You're mak - ing me like You. Je - sus, You're trans- form-ing me, that Your love - li-ness may be seen in all I do.

312.　Jesus, You are the radiance

Heb 1:2–3; 2:9

Capo 5(C)

David Fellingham

313.

Join all the glorious names

Josh 5:14; Acts 3:22;
Rom 8:38–39;
Heb 10:19–22; Rev 2:26; 4:4

ST GODRIC

John Bacchus Dykes (1823-76)

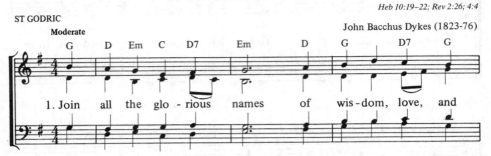

1. Join all the glo - rious names of wis - dom, love, and

pow'r, that e - ver mor - tals knew, that

an - gels e - ver bore: all are too mean to

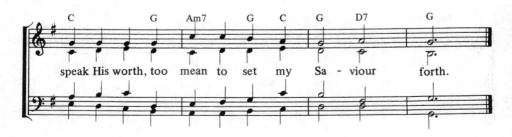

speak His worth, too mean to set my Sa - viour forth.

Alternative tunes: DARWALL'S 148th & GOSPAL

2. Great Prophet of my God,
   My tongue would bless Thy name:
   By Thee the joyful news
   Of our salvation came:
   The joyful news of sins forgiven,
   Of hell subdued and peace with heaven.

3. Jesus, my great High Priest,
   Offered His blood, and died;
   My guilty conscience seeks
   No sacrifice beside:
   His powerful blood did once atone,
   And now it pleads before the throne.

4. My Saviour and my Lord,
   My Conqueror and my King,
   Thy sceptre and Thy sword,
   Thy reigning grace I sing:
   Thine is the power; behold, I sit
   In willing bonds beneath Thy feet.

5. Now let my soul arise,
   And tread the tempter down:
   My Captain leads me forth
   To conquest and a crown:
   March on, nor fear to win the day,
   Though death and hell obstruct the way.

6. Should all the hosts of death,
   And powers of hell unknown,
   Put their most dreadful forms
   Of rage and malice on,
   I shall be safe; for Christ displays
   Superior power and guardian grace.

Isaac Watts (1674-1748)

314. Joy to the world

Jn 1:23

Words: I Watts (1674-1748)
Music: G F Handel (1685-1759)
arranged L Mason (1792-1872)

1. Joy to the world— the Lord has come: let earth re - ceive her King, let ev - ery heart prepare Him room and heaven and na - ture sing, and heaven and na - ture sing, and heaven, and heaven and na - ture sing!

(lower voice) and heaven and na - ture sing, and heaven and na - ture sing, and heaven and na - ture sing!

2. Joy to the earth— the Saviour reigns:
   Your sweetest songs employ,
   While fields and streams and hills and plains
   Repeat the sounding joy,
   Repeat the sounding joy,
   Repeat, repeat the sounding joy!

3. He rules the world with truth and grace,
   And makes the nations prove
   The glories of his righteousness,
   The wonders of His love,
   The wonders of His love,
   The wonders, wonders of his love.

315. Jubilate, everybody
(Jubilate Deo)

Ps 100:1–2, 4–5

Fred Dunn

316.

Just as I am
(First tune)

Mt 5:3, 11:28; Eph 3:18; 1 Jn 1:7

Capo 3(C)
WORDSWORTH

William Batchelder Bradbury (1816-68)

With feeling

1. Just as I am, with-out one plea but

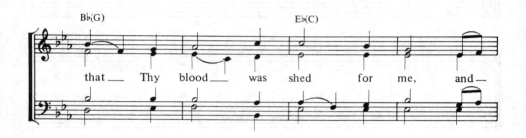

that Thy blood was shed for me, and

that Thou bid'st me come to Thee, O

Lamb of God, I come, I come.

2. Just as I am, and waiting not
   To rid my soul of one dark blot,
   To Thee, whose blood can cleanse each spot,
   O Lamb of God, I come.*

3. Just as I am, though tossed about
   With many a conflict, many a doubt,
   Fightings and fears within, without,
   O Lamb of God, I come.

4. Just as I am, poor, wretched, blind:
   Sight, riches, healing of the mind.
   Yea, all I need, in Thee to find,
   O Lamb of God, I come.

5. Just as I am, Thou wilt receive,
   Wilt welcome, pardon, cleanse, relieve,
   Because Thy promise I believe,
   O Lamb of God, I come.

6. Just as I am, Thy love unknown
   Has broken every barrier down;
   Now to be Thine, yea, Thine alone,
   O Lamb of God, I come.

7. Just as I am, of that free love
   The breadth, length, depth, and height to prove,
   Here for a season, then above,
   O Lamb of God, I come.

Charlotte Elliott (1789-1871)

* *When singing to* JUST AS I AM *sing 'I come' twice.*

Just as I am
(*Second tune*)

A.H. Brown (1830-1926)

SAFFRON WALDEN

1. Just as I am, with - out ___ one

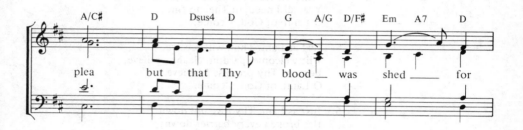

plea but that Thy blood ___ was shed ___ for

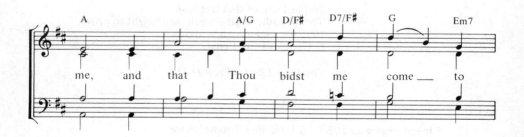

me, and that Thou bidst me come ___ to

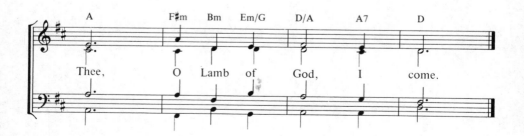

Thee, O Lamb of God, I come.

317. Just like You promised

Mt 18:20

Patty Kennedy

318.

King forever

Is 9:6; Rev 4:8; 5:12; 19:13

Jane Norton

1. King for - e - ver, Lord Mes-si - ah, He who was, and is, and is to come; Prince of glo - ry, name of Je - sus, be Your praise and wor-ship e - ver sung. — And we will sing — ho - san - na to Je - sus, we ex - alt and raise Your name a - bove; — and we pro - claim — the glo - ry of Je - sus; Prince of peace and wor-thy King of love. 2. Lord an - love.

2. Lord anointed, our salvation,
   He whom angels call the Word of God;
   True and faithful, Lamb of mercy,
   Now receive our worship and our love.

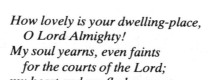

How lovely is your dwelling-place,
*   O Lord Almighty!*
My soul yearns, even faints
*   for the courts of the Lord;*
my heart and my flesh cry out
*   for the living God.*

PSALM 84:1–2

319.

King of kings
(The King of glory comes)

Ps 9:8; 24:8; 98:9; 1 Tim 6:15;
Rev 5:5; 17:14; 19:13, 16

Capo 2 (G)

Graham Kendrick

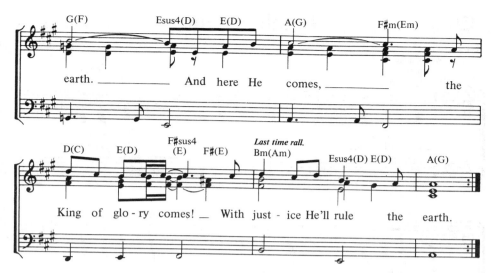

earth. _____ And here He comes, _____ the

King of glo-ry comes! _ With just-ice He'll rule the earth.

(Last time: Cheers, shouts of victory, etc.)

SHOUT

All: Almighty God, You are the Rock;
All Your works are perfect,
And all Your ways are just.
You are a faithful God who does no wrong.
Yet we Your people,
Both church and nation,
Are covered with shame
Because of our unfaithfulness to You.
We have sinned so seriously against You,
And against one another —
Therefore the foundations of our society crumble
Have mercy, Lord,
Forgive us, Lord,
Restore us, Lord,
Revive Your church again;
Let justice flow
Like rivers,
And righteousness like a never-failing stream.

320.
Lamb of God

Jn 1:29; 1 Jn 1:7; Rev 5:12

Capo 1 (A)

Chris Bowater

Lamb of God, Holy One, Jesus Christ, Son of God, lifted up willingly to die; that I the guilty one may know the blood once shed still freely flowing, still cleansing, still healing. I ex-

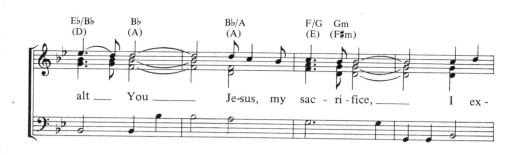

alt ___ You ___ Je-sus, my sac - ri - fice, ___ I ex-

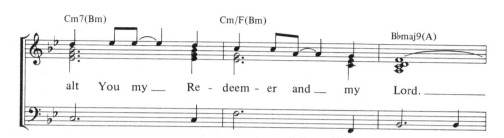

alt You my ___ Re - deem - er and ___ my Lord.

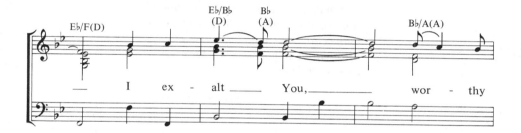

___ I ex - alt ___ You, ___ wor - thy

Lamb of God, ___ and in hon - our I ___ bow

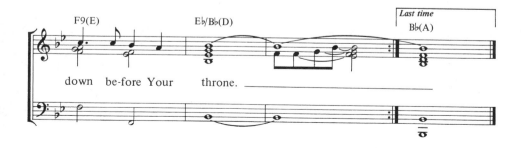

down be-fore Your throne. ___

───── □ □ □ ─────

*Now to him who is able to do
immeasurably more than all we ask or
imagine, according to his power that
is at work within us, to him be glory
in the church and in Christ Jesus
throughout all generations, for ever
and ever! Amen.*

EPHESIANS 3:20–21

───── □ □ □ ─────

321. Lead us, heavenly Father, lead us

Ps 23:2; 32:8;
Mt 4:1; Mk 1:13;
Lk 4:2; Jn 14:27

Capo 4(C)
MANNHEIM

Adapted from F. Filitz's *Choralbuch* (1847)

Boldly

1. Lead us, heav'n-ly Fa-ther, lead us o'er the world's tem-pes-tuous sea;

guard us, guide us, keep us, feed us, for we have no help but Thee;

yet pos-sess-ing ev-'ry bless-ing if our God our Fa-ther be.

2. Saviour, breathe forgiveness o'er us;
All our weakness Thou dost know,
Thou didst tread this earth before us,
Thou didst feel its keenest woe;
Tempted, taunted, yet undaunted,
Through the desert Thou didst go.

3. Spirit of our God, descending,
Fill our hearts with heavenly joy,
Love with every passion blending,
Pleasure that can never cloy;
Thus provided, pardoned, guided,
Nothing can our peace destroy.

James Edmeston (1791-1867) alt.

322.

Led like a lamb

(You're alive)

Is 53:7; Mt 28:6, 18; Mk 16:6; Lk 24:6; Jn 20:16; 21:14

Graham Kendrick

Verse **thoughtfully**
Chorus **triumphantly**

1. Led like a lamb to the slaugh-ter in si-lence and shame, there on Your back You _ car-ried a world of vio-lence and pain.

Bleeding, — dy-ing, — bleeding, —

*For the antiphonal Alleluias the congregation divide into three parts.

2. At break of dawn, poor Mary,
   Still weeping she came,
   When through her grief she heard Your voice
   Now speaking her name.
   Mary, Master, Mary, Master.

3. At the right hand of the Father
   Now seated on high
   You have begun Your eternal reign
   Of justice and joy.
   Glory, glory, glory, glory.

323.

Let God arise

Ps 68:1, 3

Graham Kendrick

Triumphantly

Chorus

Let God a - rise, and let His en - e - mies be sca - ttered; and

let those who hate Him flee be - fore ___ Him. ___

Let God a - rise, and let His en - e - mies be sca - ttered; and

let those who hate Him flee a - way. ___

324.   Let God speak

Ian Smale

Let God speak and I will lis - ten, __ let God speak, there's things I'm needing to put right. Let God speak and I will o-bey what He says, please God I want to hear Your voice to-night.

night. Lord I want to hear Your voice, _ Lord I want to hear Your voice, _

Lord I want to hear Your voice to- night, _____ to - night. _____

325.   Let Me have My way among you
(Do not strive)

Mt 28:18;
Phil: 4:7; Col 3:15;
2 Tim 2:24

Graham Kendrick

2. We'll let You have Your way among us,
   We'll not strive, we'll not strive. (*Repeat.*)
   For Yours is the power and the glory
   For ever and ever the same.
   We'll let You have Your way among us,
   We'll not strive, we'll not strive.

3. Let My peace rule within your hearts,
   Do not strive, do not strive. (*Repeat.*)
   For Mine is the power and the glory
   For ever and ever the same.
   Let My peace rule within your hearts,
   Do not strive, do not strive.

4. We'll let Your peace rule within our hearts,
   We'll not strive, we'll not strive. (*Repeat.*)
   For Yours . . . (*etc.*)

326. Let our praise to You be as incense

Ps 141:2;
Rev 4:8; 8:4

Brent Chambers

Let our praise to You be as in - cense,_____ let our

praise to You be as pil - lars of Your throne.

Let our praise to You be as in - cense,_____ as we

come be - fore You and wor - ship You a - lone.

327.

Let praises ring

Phil 2:9; 1 Pet 2:9; Rev 1:6; 5:10

Mike & Claire McIntosh

1. Let prai - ses ring, _____ let prai - ses ring, _____
lift voi - ces up to love _____ Him, lift
hearts and hands to touch _____ Him, O let prai - ses ring. _____
_____ And fill the skies with an - thems high that tell His ex -
cel - len - cies, _____ as priests and kings who rule with

2. Let praises ring, let praises ring,
   Bow down in adoration,
   Cry out His exaltation,
   O let praises ring.
   And lift the name above all names
   Till every nation knows
   The love of God has come to men,
   His mercies overflow.

328. Let there be glory and honour

Is 9:2; Mt 5:16;
Rev 5:12

James & Elizabeth Greenelsh

329.
Let there be love

1 Jn 4:7

Dave Bilbrough

Triumphantly

Let there be love shared a-mong us, let there be love in our eyes, May now Your love sweep this na-tion, Cause us O Lord ____ to a - rise. Give us a fresh un-der-stand - ing of bro-ther-ly love that is real, Let there be love shared a - mong us, Let there be love. ____

330. Let us break bread together

Mt 26:26–27;
Mk 14:22–23;
Lk 22:19–20; Acts 2:42, 46;
1 Cor 11:23–26

Capo 2 (D)

Calhoun melody,
arr. Stuart Townend

Flowing

1. Let us break bread to-geth-er, we are one. Let us break bread to-geth-er, we are one. We are one as we stand with our face to the ris-en Son. O Lord, have mer-cy on us.

2. Let us drink wine together, we are one.
   Let us drink wine together, we are one.
   We are one . . .

3. Let us praise God together, we are one.
   Let us praise God together, we are one.
   We are one . . .

331. Let us go to the house of the Lord
(Psalm 122)

Ps 122:1–4, 6–9

Ian White

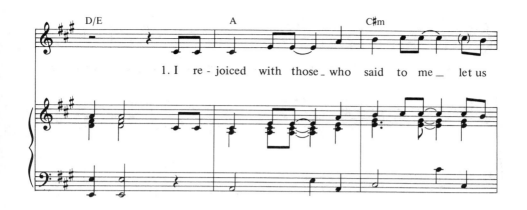

1. I re - joiced with those _ who said to me _ let us

go to the house of the Lord. Our feet are stand - ing

in your gates, Je - ru - sa - lem, like a

ci - ty built to - ge - ther, — where the peo-ple of God go up, to — praise the — name — of the Lord. Let us go —

2. For peace for all Jerusalem
   And loved ones this we pray;
   May all men be secure where they must live.
   And to all my friends and brothers
   May the peace be within you,
   For the sake of the house of the Lord.

332. Let us praise His name with dancing

2 Sam 6:14; Ps 149:3

Pale Sauni

1. Let us praise His name with dan-cing and with the tam-bour-ine. Let us praise His name with dan - cing, make a joy-ful noise and sing.

Dance, dance, dance be-fore the King.

Dance, dance, cel - e - brate and sing.

2. Let us celebrate with dancing;
The King has set us free.
Let us celebrate with dancing,
Rejoice in victory.

━━━━━━━━━━ □ ▢ □ ━━━━━━━━━━

Shout for joy to the Lord, all the
 earth,
 burst into jubilant song with
 music;
make music to the Lord with the
 harp,
 with the harp and the sound of
 singing,
with trumpets and the blast of the
 ram's horn –
 shout for joy before the Lord, the
 King.

PSALM 98:4–6

━━━━━━━━━━ □ ▢ □ ━━━━━━━━━━

333.
Capo 1(A)
MONKLAND

Let us with a gladsome mind

Ps 136:1–2, 7–9, 16, 25

John Antes (1740-1811)
Arranged by John Wilkes (1785-1869)

Joyfully

Verse

1. Let us with a glad - some mind praise the Lord, for He is kind:

Chorus

For His mer-cies shall en - dure, ev - er faith - ful, ev - er sure.

2. Let us blaze His name abroad,
   For of gods He is the God:

3. He, with all-commanding might,
   Filled the new-made world with light:

4. He the golden-tressèd sun,
   Caused all day his course to run:

5. And the silver moon by night,
   'Mid her spangled sisters bright:

6. He His chosen race did bless
   In the wasteful wilderness:

7. All things living He doth feed,
   His full hand supplies their need:

8. Let us then with gladsome mind
   Praise the Lord, for He is kind:

John Milton (1608-74)

334. Let Your living water flow

Jn 7:38; Eph 5:18;
1 Pet 5:7

John Watson

With a strong beat

1. Let Your liv-ing wa-ter flow o-ver my soul. Let Your Ho-ly Spi-rit come and take con - trol ____ of ev'-ry sit-u-a - tion that has trou-bled my mind. All my cares and bur-dens on to You I ____ roll.

To Chorus / *Last time* / *Fine*

2. Come now Holy Spirit and take control.
   Hold me in Your loving arms and make me whole.
   Wipe away all doubt and fear and take my pride
   Draw me to Your love and keep me by Your side.

3. Give your life to Jesus, let Him fill your soul.
   Let Him take you in His arms and make you whole.
   As you give your life to Him He'll set you free.
   You will live and reign with Him eternally.

4. (*As verse 1.*)

335.

Lift high the Cross

Jn 1:29; 12:32, 35; 1 Tim 2:6;
Heb 7:27; 10:1

Graham Kendrick

Lift high the cross,

lift high the cross, in ma-jes-ty,

in vic-tor-y.

1. Here raged the fight, here raged the fight, dark-ness and

(Men) (Women) (Men)

hell's pow'r is bro ken, and hea-ven stands op - en; lift high the cross! Lift high the cross, lift high the cross, in ma-jes - ty, in vic - to - ry.

2. *(Men)*   Here once for all
   (Women)   Here once for all
   (Men)   Was sacrificed
   (Women)   Was sacrificed
   (Men)   The Lamb of God,
   (Women)   The Lamb of God,
   (All)   Jesus Christ.

336.

Lift up your heads

Lk 21:28

Capo 1 (G)

Steven L. Fry

Majestically with strength

Lift up your heads to the com - ing King. Bow be-fore Him and a-dore Him, sing _____ to His maj-est - y, let your prais - es be pure and ho - ly, giv - ing glo - ry to the King of kings. kings.

1st time

Last time only

337.

Lift up your heads
(O you gates)

Ps 24:7; Eph 1:20–21

Graham Kendrick

2. Up from the dead He ascends,
   Through every rank of heavenly power.
   Let heaven prepare the highest place,
   Throw wide the everlasting doors:

3. With trumpet blast and shouts of joy,
   All heaven greets the risen King.
   With angel choirs come line the way,
   Throw wide the gates and welcome Him:

338. Lift up your heads, O ye gates

(The King of glory)

Ps 24:3–4, 7–8

Capo 2(C)

Terry Manship

Lift up your heads, O ye gates, and be ye lift-ed up, ye ev-er-last-ing doors. Lift up your heads, O ye gates, and be ye lift-ed up, ye ev-er-last-ing doors; and the King of glo-ry shall come in, the King of glo-ry shall come in, the King of glo-ry shall come

(Women)

2. Who shall ascend the hill,
   The hill of the Lord?

(Men)

Even he that hath clean hands
And a pure heart with which to praise his God.

339. Light a flame

Mt 5:14; Lk 2:10

Mick Gisbey

Light a flame with - in my heart that's burn - ing

bright; fan the fire ___ of joy in me to

set the world a - light. Let my flame be - gin to spread, my

life to glow; God of light, ___ may

I re-flect Your love to all I know.

1. From hea-ven's splen-dour He comes|to earth,
while all the an-gels ce-le-brate the
good news of His birth.

2. We too exalt You,
    Our glorious King;
    Jesus our Saviour
    Paid the price to take away our sin.

340.

Lighten our darkness

Jn 1:5; 8:12; 12:36, 46

This song can be sung in the form of a call and response.

Prayerfully

Chris Rolinson

341.

Light has dawned

Jn 1:5; 8:12; 12:36, 46; 1 Jn 1:7

Capo 2 (G)

Graham Kendrick

Heaven and earth shall bow at His feet, when He comes to reign. reign. reign.

(Women)

2. Saviour of the world is He,
   Heaven's King come down.
   Judgement, love and mercy meet
   At His thorny crown.

(Men)

3. Life has sprung from hearts of stone,
   By the Spirit's breath.
   Hell shall let its captives go,
   Life has conquered death.

4. Blood has flowed that cleanses from sin,
   God His love has proved.
   Men may mock and demons may rage,
   We shall not be moved!

(Chorus twice to end)

342.

Light of the world
(Fire of God)

Mt 3:11; Lk 3:16; Jn 8:12

Craig Musseau

1. Light of the world, ___ shine Your

light ___ in-to ___ my heart. ___

God of love, ___ pierce my soul ___

___ with Your mer - cy.

Chorus

So we might see Your glo - ry, so we might see Your face. ___ So we can feel Your heart - beat, and hear You call our name. ___

2. Fire of God,
   Burn away what is not holy.
   Jesus, take our hearts
   And make them new.

343.

Like a gentle breeze
(Holy Spirit, come)

Mt 3:11; Lk 3:16; Acts 2:2

Maggi Dawn

Tenderly

Like a gen-tle breeze,— like a might-y wind,— like a roar-ing fire,_____ You will vis-it us,— You will cleanse our souls, _ and our hearts in - spire,_____ bring-ing peace to us _ like a heal-ing balm,— or a gen-tle dove;_____ O come to us,— O bring to us _ God's

———— □ ⬜ □ ————

*Rejoice in the Lord always. I will
say it again: Rejoice!*

PHILIPPIANS 4:4

———— □ ⬜ □ ————

344.
Like a river glorious

Capo 3 (D)

WYE VALLEY

Ps 46:4–5; Is 26:3; Jas 1:2;
Rev 22:1

J. Mountain (1844-1933)

1. Like a ri - ver glo - rious is God's per - fect peace,
over all vic - tor - ious, in its bright in - crease:
per - fect, yet it flow - eth full - er ev - 'ry day;
Stayed up - on Je - ho - vah, hearts are ful - ly blest,
per - fect, yet it grow - eth deep - er all the way.
find - ing, as He pro - mised, per - fect peace and rest.

2. Hidden in the hollow of His blessèd hand,
Never foe can follow, never traitor stand;
Not a surge of worry, not a shade of care,
Not a blast of hurry touched the Spirit there.
    Stayed upon Jehovah . . .

3. Every joy or trial falleth from above,
Traced upon our dial by the sun of love.
We may trust Him fully, all for us to do;
They who trust Him wholly find Him wholly true.
    Stayed upon Jehovah . . .

Frances Ridley Havergal (1836-79)

345.

Lion of Judah

Is 9:6; 1 Tim 6:15; Rev 5:5; 17:14; 19:16; 22:20

Ted Sandquist

1. Li - on of Ju - dah on the throne, I shout Your name, let it be known that You are the King of kings, You are the Prince of Peace, may Your king - dom's reign never cease. Hail to the King!

Hail to — the King! _____

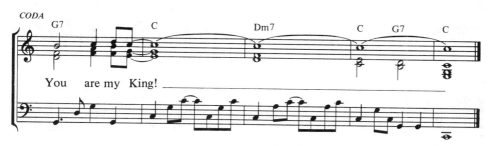

You   are my   King! _____

2.   Lion of Judah come to earth,
     I want to thank You for Your birth,
     For the living Word,
     For Your death on the tree,
     For Your resurrection victory.
     Hallelujah! Hallelujah!

3.   Lion of Judah, come again,
     Take up Your throne Jerusalem.
     Bring release to this earth
     And the consummation
     Of Your kingdom's reign, let it come!
     Maranatha! Maranatha!

4.   Lion of Judah on the throne,
     I shout Your name, let it be known
     That You are the King of kings,
     You are the Prince of Peace,
     May Your kingdom's reign never cease.
     Hail to the King!
     Hail to the King!
     You are my King!

346. Living under the shadow of His wing

Ps 57:1

David J. Hadden & Bob Silvester

1. Li-ving un - der the sha-dow of His wing we find sec-u-ri-ty. Standing in His pre - sence we will bring our wor - ship, wor - ship, wor - ship to the King.

2. Bowed in adoration at His feet
   We dwell in harmony.
   Voices joined together that repeat,
   Worthy, worthy, worthy is the Lamb.

3. Heart to heart embracing in His love
   Reveals His purity.
   Soaring in my spirit like a dove.
   Holy, holy, holy is the Lord.

---□ ▢ □---

Shout for joy to the Lord, all the
earth.
Serve the Lord with gladness;
come before him with joyful songs.

PSALM 100:1–2

---□ ▢ □---

347. Lo, He comes with clouds descending

Acts 1:11; 1 Thess 4:16–17; Rev 1:7

HELMSLEY

With strength

18th century English melody

1. Lo, He comes with clouds de-scend-ing, once for fa-vour'd sin-ners slain; Al-le-lu-ia! Al-le-lu-ia! Al-le-lu-ia! God ap-pears on earth to reign.

thou-sand thou-sand saints at-tend-ing swell the tri-umph of His train:

2. Every eye shall now behold Him
Robed in glorious majesty;
Those who set at naught and sold Him,
Pierced and nailed Him to the tree,
Deeply wailing,
Deeply wailing,
Deeply wailing,
Shall their true Messiah see.

3. Those dear tokens of His passion
Still His dazzling body bears;
Cause of endless exultation
To His ransomed worshippers:
With what rapture,
With what rapture,
With what rapture,
Gaze we on those glorious scars.

4. Yea, Amen, let all adore Thee,
High on Thine eternal throne;
Saviour, take the power and glory,
Claim the kingdom for Thine own:
Come, Lord Jesus!
Come, Lord Jesus!
Come, Lord Jesus!
Everlasting God, come down!

Charles Wesley (1707-88)

348. Look and see the glory of the King

Is 6:1;
Eph 1:20;
2:22

Joyfully with swing

Martin F. Ball

Chorus

Look and see the glo-ry of the King, — sense the presence of the Lord amongst His peo - ple. Feel Him fill the tem-ple of our lives — as He sits up-on — the throne of our praise. praise.

1st time
Last time only — Fine

Verse

1. We are His church, we are all God's own peo - ple.

We all pro - claim that He is King, He is King.

D.C. al Fine

2. At God's right hand,
   Jesus Christ is exalted,
   His rule is now and shall be for evermore.

———————— □ ▢ □ ————————

God has chosen to make known among the Gentiles the glorious riches of this mystery, which is Christ in you, the hope of glory.

COLOSSIANS 1:27

———————— □ ▢ □ ————————

349. Look, ye saints, the sight is glorious

Is 53:3;
Mt 27:29;
Mk 15:17; 1 Tim 6:15; Heb 2:9;
Rev 17:14; 19:12, 16

Capo 3(G)

REGENT SQUARE

Henry Smart (1813-79)

1. Look, ye saints, the sight is glo - rious; see the Man of

Sor - rows now, from the fight re - turn'd vic - tor - ious,

ev - 'ry knee to ___ Him shall bow: Crown Him! Crown Him!

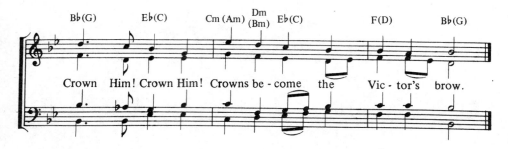

Crown Him! Crown Him! Crowns be - come the Vic - tor's brow.

Alternative tune: CWM RHONDA

2. Crown the Saviour, angels, crown Him:
   Rich the trophies Jesus brings;
   In the seat of power enthrone Him,
   While the vault of heaven rings:
   Crown Him! Crown Him!
   Crown Him! Crown Him!
   Crown the Saviour, King of kings!

3. Sinners in derision crowned Him,
   Mocking thus the Saviour's claim;
   Saints and angels throng around Him,
   Own His title, praise His name:
   Crown Him! Crown Him!
   Crown Him! Crown Him!
   Spread abroad the Victor's fame.

4. Hark, those bursts of acclamation!
   Hark, those loud triumphant chords!
   Jesus takes the highest station:
   O what joy the sight affords!
   Crown Him! Crown Him!
   Crown Him! Crown Him!
   King of kings, and Lord of lords!

Thomas Kelly (1769-1854)

350.   Lord and Father, King for ever

Noel Richards

Lord and Fath - er, _____ King for ev - er, _____

Throned with maj - es - ty _ and power, _____

we a - dore You, _____ we ex - alt You.

Wor - ship we bring, our off - er - ing,

wor - ship we bring to You _ our _____ King. _____

351. Lord, come and heal Your church

Heb: 4:16

Chris Rolinson

Worshipfully
Verse

Lord, come and heal Your church, take our lives and cleanse with your fi-re. Let Your de-li-ve-rance flow, as we lift Your name up —

Chorus

high - er; we will draw near, and sur-ren - der our — fear, lift our hands to pro-claim, ho-ly Fa - ther, You are — here.

2. Spirit of God, come in
   And release our hearts to praise You.
   Make us whole, for
   Holy we'll become, and serve You.

3. Show us Your power, we pray,
   That we might share in Your glory.
   We shall arise and go
   To proclaim Your works most holy

352. Lord, enthroned in heavenly splendour

Capo 3(G)
ST HELEN

Ex 16:15; 17:6; Ps 3:3; Is 11:1; Jn 6:58;
Heb 7:27; 1 Jn 1:7; Rev 1:5; 5:12

George C. Martin (1844-1916)

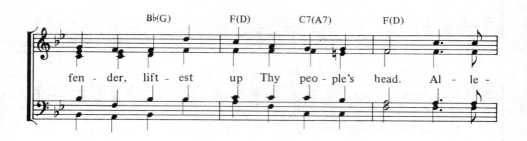

1. Lord, en - thron'd in heav'n - ly splen - dour, first be-
got - ten from the dead, Thou a - lone, our strong de-
fen - der, lift - est up Thy peo - ple's head. Al - le -
lu - ia! Al - le - lu - ia! Je - sus, true and liv - ing Bread.

2. Here our humblest homage pay we,
   Here in loving reverence bow;
   Here for faith's discernment pray we,
   Lest we fail to know Thee now.
   Alleluia! Alleluia!
   Thou art here, we ask not how.

3. Though the lowliest form doth veil Thee
   As of old in Bethlehem,
   Here as there Thine angels hail Thee
   Branch and Flower of Jesse's stem.
   Alleluia! Alleluia!
   We in worship join with them.

4. Paschal Lamb, Thine offering, finished
   Once for all when Thou wast slain,
   In its fullness undiminished
   Shall for evermore remain,
   Alleluia! Alleluia!
   Cleansing souls from every stain.

5. Life-imparting, heavenly Manna,
   Stricken Rock with streaming side,
   Heaven and earth with loud hosanna
   Worship Thee, the Lamb who died.
   Alleluia! Alleluia!
   Risen, ascended, glorified!

   G.H. Bourne (1840-1925)

353. Lord God, heavenly King

Capo 4 (C)

Worshipfully

Sue Hutchinson

Lord God, heaven-ly King, You are our God, To You we sing; Re-ceive the wor-ship of our hearts, the a-dor-a-tion of our lips; How we love You, Lord God, hea-ven-ly King.

354.

Lord, have mercy

2 Chron 7:14

Graham Kendrick

Lord, have mer-cy on us, come and heal our land. Cleanse with Your fire, heal with Your touch. Hum-bly we bow and call u-pon You now. O Lord, have mer-cy on us. O

355.

Lord, how majestic You are

(You are my everything)

Ps 3:5; 8:1; 60:4;
119:105; Mt 11:28

Stuart Townend

1. Lord how ma-jest-ic You are, — my eyes meet Your gaze and my burden is

lift - ed. Your word — is a lamp to my feet, — Your hand swift to

bless and Your ban-ner a shield. You are my

ev - 'ry - thing, You who made earth — and sky — and

sea, all that You've placed — in - side — of me calls out Your

2. Lord, how resplendent You are,
When I think of Your heavens,
The work of Your fingers —
What is man, that You are mindful of Him,
Yet You've crowned Him with glory
And caused him to reign!

356. Lord, I will celebrate Your love

Dave Bilbrough

Lord, I will cel - e - brate — Your — love,

from deep with - in — my heart, — I cel - e - brate — Your — love;

I cel - e - brate — Your — love gi - ven to me. You are the one that I — a - dore;

357.

Lord Jesus Christ

Lk 22:19; 1 Cor 11:24

LIVING LORD

With breadth

Patrick Appleford (1925-)

1. Lord Je-sus Christ, You have come to us, You are one with us, Mar - y's Son. Cleans - ing our souls from all their sin, pour-ing Your love and good-ness in; Je-sus, our love for You we sing, Liv - ing Lord. Lord.

(Optional communion verse:)

2. Lord Jesus Christ,
   Now and every day,
   Teach us how to pray,
   Son of God.
   You have commanded us to do
   This in remembrance, Lord of You:
   Into our lives Your power breaks through,
   Living Lord.

3. Lord Jesus Christ,
   You have come to us,
   Born as one of us,
   Mary's son.
   Led out to die on Calvary,
   Risen from death to set us free,
   Living Lord Jesus, help us see
   You are Lord.

4. Lord Jesus Christ,
   We would come to You,
   Live our lives for You,
   Son of God.
   All Your commands we know are true,
   Your many gifts will make us new,
   Into our lives Your power breaks through,
   Living Lord.

Patrick Appleford (1925-)

358.

Lord Jesus, here I stand

Rae Ranford

Worshipfully, with awe

Lord Je - sus, here I stand be - fore ___ You, to wor - ship You, glo - ri - fy Your name, I hum - bly bow the knee be - fore Your ma - jes - ty, give You the glo - ry, give You the praise.

--- □ ▯ □ ---

I will praise you, O Lord, among the
nations;
I will sing of you among the peoples.
For great is your love, reaching to the
heavens;
your faithfulness reaches to the
skies.
Be exalted, O God, above the heavens;
let your glory be over all the earth.

PSALM 57:9–11

--- □ ▯ □ ---

359.

Lord, keep my heart tender

Is 53:5; 1 Jn 4:19

Jesus Fellowship

Capo 2 (G)

1. Lord, keep my heart ten-der, reach-ing with out-stretched hands _ to Je-sus Christ, feel-ing my hard-ness melt, know-ing how Je-sus felt pos-sessed by love, warm Cal-v'ry love.

2. Lord, keep my heart tender,
Reaching with outstretched hands
For healing grace;
Believe the word revealed —
"By His stripes we are healed" —
Possessed by love,
Whole Calvary love.

3. Lord, keep my heart tender,
Reaching with outstretched hands
To those in need;
Finding, as tears I weep,
Compassion's well is deep,
Possessed by love,
Fresh Calvary love.

4. Lord, keep my heart tender,
Reaching with outstretched hands
To God most high;
Worshipping with desire,
My heart consumed by fire,
Possessed by love,
Strong Calvary love.

360.   Lord make me an instrument

Ps 63:4

Author unknown
Arr. Margaret Evans

Capo 3 (D)

Prayerfully

1. Lord make me an in-strument, an in-strument of wor-ship; I lift up my hands in Your name. Lord make me an in-strument, an in-stru-ment of wor-ship; I lift up my hands in Your name.

2. I'll sing You a love song,
   A love song of worship,
   I'll lift up my hands in Your name.
   I'll sing You a love song,
   A love song to Jesus,
   I'll lift up my hands in Your name.

3. For we are a symphony,
   A symphony of worship.
   We lift up our hands in Your name.
   For we are a symphony,
   A symphony of worship.
   We lift up our hands in Your name.

4. We'll sing You a love song,
   A love song of worship,
   We'll lift up our hands in Your name.
   We'll sing You a love song,
   A love song to Jesus,
   We'll lift up our hands in Your name.

361.

Lord of lords

Ex 3:14; Is 9:6; 1 Tim 6:15;
Rev 17:14; 19:16

Jessy Dixon/Randy Scruggs
John W. Thompson

2. Lord, You're righteous in all Your ways.
   We bless Your holy name and we will give You praise,
   We give You glory.
   You reign forever in majesty,
   We praise You and lift You up for eternity,
   We give You glory,
   Glory to God! Glory to God! Glory to God Almighty in the highest!

362.

Lord, the light of Your love
(Shine, Jesus, shine)

Ps 139:23; Jn 1:5; 8:12, 32;
2 Cor 3:18; Rev 22:1

Capo 2(G)

Graham Kendrick

Fa-ther's glo-ry; blaze Spi-rit, blaze,__ set our hearts on fire. Flow, ri-ver, flow,__ flood the na-tions with grace and mer-cy; send forth Your word, __ Lord, and let there be light.

2. Lord, I come to Your awesome presence,
   From the shadows into Your radiance;
   By the blood I may enter Your brightness,
   Search me, try me, consume all my darkness.
   Shine on me, shine on me.

3. As we gaze on Your kingly brightness
   So our faces display Your likeness,
   Ever changing from glory to glory,
   Mirrored here may our lives tell Your story.
   Shine on me, shine on me.

(Chorus twice to end.)

363.

Lord, we come
(Join our hearts)

Ps 133

Graham Kendrick

Gently

Verse

1. Lord, we come in Your name, gath-ered here to wor-ship You. Join us all in har-mo-ny, Spi - rit come. *(Men)* So

And
And

Chorus

join our __ hearts __ to-geth-er in love. *(Women)* Join our __ hearts __ to-geth-er in

Join our __ hearts __ to-geth-er in love,
love. Join our __ hearts, __

(All) and come like the dew __ on the moun-tains __
for there the Lord __ has com-mand-ed __

1st time

des - cend - ing.

2nd time

__ the

bless - ing. __

2. O how good, how beautiful, } *(Women)*
   When we live in unity;
   Flowing like anointing oil } *(Men)*
   On Jesus' head.

3. So let us all agree
   To make strong our bonds of peace.
   Here is life forever more,
   Spirit, come.

—————— □ ▢ □ ——————

For God did not give us a spirit of timidity, but a spirit of power, of love and of self-discipline.

2 TIMOTHY 1:7

—————— □ ▢ □ ——————

364.

Lord we give You praise

Heb 13:8

Worshipfully

Mick Ray

Lord, we give You praise; our prayer of thanks to You we bring. We sing our songs to You, for praise be-longs to You; Lord, we give You praise. Your love goes on and on; You ne-ver change, You never turn. Our hands we raise to You, and bring our praise to You; Lord, we give You praise.

365.

Lord we long for You
(Heal our nation)

2 Chron 7:14

Trish Morgan/Ray Goudie/
Ian Townend/Dave Bankhead

Prayerfully, with feeling

1. Lord we long for you to move in pow-er. There's a hun-ger deep with-in our hearts to see heal-ing in our na-tion. Send Your Spi-rit to re-vive us:

Chorus

Heal our na-tion! Heal our na-tion! Heal our na-tion! Pour out Your Spi-rit on this land!

2. Lord we hear Your Spirit coming closer,
   A mighty wave to break upon our land,
   Bringing justice, and forgiveness,
   God we cry to You 'revive us':

366.

Lord, we worship You

Dave Bilbrough

Lord, we wor-ship You, __ Lord, we wor-ship You, Lord, we wor-ship You, __ Lord, we wor-ship You. In hum-ble ad-or-a - tion we lift our voi - ces to You, and sing in acc-la-ma-tion our song of praise __ to You. You.

367.

Lord, You are calling
(Let Your kingdom come)

Mt 6:10; Lk 11:2; Phil 2:10; Rev 5:10

Simon & Lorraine Fenner

1. Lord, You are call-ing the peo-ple of Your king-dom to battle in Your name a-gainst the e-ne-my; to stand be-fore You, a peo-ple who will serve You, till Your king-dom is re-leased through-out the earth. Let Your king-dom come, let Your will be done on

368.   Lord, You are more precious

Ps 73:25; 119:72;
Prov 3:14–15; 8:11

Lynn DeShazo

Prayerfully

Lord, You are more precious than sil - ver,

Lord, You are more cost - ly than gold.

Lord, You are more beau - ti - ful _ than diamonds, and

no - thing I de - sire com - pares with You.

369.   Lord, You are so precious to me

1 Jn 4:19

Capo 2 (G)

Graham Kendrick

Tenderly

1. Lord, You are so precious to me,
Lord, You are so precious to me and I
love You, yes, I love ____ You be-
cause You first lov'd me. ____

2. Lord, You are so gracious to me,
Lord, You are so gracious to me
And I love You,
Yes, I love You
Because You first loved me.

370. Lord, You put a tongue in my mouth

Ian Smale

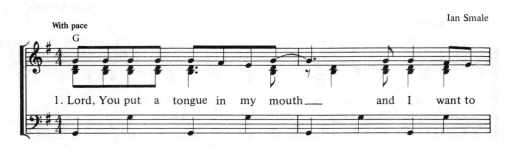

1. Lord, You put a tongue in my mouth___ and I want to

sing to You, Lord, You put a tongue in my mouth

___ and I want to sing to You,

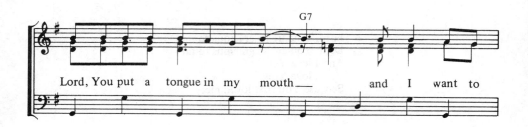

Lord, You put a tongue in my mouth___ and I want to

sing on-ly to You. Lord Je - sus,

free us in our praise;

Lord Je - sus, free us in our

praise.

1st and 2nd times   *Last time only*

2. Lord, You put some hands on my arms
   Which I want to raise to You. . . *(etc)*.

3. Lord, You put some feet on my legs
   And I want to dance to You. . . *(etc)*.

371.
Lord, You're faithful and just
(Faithful and just)

Ex 3:14; Is 9:6; 40:8;
Mt 24:35; Mk 13:31;
Lk 21:33; 1 Pet 1:25

Don Moen

Capo 3(Am)

With feeling

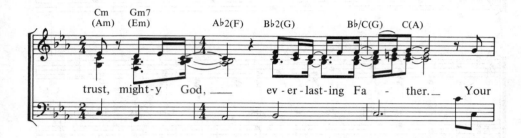

Lord, You're faith-ful _ and _ just, in You I put _ my _

trust, might-y God, _ ev-er-last-ing Fa - ther. _ Your

word is faith-ful _ and _ true, what You pro-mised You _ will _

do, oh _ Lord, _ Your word en-dures _ for - ev-

372. Lord, Your glory fills my heart
(Above all others)

Ps 8:1; Rev 5:12

Capo 2(D)

Craig Musseau

With strength
Verse

Lord, Your glo - ry fills my heart, Your pre sence deep with-in me stirs my soul. O Lord, how awe- some are Your ways, Your ma - jes - ty sur - round- ing all the earth. All wis-

2. Lord, Your Spirit moves me now,
   I see a picture of Your holiness.
   O Lord, I look into Your eyes,
   And feel a fire burn into my heart.

——— □ □ □ ———

Praise the Lord, you his angels,
  you mighty ones who do his
    bidding,
  who obey his word.
Praise the Lord, all his heavenly
    hosts,
  you his servants who do his will.
Praise the Lord, all his works
  everywhere in his dominion.

PSALM 103:20–22

——— □ □ □ ———

373. Lord, Your name is holy

Tom Shirey

374. Lord, Your name is wonderful

Is 61:1; Lk 4:18; 10:17

Barry Taylor

Lord, Your name is won-der-ful, __ at Your name the cap-tives shall_go __ free. We de-clare the might-y name_of Je - sus, and pro-claim Your ho-ly vic-to-ry. __ At Your name_ the king-doms __ fall; we de-clare_

375.

Love beyond measure

Eph 3:19

Dave Bilbrough

Love be-yond mea-sure,___ mer-cy so free.

Your end-less re-sour-ces ___ giv-en to me.

Strength to the wea-ry, ___ heal-ing our lives,

Your love be-yond mea-sure ___ has op-en'd my eyes,

op-en'd my eyes.

Last time only

376. Love came down at Christmas

Capo 3 (D)

GARTAN

Mt 2:2; 1 Jn 4:8

Irish Traditional Air

1. Love came down at Christ - mas, Love all love - ly, Love di - vine. Love was born at Christ - mas, stars and an - gels gave the sign.

2. Worship we the Godhead,
   Love incarnate, Love divine,
   Worship we our Jesus;
   But wherewith for sacred sign?

3. Love shall be our token,
   Love be yours and love be mine,
   Love to God and all men,
   Love for plea and gift and sign.

Christina Rossetti (1830-94)

377.

Love divine
(First time)

2 Cor 3:18; 5:17; Heb 4:11; 12:2;
1 Jn 4:7; Rev 1:8, 18

BLAENWERN

With strength

William Penfro Rowlands (1860-1937)

1. Love di - vine, all loves ex - cell - ing,
joy of heav'n to earth come down!
Fix in us Thy hum - ble dwell - ing,
all Thy faith - ful mer - cies crown.
Je - sus, Thou art all com - pas - sion,

pure un - boun - ded love — Thou art;

vis - it us with Thy — sal - va - tion,

en - ter ev - 'ry tremb - ling heart.

Alternative tune: HYFRYDOL (266)

2. Breathe, O breathe, Thy loving Spirit
Into every troubled breast!
Let us all in Thee inherit,
Let us find Thy promised rest;
Take away the love of sinning;
Alpha and Omega be;
End of faith, as its beginning,
Set our hearts at liberty.

3. Come, Almighty to deliver,
Let us all Thy grace receive;
Suddenly return, and never,
Never more Thy temples leave.
Thee we would be always blessing,
Serve Thee as Thy hosts above,
Pray and praise Thee without ceasing,
Glory in Thy perfect love.

4. Finish then Thy new creation,
Pure and spotless let us be;
Let us see Thy great salvation,
Perfectly restored in Thee!
Changed from glory into glory,
Till in heaven we take our place;
Till we cast our crowns before Thee,
Lost in wonder, love and praise.

Charles Wesley (1707-88)

Love divine
(Second tune)

LOVE DIVINE
Flowing

John Stainer (1840-1901)

1. Love di - vine, all loves ex - cell-ing, joy of heav'n to earth come down! Fix in us Thy hum-ble dwell-ing, all Thy faith-ful mer-cies crown.

2. Jesus, Thou art all compassion,
Pure, unbounded love Thou art;
Visit us with Thy salvation,
Enter every trembling heart.

3. Breathe, O breathe, Thy loving Spirit
Into every troubled breast!
Let us all in Thee inherit,
Let us find Thy promised rest.

4. Take away the love of sinning;
Alpha and Omega be;
End of faith, as its beginning,
Set our hearts at liberty.

5. Come, Almighty to deliver.
Let us all Thy grace receive.
Suddenly return, and never,
Never more Thy temples leave.

6. Thee we would be always blessing,
Serve Thee as Thy hosts above,
Pray and praise Thee without ceasing,
Glory in Thy perfect love

7. Finish then Thy new creation,
Pure and spotless let us be;
Let us see Thy great salvation,
Perfectly restored in Thee!

8. Changed from glory into glory,
Till in heaven we take our place;
Till we cast our crowns before Thee,
Lost in wonder, love and praise.

Charles Wesley (1707-88)

—— □ ▢ □ ——

Let us then approach the throne of grace with confidence, so that we may receive mercy and find grace to help us in our time of need.

HEBREWS 4:16

—— □ ▢ □ ——

378.

Low in the grave He lay

Mt 27:60; 28:6; Mk 15:46;
16:6; Lk 23:53; 24:6;
Jn 19:42; 21:14

Capo 3(G)
CHRIST AROSE!

Robert Lowry (1826-99)

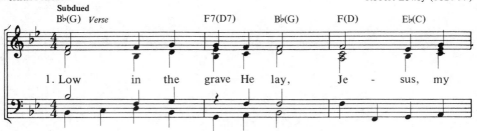

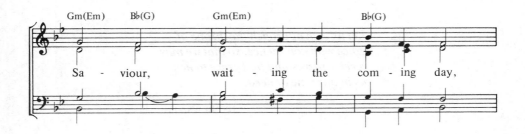

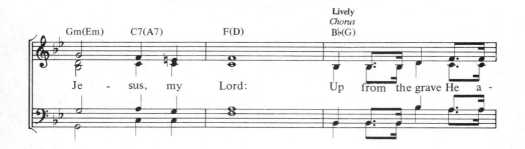

1. Low in the grave He lay, Je - sus, my Sa - viour, wait - ing the com - ing day, Je - sus, my Lord: Up from the grave He a - rose, with a migh- ty tri-umph o'er His foes; He a-

rose a Vic - tor from the dark do - main, and He
lives for ev - er with His saints to reign: He a - rose!
He a - rose! Al - le - lu - ia! Christ a - rose!

2. Vainly they watch His bed,
   Jesus, my Saviour;
   Vainly they seal the dead,
   Jesus, my Lord:

3. Death cannot keep his prey,
   Jesus, my Saviour;
   He tore the bars away,
   Jesus, my Lord:

Robert Lowry (1826-99)

379.

Majesty

Rev 1:6; 5:13

Jack W. Hayford

380.   Make a joyful melody

Eph 1:14

Dave Bilbrough

Lively, with a 'rock' feel

Make a joy - ful mel - o - dy, ___ join to - geth - er in har - mon - y, ___ we ___ are a part of a fam - i - ly, ___ the fam - i - ly of God. ___ His Spi - rit is our ___ gua - ran - tee ___ that He lives in

381.   Make me a channel of Your peace

Lk 6:38

Sebastian Temple

1. Make me a chan-nel of Your peace. _____ Where
there is hat-red let me bring Your love; _____ where
there is in-ju-ry, Your par-don Lord; _____ and _
where there's doubt, true faith _ in _ You. _____ Oh,
Mas-ter, grant that I may ne-ver seek _____ so

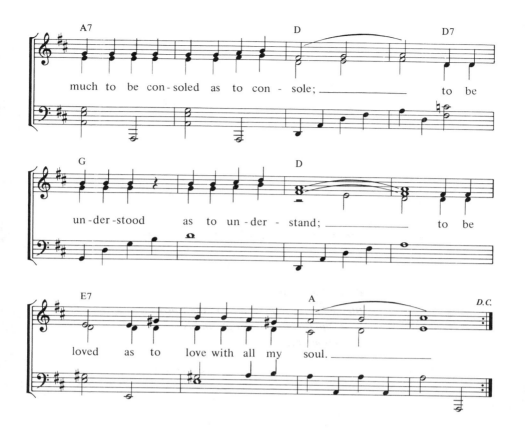

much to be con-soled as to con - sole; _____ to be
un-der-stood as to un-der - stand; _____ to be
loved as to love with all my soul. _____

2. Make me a channel of Your peace.
   Where there's despair in life let me bring hope;
   Where there is darkness, only light;
   And where there's sadness, ever joy.

3. Make me a channel of Your peace.
   It is in pardoning that we are pardoned,
   In giving to all men that we receive,
   And in dying that we're born to eternal life.

— □ ▢ □ —

Praise the Lord.

Blessed is the man who fears the Lord,
who finds great delight in his
commands.

PSALM 112:1

— □ ▢ □ —

382.
Make me, Lord, a dreamer
(For Your kingdom)

Prov 29:18; Joel 2:28;
Acts 2:17

Chris Bowater

Prayerfully

1. Make me, Lord, a dream-er for Your king-dom; plant in my heart hea-ven-ly de-sires. Grant faith that can say; im-pos-si-bi-li-ties shall be; _____ and vi-sion lest a world should per-ish _____ not know-ing Thee.

2. Make me, Lord, a dreamer for Your kingdom;
   I would aspire to greater goals in God.
   So cause faith to rise, to motivate each word and deed,
   A faith that's well convinced that Jesus meets every need.

3. Make me, Lord, a dreamer for Your kingdom,
   Dreams that will change a world that's lost its way.
   May dreams that first found their birth in Your omnipotence,
   Come alive in me, becoming reality.

4. *As verse 1.*

383.

Make us one, Lord

1 Cor 12:12

Maldwyn Pope

Make us one, ___ Lord, ___ make us one, ___ Lord, ___

___ by Your Spi - rit, ___ make us one, ___ Lord. ___

___ We are mem - bers ___ of one bod - y, ___

___ make us one, ___ Lord, ___ we pray. ___

384.   Make way

Is 40:3; 61:1; Mt 3:3; 11:5; Mk 1:3;
Lk 3:4; 4:18; 7:22; Jn 1:23; Acts 3:8

Graham Kendrick

Triumphantly

1. Make way, make way, for Christ the King in splen - dour ar - rives. Fling
wide the gates and wel - come_Him in - to your lives. Make _

way! Make way! for the King of kings. Make _
(*Ladies*:Make_way!) (Make_way!) (for the King of kings.)

way! Make_way! And_ let His king - dom in.
(Make_way!) (Make_way!)

2. He comes the broken hearts to heal
The prisoners to free.
The deaf shall hear, the lame shall dance,
The blind shall see.

3. And those who mourn with heavy hearts,
Who weep and sigh;
With laughter, joy and royal crown
He'll beautify.

4. We call you now to worship Him
As Lord of all.
To have no gods before Him
Their thrones must fall!

385.

Man of Sorrows

Is 53:3; Jn 19:30; Eph 1:20

Capo 3(G)
GETHSEMANE

Philipp Bliss (1838-76)

1. Man of Sor-rows! what a name for the Son of God, who came
ru-in'd sin-ners to re-claim! Hal-le-lu -jah! what a Sa-viour!

2. Bearing shame and scoffing rude,
   In my place condemned He stood;
   Sealed my pardon with His blood:
   Hallelujah! what a Saviour!

3. Guilty, vile, and helpless, we;
   Spotless Lamb of God was He:
   Full atonement — can it be?
   Hallelujah! what a Saviour!

4. Lifted up was He to die,
   'It is finished!' was His cry:
   Now in heaven exalted high:
   Hallelujah! what a Saviour!

5. When He comes, our glorious King,
   All His ransomed home to bring,
   Then anew this song we'll sing:
   'Hallelujah! what a Saviour!'

Philipp Bliss (1838-76)

─────── □ ▢ □ ───────

*You also, like living stones, are
being built into a spiritual house to
be a holy priesthood, offering
spiritual sacrifices acceptable to God
through Jesus Christ.*

1 PETER 2:5

─────── □ ▢ □ ───────

386. Master, speak! Thy servant heareth

I Sam 3:10;
Jn 10:11, 14

Capo 3(D)
OTTAWA

Lowell Mason (1792-1872)

Prayerfully

2. Speak to me by name, O Master,
   Let me know it is to me;
   Speak, that I may follow faster,
   With a step more firm and free,
   Where the Shepherd leads the flock
   In the shadow of the rock.

3. Master, speak! though least and lowest,
   Let me not unheard depart;
   Master, speak! for O Thou knowest
   All the yearning of my heart,
   Knowest all its truest need;
   Speak, and make me blessed indeed.

4. Master, speak! and make me ready,
   When Thy voice is truly heard,
   With obedience glad and steady
   Still to follow every word.
   I am listening, Lord, for Thee:
   Master, speak! O speak to me!

Frances Ridley Havergal (1836-79)

387.

May my life
(Sacrificial love)

Rom 12:1; Rev 5:12

Dave Bilbrough

1. May my life de-clare the hon - our of Your name,

re - veal the heart of Christ who came

to light the dark - est place with sac - ri - fi - cial

love.   2. Cause me

Teach me, Lord, to make my life as an

of - fer - ing, to tell the world that Je - sus

Christ is King, for the glo - ry of God.

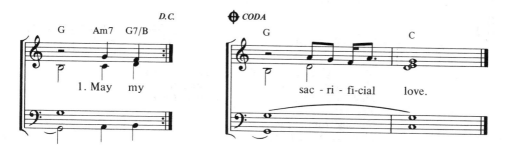

1. May my

sac - ri - fi-cial love.

2. Cause me Lord to reach out in the Father's name,
   To glorify the Lamb once slain,
   To light the darkest place
   With sacrificial love.

388.   May the fragrance

2 Cor 2:14; 3:18; Eph 5:2

Graham Kendrick

Worshipfully

2. May the glory of Jesus fill His church. *(men)*
    May the glory of Jesus fill His church. *(ladies)*
    May the glory of Jesus fill His church. *(men)*
    Radiant glory of Jesus, *(ladies)*
    Shining from our faces }
    As we gaze in adoration. } *(all)*

3. May the beauty of Jesus fill my life. *(men)*
    May the beauty of Jesus fill my life. *(ladies)*
    May the beauty of Jesus fill my life. *(men)*
    Perfect beauty of Jesus, *(ladies)*
    Fill my thoughts my words my deeds }
    My all I give in adoration. } *(All — twice.)*

———————— □ ▢ □ ————————

Though the fig-tree does not bud
* and there are no grapes on the*
*   vines,*
though the olive crop fails
* and the fields produce no food,*
though there are no sheep in the
*   pen*
and no cattle in the stalls,
yet I will rejoice in the Lord,
* I will be joyful in God my*
*   Saviour.*

HABAKKUK 3:17–18

———————— □ ▢ □ ————————

389.

May we be a shining light
(song for the nations)

Mt 5:16; 6:10; Lk 11:2;
Rev 22:2

Chris Christenson

1. May we be a shin - ing light to the na - tions, a

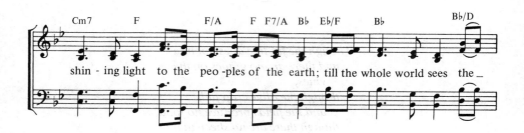

shin - ing light to the peo -ples of the earth; till the whole world sees the _

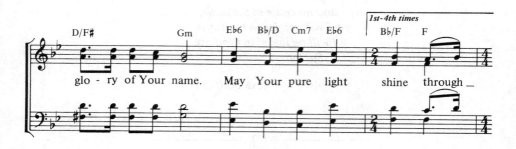

glo - ry of Your name. May Your pure light shine through _

us.
2. May we bring a
3. May we be a   come in _ us.   May Your king-dom come in _ us.
4. May we sing a
5. May _ Your _

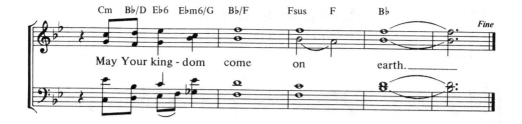

May Your king-dom come on earth.

2. May we bring a word of hope to the nations,
   A word of life to the peoples of the earth;
   Till the whole world knows there's salvation through Your name.
   May Your mercy flow through us.

3. May we be a healing balm to the nations,
   A healing balm to the peoples of the earth;
   Till the whole world knows the power of Your name.
   May Your healing flow through us.

4. May we sing a song of joy to the nations,
   A song of praise to the peoples of the earth;
   Till the whole world rings with the praises of Your name.
   May Your song be sung through us.

5. May Your kingdom come to the nations,
   Your will be done in the peoples of the earth;
   Till the whole world knows that Jesus Christ is Lord.
   May Your kingdom come in us.
   May Your kingdom come in us.
   May Your kingdom come on earth.

390.

Meekness and majesty
(This is your God)

Mt 11:29; Lk 23:34;
Jn 13:5; Phil 2:6–9

Graham Kendrick

Majestically

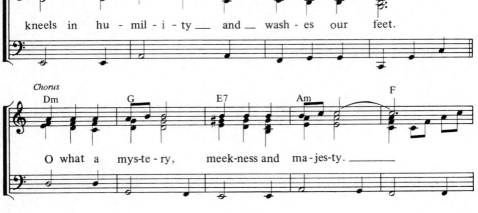

1. Meek-ness and ma-jes-ty, man-hood and de-i-ty, in per-fect har-mo-ny, the Man who is God. Lord of e-ter-ni-ty dwells in hu-man-i-ty, kneels in hu-mil-i-ty ___ and ___ wash-es our feet.

Chorus

O what a mys-te-ry, meek-ness and ma-jes-ty. _____

Bow down and wor-ship _____ for this is your God, _____ this is your God. ____

God, _____ this is your God. ____

2. Father's pure radiance,
   Perfect in innocence,
   Yet learns obedience
   To death on a cross.
   Suffering to give us life,
   Conquering through sacrifice,
   And as they crucify
   Prays: "Father forgive."

3. Wisdom unsearchable,
   God the invisible,
   Love indestructable
   In frailty appears.
   Lord of infinity,
   Stooping so tenderly,
   Lifts our humanity
   To the heights of His throne.

391. Mighty God

Ps 24:8

Maggi Dawn

Migh-ty God, gra-cious King, strong de - li - ve-rer;

You have heard all our prayers, and You've an - swered;

so we give to You our deep ap-pre - ci - a-tion, You're the li - ving God, You are Lord;

You're the li - ving God, You are Lord.

You are worthy, our Lord and God,
to receive glory and honour and
power,
for you created all things,
and by your will they were created
and have their being.

REVELATION 4:11

392.

More love, more power

Deut 6:5; Mt 22:37;
Mk 12:30; Lk 10:27

Jude del Hierro

Capo 3 (Em)

More love, _____ more pow-er, _____

More love, _____ more pow-er, _____

_____ more of You _____ in my _____ life.

more of You _____ in my _____ life.

And I will {wor-ship You / seek Your face} with all of my heart, _____

393.

Morning has broken

Gen 3:8; Ps 118:24; Jn 1:1, 3

Gaelic melody

1. Morn-ing has bro - ken like the first morn - ing; black-bird has
spo - ken like the first bird. Praise for the sing - ing! Praise for the
morn - ing! Praise for them spring - ing fresh from the Word!

2. Sweet the rain's new fall
   Sunlit from heaven,
   Like the first dewfall
   On the first grass.
   Praise for the sweetness
   Of the wet garden,
   Sprung in completeness
   Where His feet pass.

3. Mine is the sunlight!
   Mine is the morning
   Born of the one light
   Eden saw play!
   Praise with elation,
   Praise every morning,
   God's re-creation
   Of the new day!

Eleanor Farjeon (1881-1965)

394.

Move Holy Spirit

Eph 5:18

Patricia Morgan

Move Ho - ly Spi - rit, we ask You to fill us a - fresh. We re - ceive You.

────── □ ▯ □ ──────

*Father, I want those you have given me
to be with me where I am, and to see
my glory, the glory you have given me
because you loved me before the
creation of the world.*

JOHN 17:24

────── □ ▯ □ ──────

395. My God, how wonderful Thou art

Lev 16:2;
Rev 22:4

WESTMINSTER
Joyfully

James Turle (1802-82)

1. My God, how won-der-ful Thou art, Thy maj-es-ty how bright! How
beau-ti-ful Thy mer-cy-seat, in depths of burn-ing light!

2. How dread are Thine eternal years,
O everlasting Lord,
By prostrate spirits day and night
Incessantly adored!

3. How beautiful, how beautiful
The sight of Thee must be,
Thine endless wisdom, boundless power
And awesome purity!

4. O how I fear Thee, Living God,
With deepest, tenderest fears,
And worship Thee with trembling hope
And penitential tears!

5. Yet I may love Thee too, O Lord,
Almighty as Thou art,
For Thou hast stooped to ask of me
The love of my poor heart.

6. No earthly father loves like Thee;
No mother e'er so mild,
Bears and forbears as Thou hast done
With me, Thy sinful child.

7. Father of Jesus, love's reward,
What rapture will it be
Prostrate before Thy throne to lie,
And gaze, and gaze on Thee.

Frederick William Faber (1814-63)

396.

My heart is full
(All the glory)

Ps 45:1, 4, 6–8; Heb 1:8–9;
Rev 4:11; 5:12

Graham Kendrick

1. (Men) My heart is full of ad - mir - a - tion for You, my Lord, my God and King.

(All) Your ex - cel - lence, my in - spi - ra - tion, Your words of grace have made my spi - rit sing.

All — the glo - ry, hon - our and

2. You love what's right and hate what's evil, *(Men)*
   Therefore Your God sets You on high,
   And on Your head pours oil of gladness, *(Women)*
   While fragrance fills Your royal palaces.

3. Your throne, O God, will last forever, *(All)*
   Justice will be Your royal decree.
   In majesty, ride out victorious,
   For righteousness, truth and humility.

397. My Lord, He is the fairest of the fair

Song 5:10, 13; Jn 4:14; 2 Pet 1:19

Joan Parsons

398.

My Lord, what love is this
(Amazing love)

Is 53:3; Rom 5:8;
Eph 5:2

Graham Kendrick

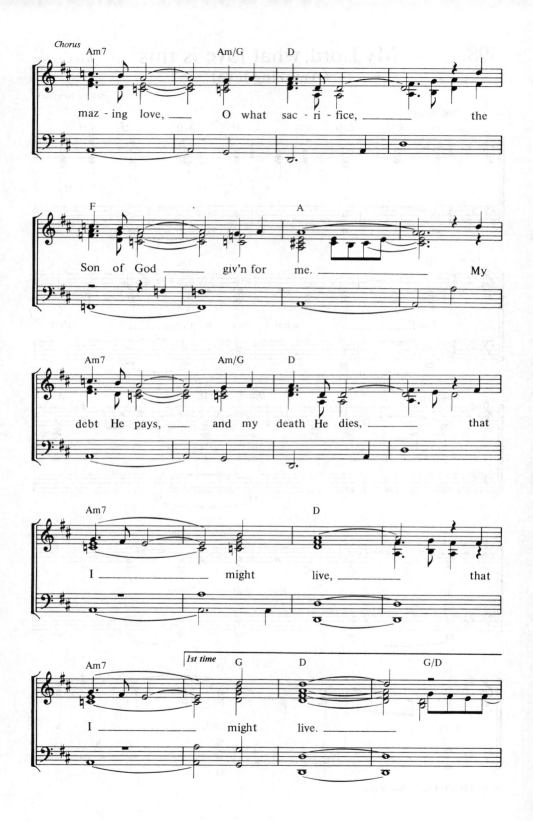

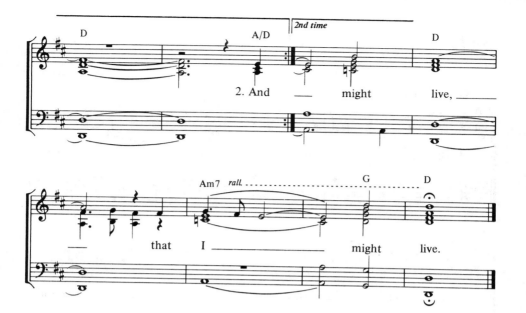

2. And so they watched Him die,
   Despised, rejected;
   But oh, the blood He shed
   Flowed for me!

3. And now this love of Christ
   Shall flow like rivers;
   Come wash your guilt away,
   Live again!

399.

My peace

Jn 14:27; 15:9, 11

Keith Routledge

Gently ♪= 120

1. My peace ___ I give ___ un-to you, ___ It's a peace ___ that the world ___ can-not give, ___ It's a peace ___ that the world ___ can-not un - der - stand. Peace to know, peace to live. ___ My peace ___ I give ___ un-to you. ___

2. My joy I give unto you,
    It's a joy that the world cannot give,
    It's a joy that the world cannot understand.
    Joy to know, joy to live.
    My joy I give unto you.

3. My love I give unto you,
    It's a love that the world cannot give,
    It's a love that the world cannot understand.
    Love to know, love to live.
    My love I give unto you.

— □ ▢ □ —

The eternal God is your refuge,
and underneath are the
everlasting arms.
He will drive out your enemy
before you,
saying, 'Destroy him!'

DEUTERONOMY 33:27

— □ ▢ □ —

400.

My song is love unknown

Mt 21:9; 27:22; Mk 11:9; 15:13; Lk 19:38; 23:21; Jn 12:13; 19:6; Rom 5:8

Capo 2(C)
LOVE UNKNOWN
With feeling

John Ireland (1879-1962)

1. My song is love un - known, my Sa - viour's love to me: love to the love - less shown, that they might love - ly be. O who am I, that for my sake my Lord should take frail flesh, and die?

2. He came from His blessed throne
   Salvation to bestow;
   But men made strange, and none
   The longed-for Christ would know:
   But O! my Friend, my Friend indeed,
   Who at my need His life did spend.

3. Sometimes they strew His way,
   And His sweet praises sing;
   Resounding all the day
   Hosannas to their King:
   Then 'Crucify!' is all their breath,
   And for His death they thirst and cry.

4. They rise and needs will have
   My dear Lord made away;
   A murderer they save,
   The Prince of Life they slay,
   Yet cheerful He to suffering goes,
   That He His foes from thence might free.

5. In life no house, no home
   My Lord on earth might have;
   In death, no friendly tomb,
   But what a stranger gave.
   What may I say? Heaven was His home;
   And mine the tomb wherein He lay.

6. Here might I stay and sing,
   No story so divine,
   Never was love, dear King!
   Never was grief like Thine.
   This is my Friend, in whose sweet praise
   I all my days could gladly spend.

Samuel Crossman (c. 1624-83)

401.

My soul longs for You

Ps 42:2

David Fellingham

My soul longs for You, O my God; I seek You with all of my heart. In this dry and thirs-ty land my voice cries out to You; on-ly Your pre-sence can sa-tis-fy my

402.

No-one but You, Lord
(Only You)

Ps 42:1

Andy Park

1. No - one _____ but You, Lord, __ can

sat - is - fy __ the long - ing in __ my heart. __

No - thing _____ I do, Lord, __ can

take the place __ of draw - ing near __ to You. On - ly

You can fill my deep-est long-ing, ___ on-ly

You. can breathe in me __ new life; ___ on-ly

You can fill my heart _ with laugh-ter, ___ on-ly

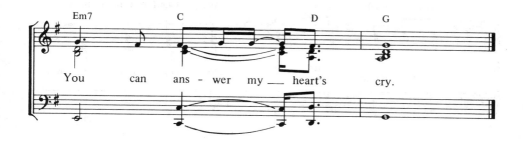

You can ans-wer my ___ heart's cry.

2. Father, I love You,
   Come satisfy the longing in my heart.
   Fill me, overwhelm me,
   Until I know Your love deep in my heart.

403.

Not unto us

Rev 5:12

Capo 2 (D)

Philip Lawson Johnston

pow - er. You a-lone de-serve all the

fame. Yours is the splen - dour and

ma - jes - ty.

From ev - er - last - ing You're the same.

2. Yours is the glorious kingdom.
   You alone are the King over all.
   The earth is under Your dominion now.
   You say when nations rise or fall.

404.

Not without a cause

Josh 6:16; Ps 149:6; 2 Cor 10:4;
Eph 6:12; 1 Tim 1:18; 6:12

Bill Anderson

Capo 2(C)

Triumphantly

1. Not with-out a cause ___ do we go march-ing forth to war, ___ not with-out a cause ___ that we'll see right - eous-ness re - stor'd. ___ Clean your weap - ons, stir your hearts, ___ shed all fears be-fore ___ we start, when we stand to do our part ___

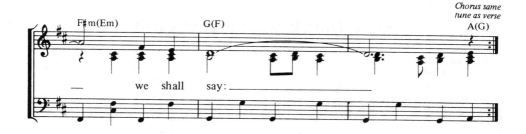

we shall say:

'Not without a right do we unsheath our silent swords,
Not without a fight but we will crown Him Lord of lords.
Lift your banner, lift it high, Jesus is our battle cry.
As we've lived, so we shall die, by His side.'

2. Not without a foe do we prepare ourselves to fight,
   Not without a shout will we scale hell's unconquered height.
   Let the hosts of Satan pray, when we rise as one that day,
   Let them run in disarray, when we say:

3. Not without a cheer will we hear bells and trumpets ring,
   Not without a tear we'll set Him on the throne of kings.
   Eyes on fire and faces grim, we will free Jerusalem,
   Through the gates we'll follow Him, as we say:

405.
Now thank we all our God

Rev 1:8

Capo 3(C)
NUN DANKET

Johann Crüger(1598-1662)

1. Now thank we all our God, with hearts and hands and voi - ces; who won-drous things has done, in whom His world re - joi - ces; who from our moth-er's arms has bless'd us on our way with count-less gifts of love, and still is ours to - day.

2. O may this bounteous God
   Through all our life be near us,
   With ever joyful hearts
   And blessèd peace to cheer us;
   And keep us in His grace,
   And guide us when perplexed,
   And free us from all ills
   In this world and the next.

3. All praise and thanks to God
   The Father now be given,
   The Son, and Him who reigns
   With them in highest heaven,
   The one eternal God,
   Whom earth and heaven adore;
   For thus it was, is now
   And shall be evermore.

Martin Rinkart (1586-1649)
Tr. Catherine Winkworth (1829-78)

406.

Now unto the King
(Unto the King)

1 Tim 1:17

Joey Holder

407. O Breath of Life, come sweeping through us

Mt 9:37–38;
Lk 10:2; Jn 4:35;
20:22; Acts 2:2

SPIRITUS VITAE

Mary J. Hammond (1878-1964)

With strength

1. O Breath of Life, come sweep-ing through us, re - vive Thy church with life and pow'r. O Breath of Life, come, cleanse, re-new us, and fit Thy church to meet this hour.

2. O Wind of God, come, bend us, break us,
   Till humbly we confess our need;
   Then in Thy tenderness remake us,
   Revive, restore; for this we plead.

3. O Breath of Love, come, breathe within us,
   Renewing thought and will and heart:
   Come, love of Christ, afresh to win us,
   Revive Thy church in every part.

4. Revive us, Lord! is zeal abating
   While harvest fields are vast and white?
   Revive us, Lord, the world is waiting,
   Equip Thy church to spread the light.

Elizabeth Porter Head (1850-1936)

408.   O come, all ye faithful

Lk 2:14

J.F. Wade (1711-86)
Arranger W.H. Monk (1823-89)

ADESTE FIDELES

1. O come, all ye faith-ful, joy-ful and tri-um-phant, O come ye, O

come ye to Beth-le-hem; come and be-hold Him,

born the King of an-gels; O come, let us a-dore Him, O come, let us a-

dore Him, O come, let us a-dore Him, Christ the Lord!

2. God of God,
   Light of light,
   Lo, He abhors not the virgin's womb;
   Very God,
   Begotten, not created:

3. Sing, choirs of angels,
   Sing in exultation,
   Sing, all ye citizens of heaven above;
   Glory to God
   In the highest:

4. Yea, Lord, we greet Thee,
   Born this happy morning,
   Jesus, to Thee be glory given;
   Word of the Father
   Now in flesh appearing:

Latin, before 18th century
Tr. Frederick Oakeley (1802-80) altd.

409.   O come let us adore Him

'ADESTE FIDELES'

J. F. Wade (1711-86)

Majestically

1. O come let us a - dore Him, O come let us a - dore Him, O come let us a - dore Him, ___ Christ ___ the Lord.

2. For He alone is worthy... *(etc).*

3. We'll give Him all the glory... *(etc).*

410.

O come, O come Immanuel

Ex 19:6; Deut 5:4; Is 7:14; 11:1, 10; 22:22; Lk 1:78–79; Rom 15:12; Heb 12:18; Rev 3:7

VENI IMMANUEL

In free rhythm

15th century plainsong melody

1. O come, O come, Im - man - u - el, and ran-som cap-tive Is - ra - el,

that mourns in lone-ly ex - ile here un-til the Son of God — ap -pear.

Refrain

Re-joice! Re-joice! Im-man - u - el shall come to thee, O Is - ra - el.

2. O come, O come Thou Lord of might
Who to Thy tribes on Sinai's height
In ancient times didst give the law
In cloud, and majesty, and awe.

3. O come, Thou Rod of Jesse, free
Thine own from Satan's tyranny;
From depths of hell Thy people save
And give them victory o'er the grave.

4. O come, Thou Dayspring, come and cheer
Our spirits by Thine advent here;
Disperse the gloomy clouds of night,
And death's dark shadows put in flight.

5. O come, Thou Key of David, come
And open wide our heavenly home;
Make safe the way that leads on high,
And close the path to misery.

Latin, 12th century
Tr. J.M. Neale (1818-66) altd.

411. O for a heart to praise my God

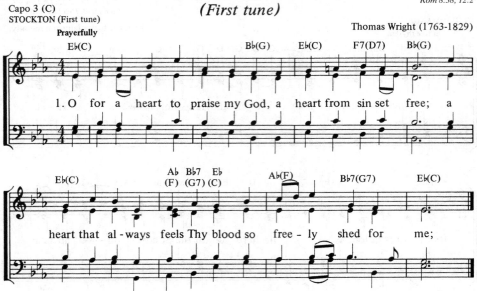

(First tune)

Capo 3 (C)
STOCKTON (First tune)

Ps 51:17;
Rom 8:38; 12:2

Thomas Wright (1763-1829)

Prayerfully

1. O for a heart to praise my God, a heart from sin set free; a
heart that al-ways feels Thy blood so free-ly shed for me;

2. A heart resigned, submissive, meek,
My great Redeemer's throne,
Where only Christ is heard to speak,
Where Jesus reigns alone;

3. A humble, lowly, contrite heart,
Believing true, and clean;
Which neither life nor death can part
From Him who dwells within;

4. A heart in every thought renewed,
And full of love divine;
Perfect and right, and pure, and good:
A copy, Lord, of Thine.

5. Thy nature, gracious Lord, impart;
Come quickly from above;
Write Thy new name upon my heart,
Thy new best name of love.

Charles Wesley (1707-88)

O for a heart to praise my God
(Second tune)

ABRIDGE

With strength

Isaac Smith (1734-1805)

2. A heart resigned, submissive, meek,
   My great Redeemer's throne,
   Where only Christ is heard to speak,
   Where Jesus reigns alone;

3. A humble, lowly, contrite heart,
   Believing, true and clean;
   Which neither life nor death can part
   From Him who dwells within;

4. A heart in every thought renewed,
   And full of love divine,
   Perfect and right, and pure, and good:
   A copy, Lord, of Thine.

5. Thy nature, gracious Lord, impart;
   Come quickly from above;
   Write Thy new name upon my heart,
   Thy new best name of love.

Charles Wesley (1707-88)

412. O for a thousand tongues

Is 61:1; Lk 4:18;
1 Tim 2:6; 1 Jn 1:7;
Rev 5:9, 12; 7:9

LYNGHAM

Thomas Jarman (1782-1862)

Triumphantly

1. O for a thou - sand tongues to sing my
great Re-deem-er's praise, my great Re - deem - er's praise!
The glo - ries of my God and King,
(Men) the
(Women) the tri-umphs of His grace, the tri-umphs of His
tri-umphs of His grace, the tri-umphs of His grace, the
grace, the tri - umphs of His grace!
tri-umphs of His grace, the tri-umphs of His grace!

2. Jesus! the name that charms our fears,
   That bids our sorrows cease,
   That bids our sorrows cease;
   'Tis music in the sinner's ears,
   'Tis life, and health, and peace.

3. See all your sins on Jesus laid;
   The Lamb of God was slain,
   The Lamb of God was slain;
   His soul was once an offering made
   For every soul of man.

4. He breaks the power of cancelled sin,
   He sets the prisoner free,
   He sets the prisoner free;
   His blood can make the foulest clean,
   His blood availed for me.

5. He speaks and, listening to His voice,
   New life the dead receive,
   New life the dead receive;
   The mournful, broken hearts rejoice,
   The humble poor believe.

6. Hear Him, ye deaf; His praise, ye dumb,
   Your loosened tongues employ,
   Your loosened tongues employ;
   Ye blind, behold your Saviour come;
   And leap, ye lame, for joy!

7. My gracious Master and my God,
   Assist me to proclaim,
   Assist me to proclaim;
   To spread through all the earth abroad
   The honours of Thy name.

Charles Wesley (1707-88)

———————— □ ☐ □ ————————

*Oh, the depths of the riches of the
wisdom and knowledge of God!
How unsearchable his judgments,
and his paths beyond tracing out!*

ROMANS 11:33

———————— □ ☐ □ ————————

413.

O give thanks

Ps 136:1

Joanne Pond

O give thanks to the Lord, all you His peo-ple, O give thanks to the Lord for He is good. Let us praise, let us thank, let us ce - le - brate and dance, O give thanks to the Lord for He is good.

414.

O God my Creator

Jn 4:14; Rev 22:1

Graham Kendrick

Capo 2(C)

Worshipfully

1. O God my Cre-a-tor, cre-ate in

me that ri – ver of wa-ter that

flows full and free. Let it bring life to the

dead and stag-nant sea; spring up O

2. O God my Creator, create in me
   That new way of living that flows full and free.
   Let it bring life to the wilderness of man;
   Spring up O well and flood this thirsty land.

415. O God, our help in ages past
Ps 90:1–4; 2 Pet 3:8

ST. ANNE

William Croft (1678-1727)

Steadily

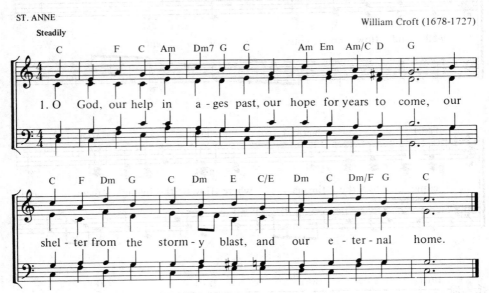

1. O God, our help in a - ges past, our hope for years to come, our shel - ter from the storm - y blast, and our e - ter - nal home.

2. Under the shadow of Thy throne
   Thy saints have dwelt secure;
   Sufficient is Thine arm alone,
   And our defence is sure.

3. Before the hills in order stood,
   Or earth received her frame,
   From everlasting Thou art God,
   To endless years the same.

4. A thousand ages in Thy sight
   Are like an evening gone,
   Short as the watch that ends the night
   Before the rising sun.

5. Time, like an ever-rolling stream,
   Bears all its sons away;
   They fly forgotten, as a dream
   Dies at the opening day.

6. O God, our help in ages past,
   Our hope for years to come,
   Be Thou our guard while troubles last,
   And our eternal home.

Isaac Watts (1674-1748)

— □ ▢ □ —

I will extol the Lord with all my
heart
in the council of the upright and
in the assembly.

PSALM 111:1

— □ ▢ □ —

416.
O, heaven is in my heart
(Heaven is in my heart)

Ps 16:11; Lk 17:20;
1 Cor 3:11; Eph 2:20–22;
1 Thess 4:16; Heb 10:19;
Rev 22:17

Graham Kendrick

Lively

O, _____ heav-en is in __ my heart..

_____ O, _____

heav-en is in __ my heart. _ 1. (Leader) The

king-dom of __ our God __ is here, __ (All) heav-en is in __ my heart..

_ (Leader) The pres-ence of __ His maj - es - ty, __

(All) heav-en is in _ my heart. _ (Leader) And in His pres-ence joy _
_ a - bounds, _ (All) heav -en is in _ my heart. _
_ (Leader) The light of ho - li - ness _ sur - rounds, _
(All) heav-en is in _ my heart. _ ("Everybody sing!")

Last time only
D.C.

2. His precious life on me He spent.   (All)
   Heaven is in my heart.
   To give me life without an end,
   Heaven is in my heart.
   In Christ is all my confidence,
   Heaven is in my heart.
   The hope of my inheritance,
   Heaven is in my heart.

3. We are a temple for His throne,   (Women)
   Heaven is in my heart.   (All)
   And Christ is the foundation stone,   (Women)
   Heaven is in my heart.   (All)
   He will return to take us home,   (Women)
   Heaven is in my heart.   (All)
   The Spirit and the Bride say "Come!"   (Women)
   Heaven is in my heart.   (All)

417.
O I will sing unto You with joy
(Rock of my salvation)

Ps 95:1–4
Shona Sauni

Capo 5(C)

O I will sing un-to You with joy, O Lord, for You're the
rock of my sal - va - tion, come be-fore You with thanks -
giv - ing and ex - tol You with a song. For You're the great - est King a - bove all else, You hold the depths of the earth in Your hand.

418.

Capo 4 (C)
DAY OF REST

O Jesus, I have promised
(First tune)

Ps 31:3; 91:14; Is 30:21;
Jn 14:3; 15:15;
1 Cor 9:24; Heb 12:2

James William Elliott (1833-1915)

1. O Jesus, I have prom-is'd to serve Thee to the end; be Thou for e-ver near me, my Mas-ter and my Friend; I shall not fear the bat-tle if Thou art by my side, nor wan-der from the path-way if Thou wilt be my Guide.

Alternative tune: PENLAN

2. O let me feel Thee near me;
   The world is ever near;
   I see the sights that dazzle,
   The tempting sounds I hear;
   My foes are ever near me,
   Around me and within;
   But Jesus, draw Thou nearer,
   And shield my soul from sin.

3. O let me hear Thee speaking
   In accents clear and still,
   Above the storms of passion,
   The murmurs of self-will;
   O speak to reassure me,
   To hasten, or control;
   O speak, and make me listen,
   Thou Guardian of my soul.

4. O Jesus, Thou hast promised
   To all who follow Thee
   That where Thou art in glory
   There shall Thy servants be;
   And, Jesus, I have promised
   To serve Thee to the end;
   O give me grace to follow
   My Master and my Friend.

5. O let me see Thy footmarks,
   And in them plant mine own;
   My hope to follow duly
   Is in Thy strength alone.
   O guide me, call me, draw me,
   Uphold me to the end;
   And then in heaven receive me,
   My Saviour and my Friend.

John Ernest Bode (1816-74)

O Jesus, I have promised
(Second tune)

Capo 2 (C)
THORNBURY

Basil Harwood (1859-1949)

1. O Je-sus, I have prom-is'd to serve Thee to __ the end; be Thou for e-ver near me, my Mas-ter and __ my Friend; I shall not fear the bat __ tle if Thou art by my side, nor wan-der __ from the path-way if Thou wilt be my Guide. __

2. O let me feel Thee near me;
   The world is ever near;
   I see the sights that dazzle,
   The tempting sounds I hear;
   My foes are ever near me,
   Around me and within;
   But Jesus, draw Thou nearer,
   And shield my soul from sin.

3. O let me hear Thee speaking
   In accents clear and still,
   Above the storms of passion,
   The murmurs of self-will;
   O speak to reassure me,
   To hasten, or control;
   O speak, and make me listen,
   Thou Guardian of my soul.

4. O Jesus, Thou hast promised
   To all who follow Thee
   That where Thou art in glory
   There shall Thy servants be;
   And, Jesus, I have promised
   To serve Thee to the end;
   O give me grace to follow
   My Master and my Friend.

5. O let me see Thy footmarks,
   And in them plant mine own;
   My hope to follow duly
   Is in Thy strength alone.
   O guide me, call me, draw me,
   Uphold me to the end;
   And then in heaven receive me,
   My Saviour and my Friend.

John Ernest Bode (1816-74)

419. O let the Son of God enfold you
(Spirit song)

Ps 90:14; 107:9;
Jn 10:11, 14; 21:15

Capo 2(C)

John Wimber

Worshipfully

Verse

1. O let the Son of God en-fold you with His Spi-rit and His love, let Him fill your heart and sat-is-fy your soul. O let Him have the things that hold you, and His Spi-rit like a dove will de-scend up-on your life and make you whole.

Chorus

Gmaj7(Fmaj7) A7(G7) F#m7(Em7) Bm(Am)

Je - sus, O Je - sus,

Em7(Dm7) A7(G7) Dmaj7(Cmaj7) C/D(C7) D(C)

come and fill Your lambs.

Gmaj7(Fmaj7) A7(G7) F#m7(Em7) Bm(Am)

Je - sus, O Je - sus,

Em7(Dm7) Em7/A(G) D(C)

1st time
Dmaj7 Em7 F#m7
(Cmaj7) (Dm7) (Em7)

Last time only
D(C)

come and fill Your lambs. 2. O come and

2. O come and sing this song with gladness
As your hearts are filled with joy,
Lift your hands in sweet surrender to His name.
O give Him all your tears and sadness,
Give Him all your years of pain,
And you'll enter into life in Jesus' name.

420.

O little town of Bethlehem

English traditional melody
arranged by R. Vaughan Williams (1872-1958)

Lk 2:4

Capo 3 (D)

FOREST GREEN

1. O lit-tle town of Beth-le-hem, how still we __ see thee lie! A-bove thy deep and dream-less __ sleep the si-lent __ stars go by. Yet __ in thy dark __ streets __ shin - eth the ev-er-last-ing Light; the

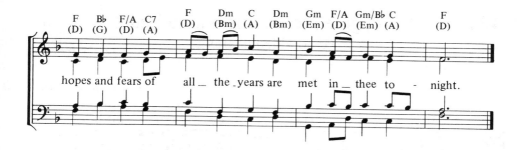

hopes and fears of all __ the __ years are met in __ thee to - night.

2. O morning stars, together
   Proclaim the holy birth,
   And praises sing to God the King,
   And peace to men on earth;
   For Christ is born of Mary,
   And gathered all above,
   While mortals sleep, the angels keep
   Their watch of wondering love.

3. How silently, how silently
   The wondrous gift is given!
   So God imparts to human hearts
   The blessings of His heaven.
   No ear may hear His coming;
   But in this world of sin,
   Where meek souls will receive Him, still
   The dear Christ enters in.

4. O holy Child of Bethlehem,
   Descend to us, we pray;
   Cast out our sin, and enter in;
   Be born in us today.
   We hear the Christmas angels
   The great glad tidings tell;
   O come to us, abide with us,
   Our Lord Immanuel!

   Phillips Brooks (1835-93)

421. O Lord, give me an undivided heart
(Undivided heart)

1 Sam 13:14;
Jer 31:33;
Ezek 11:19;
Jn 4:23; 5:19; Acts 13:22

Chris Roe/Dave Markee

O Lord, give me ___ an un-di-vi-ded heart
Lord, give me ___ an un-re-lent-ing mind

to fol-low You. O
to seek Your face. O

Lord, give me ___ an un-di-min-ished love,
Lord, give me ___ an un-de-feat-ed faith,

to see what You see, to do what You do, O
to see vic-to-ry in all that I do, to

——————— □ ☐ □ ———————

Listen, I tell you a mystery: We will not all sleep, but we will all be changed—in a flash, in the twinkling of an eye, at the last trumpet.

1 CORINTHIANS 15:51–52

——————— □ ☐ □ ———————

422.   O Lord, have mercy on me

Ps 40:2–3, 11

Carl Tuttle

423. O Lord, hear my prayer

Ps 4:1; 17:6; 39:12; 54:2; 102:1; 143:1

Taizé

O Lord, hear my prayer, O Lord, hear my prayer: when I call ans - wer me. O Lord, hear my prayer, O Lord, hear my prayer: come and lis - ten to me.

424.

O Lord most Holy God

Mt 6:10; Lk 11:2; 1 Pet 2:5

Wendy Churchill

Worshipfully

1. O Lord most Ho - ly God, Great are Your pur - po - ses,

Great is Your will for us, Great is Your love.

And we re - joice in You, And we will sing to You,

O Fa - ther have Your way, Your will be done.

2. For You are building
A temple without hands,
A city without walls
Enclosed by fire.
A place for You to dwell,
Built out of living stones,
Shaped by a Father's hand
And joined in love.

425.

O Lord my God!

(How great Thou art)

Ps 8:1, 3; Rom 5:9;
8:32; 1 Thess 4:16–17

HOW GREAT THOU ART

Stuart K. Hine

1. O Lord my God! when I in awe-some won – der___ con – si – der all the works Thy hand hath made, I see the stars, I hear the migh-ty thun – der,___ Thy pow'r through-out the u – ni verse dis-play'd: then sings my soul, my Sa-viour God, to Thee, how great Thou art! How great Thou art! Then sings my soul, my Sa-viour God, to

Alternative ending

2. When through the woods and forest glades I wander
   And hear the birds sing sweetly in the trees;
   When I look down from lofty mountain grandeur,
   And hear the brook, and feel the gentle breeze;

3. And when I think that God His Son not sparing,
   Sent Him to die — I scarce can take it in.
   That on the cross my burden gladly bearing,
   He bled and died to take away my sin:

4. When Christ shall come with shout of acclamation
   And take me home — what joy shall fill my heart!
   Then shall I bow in humble adoration
   And there proclaim, my God, how great Thou art!

   Russian hymn

426.

O Lord our God
(We will magnify)

Ps 8:1–2, 9:7–8; Col 1:17;
Rev 5:13

Phil Lawson Johnston

Flowing

Verse

1. O Lord our God, — how ma-jest - ic is Your—
name, _____ the earth _ is filled with Your glo - ry.—
_ O Lord our God, — You are robed in ma-jes -
ty, _____ You've set Your glo-ry a-bove_ the hea -
vens. *Chorus* We will mag - ni-fy, _____ we will mag - ni-fy _____

2. O Lord our God, You have established a throne,
   You reign in righteousness and splendour.
   O Lord our God, the skies are ringing with Your praise,
   Soon those on earth will come to worship.

3. O Lord our God, the world was made at Your command,
   In You all things now hold together.
   Now to Him who sits on the throne and to the Lamb,
   Be praise and glory and power for ever.

———— □ ▯ □ ————

O Lord, open my lips,
  and my mouth will declare your
    praise.
You do not delight in sacrifice, or I
    would bring it;
  you do not take pleasure in burnt
    offerings.
The sacrifices of God are a broken
    spirit;
  a broken and contrite heart,
  O God, you will not despise.

PSALM 51:15–17

———— □ ▯ □ ————

427. O Lord our God, You are a great God   *Ex 15:11*

Worshipfully

Mike Kerry

O Lord our God, You are a great God, ___ Your maj - est -
y be-yond com-pare. ___ Who is a God like un - to
You, and who like me could know Your care? ___ It's
good, dear Lord, to know Your great - ness, ___ it's good, dear
Lord, to know Your care. ___ It's good just to be in Your
presence, it's good just to know that You are there. ___

428.

O Lord, our Lord

Ps 8:1–4, 6

Hilary Davies

O Lord, our Lord, how

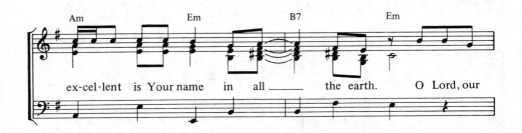

ex-cel-lent is Your name in all ___ the earth. O Lord, our

Lord, how ex-cel-lent is Your name in all ___

___ the earth. ___ You have set Your glo -

2. What is man, that You are mindful of him;
   The son of man that You take care of him?
   You have put everything beneath his feet,
   And made him ruler of Your works.

429.   O Lord, the clouds are gathering

Lam 4:4;
Amos 5:24;
Mt 6:10; Lk 11:2

N.B. Some congregations may find this song more comfortable to sing
in a slightly lower key, e.g. B major.

Graham Kendrick

1. O Lord, the clouds are gath-er-ing, the fire of judge-ment burns, how we have fall - en! O Lord, You stand a - pall'd to see Your laws of love so scorn'd and lives so bro - ken. Have

(Women) Have mer - cy, Lord, for - give us, Lord, re -

(Men) mer - cy, Lord, for - give us, Lord, re -

store us, Lord, re - vive Your church a - gain.

store us, Lord, re - vive Your church a - gain.

2. O Lord, over the nations now
   Where is the dove of peace?
   Her wings are broken.
   O Lord, while precious children starve
   The tools of war increase;
   Their bread is stolen.

3. O Lord, dark powers are poised to flood
   Our streets with hate and fear;
   We must awaken!
   O Lord, let love reclaim the lives
   That sin would sweep away
   And let Your kingdom come.

4. Yet, O Lord, Your glorious cross shall tower
   Triumphant in this land,
   Evil confounding.
   Through the fire Your suffering church display
   The glories of her Christ:
   Praises resounding!

430.

O Lord, You are my God

Is 25:1

Capo 2 (C)

David J. Hadden

Worshipfully

O Lord, You are my God, I will ex - alt You and praise Your name, I will ex - alt You and praise Your name. For in Your per - fect faith - ful - ness You have done mar - vellous things. O Lord, You are my God, I will ex - alt You and praise Your name.

431. O Lord, You are my light

Ps 40:2; Col 3:3

David Fellingham

O Lord, You are my light, O Lord, You are my sal-
va - tion. You have deliver'd me from all my fear, for You are the defence of my
life. For my life is hid-den with Christ in God.__ You have concealed me
in Your love,__ You've lift-ed me up,__ placed my feet on a rock.__
I will shout for joy in the house of God. _____ O

432.   O Lord, You're beautiful

Ps 27:4, 8; 2 Cor 9:8;
Rev 2:4–5

Keith Green

Capo 5(C)

2. O Lord, please light the fire
   That once burned bright and clear,
   Replace the lamp of my first love
   That burns with holy fear!

3. O Lord, You're beautiful,
   Your face is all I seek,
   For when Your eyes are on this child,
   Your grace abounds to me.

433.

O Lord, Your tenderness

Ps 51:1–2; Jas 5:11

Graham Kendrick

With feeling

O Lord, Your tend - er - ness, __ melt-ing all my bit - ter - ness, __ O Lord, I re - ceive Your love. __ O Lord, Your love - li - ness, __ chang-ing all my

——————— □ ▢ □ ———————

*Praise be to the God and Father of
our Lord Jesus Christ, who has
blessed us in the heavenly realms
with every spiritual blessing in
Christ. For he chose us in him
before the creation of the world to be
holy and blameless in his sight.*

EPHESIANS 1:3–4

——————— □ ▢ □ ———————

434. O love that wilt not let me go

Gen 9:16; Jn 8:12; 10:28; Rom 8:38–39

ST MARGARET

With feeling

Albert Lister Peace (1844-1912)

1. O love that wilt not let me go,____ I rest my wea-ry soul in thee: ____ I give thee back the life I owe, ____ that in thine o-cean depths its flow may rich-er, full - er be.

2. O light that followest all my way,
   I yield my flickering torch to thee:
   My heart restores its borrowed ray,
   That in thy sunshine's blaze its day
   May brighter, fairer be.

3. O joy that seekest me through pain,
   I cannot close my heart to thee:
   I trace the rainbow through the rain,
   And feel the promise is not vain,
   That morn shall tearless be.

4. O cross that liftest up my head,
   I dare not ask to fly from thee:
   I lay in dust life's glory dead,
   And from the ground there blossoms red
   Life that shall endless be.

George Matheson (1842-1906)

435.   O magnify the Lord

(Psalm 34)

Ps 34:1–4

Maggi Dawn

In a 'fiesta' style

O mag - ni - fy the Lord with_ me,_ and let us ex - alt_ His name to - ge - ther._ O mag - ni - fy the Lord with_ me,_ and let us ex - alt_ His name to - ge - ther._

Last time to Coda

1st and 2nd times

1. I called_ to the Lord and_ He an - swered,_ saved me_ from all of_ my trou - ble;_ He_ de - li - vered me_ from all my_ fear, so

2. We will boast about the Lord,
   Tell of the things He has done;
   Let the whole world hear about it,
   And they'll rejoice, they'll rejoice!

436.   O my Lord, You are most glorious   *Is 9:6; Jn 1:3*

Geoff Roberts

Oh my Lord _____ You are most glo - ri - ous, _____

King of kings _____ and Prince of Peace. _____

By Your word _____ this world was cre -

a - ted; _____ by Your love _____

I have been set free. _____ And I

437.
Capo 3 (D)

DERBY

O my Saviour, lifted

Jn 12:32; 1 Pet 5:7

Friedrich Filitz (1804-76)

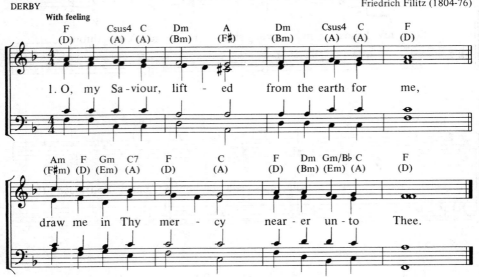

1. O, my Sa-viour, lift - ed from the earth for me, draw me in Thy mer - cy near - er un - to Thee.

2. Lift my earthbound longings,
   Fix them, Lord, above;
   Draw me with the magnet
   Of Thy mighty love.

3. And I come, Lord Jesus;
   Dare I turn away?
   No! Thy love hath conquered,
   And I come today.

4. Bringing all my burdens,
   Sorrow, sin, and care;
   At Thy feet I lay them,
   And I leave them there.

William Walsham How (1823-97)

--- □ ▢ □ ---

*Enter his gates with thanksgiving
and his courts with praise;
give thanks to him and praise his
name.*

PSALM 100:4

--- □ ▢ □ ---

438. Once in royal David's city

Lk 2:4, 7, 51; Heb 4:15

Capo 3 (D)
IRBY

Henry John Gauntlett (1805-76)

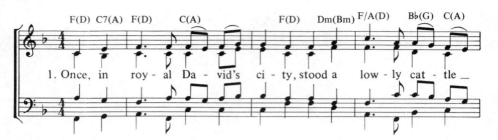

1. Once, in roy - al Da - vid's ci - ty, stood a low - ly cat - tle _

shed, where a mo - ther laid _ her _ ba - by in a

man - ger for _ His _ bed. Ma - ry was that mo - ther

mild, Je - sus Christ, her lit - tle _ child.

2. He came down to earth from heaven,
   Who is God and Lord of all,
   And His shelter was a stable,
   And His cradle was a stall:
   With the poor and meek and lowly
   Lived on earth our Saviour holy.

3. And through all His wondrous childhood
   He would honour and obey,
   Love and watch the lowly mother
   In whose gentle arms He lay.
   Christian children all should be
   Mild, obedient, good as He.

4. For He is our childhood's pattern:
   Day by day like us He grew;
   He was little, weak and helpless;
   Tears and smiles like us He knew:
   And He feeleth for our sadness,
   And He shareth in our gladness.

5. And our eyes at last shall see Him
   Through His own redeeming love;
   For that child, so dear and gentle,
   Is our Lord in heaven above;
   And He leads His children on
   To the place where He is gone.

6. Not in that poor lowly stable,
   With the oxen standing by,
   We shall see Him, but in heaven,
   Set at God's right hand on high;
   When like stars His children crowned,
   All in white shall wait around.

Cecil Frances Alexander (1823-95)

439.
One shall tell another
(The wine of the kingdom)

Joel 1:3; Mt 5:16; 9:17;
Mk 2:22; Lk 5:37; Jn 2:10;
Acts 2:46–47

Graham Kendrick

Lightly with increasing pace

Verse

1. One shall tell a-noth-er, and he shall tell his friend, hus-bands, wives and chil-dren shall come fol-low-ing on. From house to house in fam-i-lies shall **more** be gath-ered in, and lights will shine in ev'-ry street, so warm and welcom-ing.

Chorus

Come on in __ and taste the new wine, the wine of the

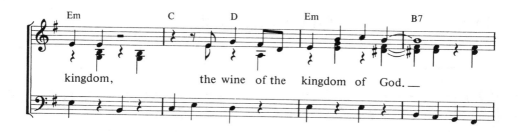

kingdom, the wine of the kingdom of God. __

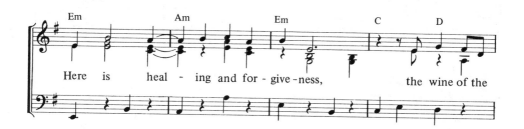

Here is heal - ing and for - give -ness, the wine of the

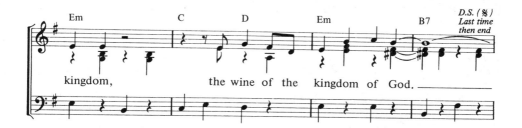

kingdom, the wine of the kingdom of God. _____

2. Compassion of the Father
   Is ready now to flow,
   Through acts of love and mercy
   We must let it show.
   He turns now from His anger
   To show a smiling face
   And longs that men should stand beneath
   The fountain of His grace.

3. He longs to do much more than
   Our faith has yet allowed,
   To thrill us and surprise us
   With His sovereign power.
   Where darkness has been darkest
   The brightest light will shine,
   His invitation comes to us,
   It's yours and it is mine.

440.

One thing I ask

Ps 27:4, 7–9

Andy Park

Prayerfully

One thing I ask, one ____ thing I
Hear me, O Lord, hear me when I

seek, that I may dwell in Your
cry; Lord, do not hide Your

house, O ____ Lord. All of my
face from ____ me. You have been my

days, all ____ of my
strength, You have been my

life, that I may see You,
shield, and You will lift me

441.

Only by grace

Jn 6:44; Eph 2:8–9; 1 Jn 1:7; Rev 12:11

Gerrit Gustafson

On - ly by grace can we en - ter, on-ly by grace can we stand; not by our hu - man en-dea- vour, but by the blood of the Lamb. In to Your pre-sence You call us, You call us to come. In - to Your pre - sence You draw us, and

now by Your grace we come, now by Your grace we come.

Lord, if You mark our trans-gres-

- sions, who would stand?

Thanks to Your grace we are cleansed by the blood of the Lamb.

442.

Onward, Christian soldiers

Mt 16:18; Eph 4:4;
Col 2:15; 2 Tim 2:3;
Jas 2:19

Capo 3 (C)
ST GERTRUDE

Arthur Seymour Sullivan (1842-1900)

1. On-ward, Christ-ian sol – diers, march-ing as to war,
with the cross of Je – sus go-ing on be – fore!
Christ, the roy-al Mas – ter, leads a-gainst the foe;
for-ward in – to bat – tle,___ see, His ban-ners go!

Chorus

On-ward, Christ-ian sol – diers, march-ing as to___ war,

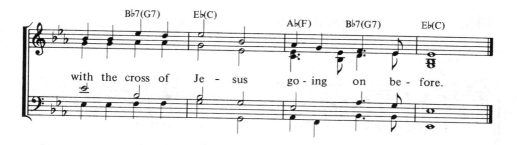

with the cross of Je - sus go - ing on be - fore.

2. At the name of Jesus
   Satan's host doth flee:
   On then, Christian soldiers,
   On to victory!
   Hell's foundations quiver
   At the shout of praise:
   Brothers, lift your voices;
   Loud your anthems raise:

3. Like a mighty army
   Moves the church of God:
   Brothers we are treading
   Where the saints have trod.
   We are not divided
   All one body we,
   One in hope and doctrine,
   One in charity.

4. Crowns and thrones may perish,
   Kingdoms rise and wane,
   But the church of Jesus
   Constant will remain;
   Gates of hell can never
   'Gainst that church prevail;
   We have Christ's own promise,
   And that cannot fail:

5. Onward, then, ye people!
   Join our happy throng;
   Blend with ours your voices
   In the triumph-song:
   Glory, laud, and honour
   Unto Christ the King!
   This through countless ages
   Men and angels sing:

Sabine Baring-Gould (1834-1924)

443.

Open our eyes, Lord

Jn 16:14

Bob Cull

O-pen our eyes, Lord, ____ we want to see Je -

- sus, ____ to reach out and touch Him ____ and

say that we love Him. ____ O-pen our ears, Lord, ____

____ and help us to lis - ten. ____ O-pen our

eyes, Lord, ____ we want to see Je - sus. ____

444.
Open your eyes

Is 6:1

Worshipfully

Carl Tuttle

O - pen your ___ eyes, see the glo - ry of the King. Lift up your ___ voice and His prai - ses ___ sing. I love You, Lord, I will pro - claim: Hal - le - lu - ia, I bless Your name.

445. O praise ye the Lord

Ps 148:1–2

Capo 3 (D)
LAUDATE DOMINUM (GAUNTLETT)
With strength

Henry John Gauntlett (1805-76)

Alternative tune: **LAUDATE DOMINUM (PARRY)**

2. O praise ye the Lord!
   Praise Him upon earth,
   In tuneful accord,
   Ye sons of new birth;
   Praise Him who hath brought you
   His grace from above,
   Praise Him who hath taught you
   To sing of His love.

3. O praise ye the Lord,
   All things that give sound;
   Each jubilant chord,
   Re-echo around;
   Loud organs, His glory
   Forthtell in deep tone,
   And sweet harp, the story
   Of what He hath done.

4. O praise ye the Lord!
   Thanksgiving and song
   To Him be outpoured
   All ages along;
   For love in creation,
   For heaven restored,
   For grace of salvation,
   O praise ye the Lord!

Henry Williams Baker (1821-77)

446.

O sacred head, once wounded

Mt 27:29; Mk 16:17;
Jn 18:2

Melody by Hans Leo Hassler (1564-1612)
arranged J.S. Bach (1685-1750)

PASSION CHORALE

1. O sa-cred head, once wound-ed, with grief and pain weighed

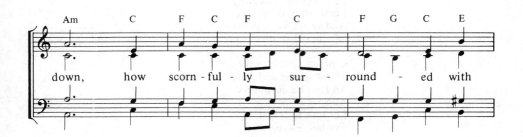

down, how scorn-ful-ly sur-round-ed with

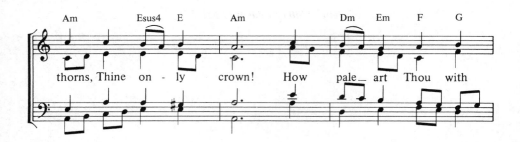

thorns, Thine on-ly crown! How pale art Thou with

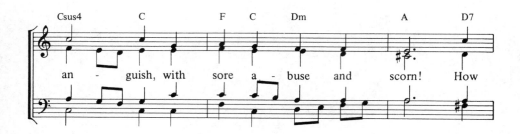

an-guish, with sore a-buse and scorn! How

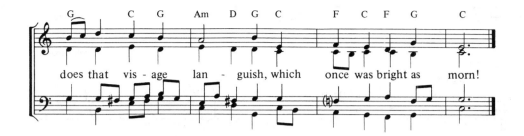

does that vis - age lan - guish, which once was bright as morn!

2. O lord of life and glory,
   What bliss till now was Thine!
   I read the wondrous story,
   I joy to call Thee mine.
   Thy grief and Thy compassion
   Were all for sinners' gain;
   Mine, mine was the transgression,
   But Thine the deadly pain.

3. What language shall I borrow
   To praise Thee, heavenly friend,
   For this, Thy dying sorrow,
   Thy pity without end?
   Lord, make me Thine for ever,
   Nor let me faithless prove;
   O let me never, never
   Abuse such dying love!

4. Be near me, Lord, when dying;
   O show Thyself to me;
   And for my succour flying,
   Come, Lord, to set me free:
   These eyes, new faith receiving,
   From Jesus shall not move;
   For he who dies believing,
   Dies safely through Thy love.

Paulus Gerhardt (1607-76),
attributed to Bernard of Clairvaux (1091-1153)
tr. James Waddell Alexander (1804-59)

447.

O taste and see

Ps 34:4, 8

Phil Rogers

Capo 5 (C)

Light 'Latin' feel

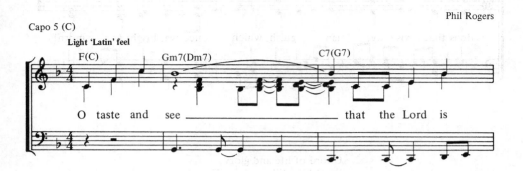

O taste and see _____ that the Lord is

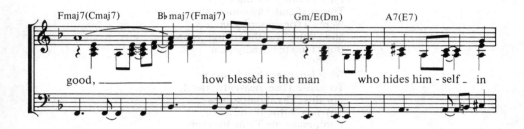

good, _____ how blessèd is the man who hides him-self _ in

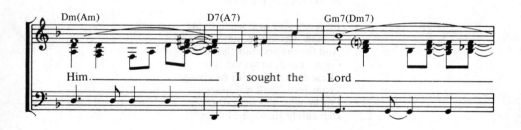

Him. _____ I sought the Lord _____

__ and He ans-wer'd _ me _____ and set _ me _

448.

O, that You would bless me

Ex 34:24; Mt 6:10, 13;
Lk 11:2, 4; Eph 5:18

Phil Rogers

1. { O, that You would bless __ me,
   { O, that You would keep __ me

and en-large my bor - ders,
keep me from all ev - il,

that Your hand would be with __ me, O
so that I may not be a-shamed O

Lord,   O __ Lord.   Lord.   May Your
Lord   O __

king - dom come,— may Your will be - done— on

earth as it is in hea - ven; may Your

king-dom come,— may Your will be-done,— through me, O —

Lord, O — Lord.

2 O that You would fill me,
   Fill me with Your Spirit,
   So that I may know Your power,
   O Lord, O Lord.
   O that you would use me
   To fulfil Your purposes,
   That through me Your glory would shine,
   O Lord, O Lord.

449.   O, the joy of Your forgiveness

Capo 3 (G)

Dave Bilbrough

450. O the valleys shall ring

Is 9:7; 11:6; Mt 6:10; Lk 11:2

Capo 3 (D)

Dave Bilbrough

O the val - leys shall ring with the sound of praise, and the li - on shall lie with the lamb. Of His gov - ern - ment there shall be no end, and His glo - ry shall fill the earth. May Your will be done, may Your king - dom come! Let it rule, let it reign in our lives. There's a shout in the camp as we ans - wer the call, Hail the King! Hail the Lord of lords!

451.　O Thou who camest from above

Mt 3:11; Lk 3:16;
2 Tim 1:6;
Heb 12:29

Capo 3 (C)
HEREFORD

(First tune)

Samuel Sebastian Wesley (1810-76)

1. O Thou who cam-est from above the pure ce-

les - tial fire to im - part, kin - dle a flame of

sa - cred love on the mean al - tar of my heart.

2. There let it for Thy glory burn
   With inextinguishable blaze,
   And trembling to its source return,
   In humble prayer and fervent praise.

3. Jesus, confirm my heart's desire
   To work, and speak, and think for Thee;
   Still let me guard the holy fire,
   And still stir up Thy gift in me;

4. Ready for all Thy perfect will,
   My acts of faith and love repeat,
   Till death Thy endless mercies seal,
   And make the sacrifice complete.

Charles Wesley (1707-88)

O Thou who camest from above
(Second tune)

WILTON

Samuel Stanley (1767-1822)

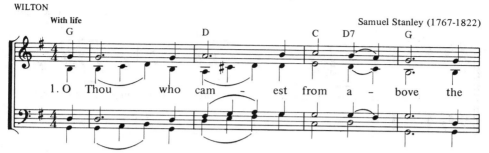

1. O Thou who cam - est from a - bove the

pure ce - les - tial fire to im - part, kin -

dle a flame of sa - cred love on

the mean al - tar of my heart.

452.
Our confidence is in the Lord

Ps 62:1–2; 91:2;
Mt 11:28; Heb 4:16

Noel & Tricia Richards

With strength

Our con-fi-dence is in the Lord, the source of our sal-va-tion. Rest is found in Him a-lone, the Auth-or of cre-a-tion. We will not fear the ev-il day, be-cause we have a ref-uge; in ev-'ry circ-um-stance we say, our hope is built on Je-sus.

─────────── □ ▢ □ ───────────

Speak to one another with psalms,
hymns and spiritual songs. Sing and
make music in your heart to the Lord,
always giving thanks to God the Father
for everything, in the name of our
Lord Jesus Christ.

EPHESIANS 5:19–20

─────────── □ ▢ □ ───────────

453. Our God is an awesome God
(Awesome God)

Rich Mullins

With strength

Our God __ is an awe-some God, He reigns __ from

hea-ven a-bove, with wis - dom, __ pow'r and love, our

God is an awe-some God! __ Our God __ is an

awe-some God, He reigns __ from __ hea-ven a-bove, with

wis - dom __ pow'r and love, our God is an awe-some God! __

454. Out of Your great love

Patricia Morgan

Out of Your great love, ___

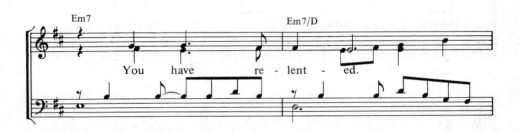

You have re - lent - ed.

Out of Your great love, ___

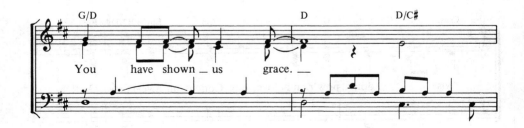

You have shown us grace. ___

Though we've caused You pain, ___

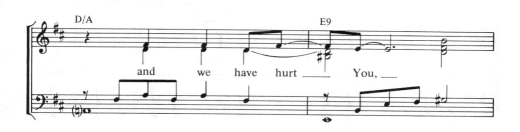

and we have hurt ___ You, ___

out of Your great love ___ You've turned a -

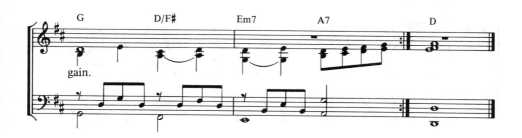

gain.

455. O, we are more than conquerors
(We are more than conquerors)

Ps 147:11;
Rom 8:35, 37;
Eph 1:3; Phil 1:6

Steven Fry

(O,) we are more than con-quer-ors.

O, we are more than con-quer - ors, _____ and

who _____ can se - pa - rate us from the

love, the love _ of God. _ O yes, _ we are,

1. For He _ has pro - mised to ful-fill _ His will _ in us, _

2. For He's within to finish what's begun in me,
   He opens doors than no one can deny;
   He makes a way where there's no other way,
   And gives me wings to fly.

456.

O worship the King

Ps 18:2, 10–12; Dan 7:9

HANOVER

William Croft (1678-1727)

Triumphantly

1. O wor - ship the King, all glor - ious a - bove; O grate - ful - ly sing His pow'r and His love: our Shield and De - fend - er, the An - cient of days, pav - il - ion'd in splen - dour and gird - ed with praise.

Alternative tune: PADERBORN

2. O tell of His might,
   O sing of His grace,
   Whose robe is the light,
   Whose canopy space;
   His chariots of wrath
   The deep thunder-clouds form,
   And dark is His path
   On the wings of the storm.

3. The earth, with its store
   Of wonders untold,
   Almighty, Thy power
   Hath founded of old;
   Hath 'stablished it fast,
   By a changeless decree,
   And round it hath cast,
   Like a mantle, the sea.

4. Thy bountiful care
   What tongue can recite?
   It breathes in the air,
   It shines in the light;
   It streams from the hills,
   It descends to the plain,
   And sweetly distils
   In the dew and the rain.

5. Frail children of dust,
   And feeble as frail,
   In Thee do we trust,
   Nor find Thee to fail;
   Thy mercies how tender,
   How firm to the end,
   Our Maker, Defender,
   Redeemer, and Friend!

Robert Grant (1779-1838)

457. O worship the Lord

1 Chron 16:29; Ps 29:2; 96:9;
Hos 6:6; Rom 12:1;
1 Pet 2:5; 5:7

WAS LEBET, WAS SCHWEBET

Rheinhardt manuscript, Üttingen (1754)

With strength

1. O worship the Lord in the beau-ty of hol-i-ness, bow down be-fore Him, His glo-ry pro-claim; with gold of o-be-dience and in-cense of low-li-ness, kneel and a-dore Him: the Lord is His name.

2. Low at His feet lay thy burden of carefulness,
   High on His heart He will bear it for thee,
   Comfort thy sorrows, and answer thy prayerfulness,
   Guiding thy steps as may best for thee be.

3. Fear not to enter His courts in the slenderness
   Of the poor wealth thou wouldst reckon as thine;
   Truth in its beauty, and love in its tenderness,
   These are the offerings to lay on His shrine.

4. These, though we bring them in trembling and fearfulness,
   He will accept for the name that is dear;
   Mornings of joy give for evenings of tearfulness,
   Trust for our trembling, and hope for our fear.

5. O worship the Lord in the beauty of holiness,
   Bow down before Him, His glory proclaim;
   With gold of obedience and incense of lowliness,
   Kneel and adore Him: the Lord is His name.

John Samuel Bewley Monsell (1811-75)

458.   Peace is flowing like a river

Is 43:19; Jn 14:27;
Rev 22:1

Author unknown
Arr. Margaret Evans

Capo 3(C)

Flowing

1. Peace is flow-ing like a riv - er, flow - ing out through you and me, spread - ing out in - to the des - ert, set - ting all the cap-tives free. Let it flow through me, let it flow through me, let the

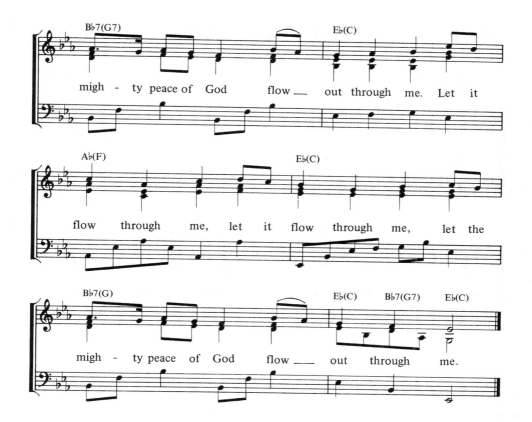

mighty peace of God flow — out through me. Let it

flow through me, let it flow through me, let the

mighty peace of God flow — out through me.

2. Love is flowing. . . *(etc)*.

3. Joy is flowing. . . *(etc)*.

4. Faith is flowing. . . *(etc)*.

5. Hope is flowing. . . *(etc)*.

459.

Peace like a river

Jn 3:8; 4:14; Acts 2:2

Slowly, with feeling

John Watson

Peace like a ri - ver, love like a mount-ain, the wind of Your Spi - rit is blow-ing ev - 'ry - where. Joy like a fount - ain, heal - ing spring of life; come, Ho - ly Spi - rit, let Your fi - re fall.

460.

Peace to you

Is 9:6; Jn 14:27; 20:19

Graham Kendrick

Peace to you. We bless you now in the name of the Lord. Peace to you. We bless you now in the name of the Prince of Peace.

Repeat verse 3 times   4th time only

Peace to you. Peace to you. Peace to you Peace to you.

(rit. . . . . . .)

461.

Praise God for the body

Mt 10:10; Mk 6:8–9;
Lk 9:3; 10:4; 1 Cor 12:12;
Eph 4:3–4

Anne Ortlund

Capo 3(Em)

1. Praise God for the bo - dy,— praise God for the Son;—
praise God for the life that binds our hearts in one.

Joy is the food we share; love is our home, bro-thers.

Praise God for the bo-dy; Sha-lom, Sha - lom.

2. Guard your circle, brothers,
   Clasp your hand in hand;
   Satan cannot break
   The bond in which we stand.

3. Shed your extra clothing,
   Keep your baggage light;
   Rough will be the battle,
   Long will be the fight, but

4. Praise God for the body,
   Praise God for the Son;
   Praise God for the life
   That binds our hearts in one.

462. Praise God from whom all blessings flow
(Doxology)

Jimmy Owens
Traditional words by
Thomas Ken

463. Praise Him

Twila Paris

1. Praise Him, praise Him, praise Him with your song. Praise Him, praise Him, praise Him all day long! For the Lord is wor-thy, wor-thy to re-

ceive our praise. For the Lord is

wor - thy, _____ wor-thy to rem -

ceive our praise.

2. Praise Him, praise Him,
   Praise Him with your heart.
   Praise Him, praise Him,
   Give Him all you are.

3. Praise Him, praise Him,
   Praise Him with your life.
   Praise Him, praise Him,
   Lift His name up high.

464. Praise Him on the trumpet

Ps 150:3–6

John Kennett

Praise Him on the trumpet, the psaltery and harp, __ praise Him on the timbrel __ and the dance, __ praise Him __ with stringed in - struments too.

Praise Him on the loud cym - bals, __ praise Him on the loud cym - bals, __ let

Praise Him, praise Him!
Jesus our blessèd Redeemer

Is 53:3; Mt 27:29;
Mk 15:17; Jn 10:11, 14;
1 Cor 15:55; 1 Pet 2:24

PRAISE HIM! PRAISE HIM!
Triumphantly

Chester G. Allen (1838-78)

Praise Him, praise Him! Je-sus, our bless-èd Re-deem - er;

sing, O earth, His won-der -ful love pro - claim! __

Hail Him, hail Him! high-est arch-an -gels in glo - ry,

strength and honour give to His ho - ly name. __

Like a shep - herd, Je - sus will guard His child - ren,

in His arms He car - ries them all day long; —

O ye saints that dwell in the moun-tains of Zi - on,

praise Him, praise Him! ev - er in joy - ful song. —

2. Praise Him, praise Him! Jesus, our blessèd Redeemer;
For our sins He suffered and bled and died.
He, our Rock, our hope of eternal salvation,
Hail Him, hail Him! Jesus the Crucified.
Loving Saviour, meekly enduring sorrow,
Crowned with thorns that cruelly pierced His brow;
Once for us rejected, despised, and forsaken,
Prince of glory, ever triumphant now.

3. Praise Him, praise Him! Jesus, our blessèd Redeemer;
Heavenly portals loud with hosannas ring!
Jesus, Saviour, reigneth for ever and ever,
Crown Him, crown Him! Prophet and Priest and King!
Death is vanquished, tell it with joy, ye faithful!
Where is now thy victory, boasting grave?
Jesus lives, no longer thy portals are cheerless;
Jesus lives, the mighty and strong to save.

Fanny J. Crosby (1820-1915)

466. Praise, my soul, the King of heaven

Capo 2 (C)

PRAISE, MY SOUL

Ps 103:7–8, 13–14, 20

John Goss (1800-80)

1. Praise, my soul, the King of hea - ven; to His feet thy trib - ute bring. Ran - som'd, heal'd, re - stor'd, for - gi - ven, who like thee His praise should sing? Praise Him! Praise Him! Praise Him! Praise Him! Praise the ev - er - last - ing King.

2. Praise Him for His grace and favour
   To our fathers in distress;
   Praise Him, still the same for ever,
   Slow to chide, and swift to bless.
   Praise Him! Praise Him!
   Praise Him! Praise Him!
   Glorious in His faithfulness.

3. Father-like, He tends and spares us;
   Well our feeble frame He knows;
   In His hands He gently bears us,
   Rescues us from all our foes.
   Praise Him! Praise Him!
   Praise Him! Praise Him!
   Widely as His mercy flows.

4. Angels in the height, adore Him;
   Ye behold Him face to face;
   Sun and moon, bow down before Him,
   Dwellers all in time and space.
   Praise Him! Praise Him!
   Praise Him! Praise Him!
   Praise with us the God of grace!

   Henry Francis Lyte (1793-1847)

467.

Praise the Lord

Ps 150:1–2

David Fellingham

Praise the Lord, praise Him in His tem-ple, praise Him in the sanc-tu-a-ry of His pow'r.

Lift your voi-ces with great re-joi-cing for God is great in all the earth.

Praise Him for His ex-cell-ence, _____ praise Him

for His love, _____ praise Him for His

mer - cy _ giv - ing us new life. _____

468. Praise the name of Jesus

Ps 18:2

Capo 3 (C)

Roy Hicks

Worshipfully

Praise the name of Je - sus, praise the name of Je - sus, He's my rock, He's my fort-ress, He's my de-liv-er-er, in Him will I trust. Praise the name of Je - sus.

469.   Praise to the Holiest in the height

Ps 148: 1, 7;
1 Cor 15:45, 47

GERONTIUS

John Bacchus Dykes (1823-76)

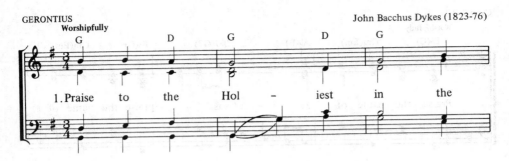

1. Praise to the Hol – iest in the

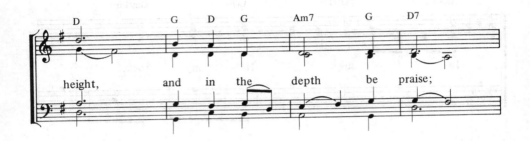

height, and in the depth be praise;

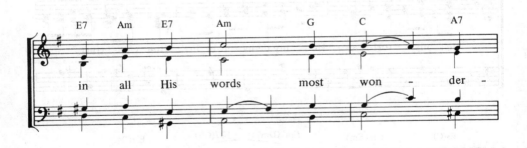

in all His words most won – der –

ful, most sure in all His ways.

2. O loving wisdom of our God!
   When all was sin and shame,
   A second Adam to the fight
   And to the rescue came.

3. O wisest love! that flesh and blood,
   Which did in Adam fail,
   Should strive afresh against the foe,
   Should strive and should prevail;

4. And that a higher gift than grace
   Should flesh and blood refine,
   God's presence and His very self,
   And essence all-divine.

5. O generous love! that He, who smote
   In Man for man the foe,
   The double agony in Man
   For man should undergo;

6. And in the garden secretly,
   And on the cross on high,
   Should teach His brethren, and inspire
   To suffer and to die.

7. Praise to the Holiest in the height,
   And in the depth be praise;
   In all His words most wonderful,
   Most sure in all His ways.

   John Henry Newman (1801-90)

470. Praise to the Lord, the Almighty

Ps 150:6;
Mt 8:26;
Mk 4:39; Lk 8:24;
Jn 8:12; Phil 4:19

Capo 5 (C)
LOBE DEN HERREN

Stralsund Gesangbuch (1665)

1. Praise to the Lord, the Al - migh - ty, the King of cre - a - tion! O my soul, praise Him, for He is thy health and sal - va - tion! All ye who hear, bro- thers and sis - ters, draw near, praise Him in glad ad - or - a - tion.

2. Praise to the Lord, who doth prosper thy work and defend thee;
   Surely His goodness and mercy here daily attend thee:
   Ponder anew
   What the Almighty can do,
   Who with His love doth befriend thee.

3. Praise to the Lord, who doth nourish thy life and restore thee,
   Fitting thee well for the tasks that are ever before thee,
   Then to thy need
   He like a mother doth speed,
   Spreading the wings of grace o'er thee.

4. Praise to the Lord, who when tempests their warfare are waging,
   Who, when the elements madly around thee are raging,
   Biddeth them cease,
   Turneth their fury to peace,
   Whirlwinds and waters assuaging.

5. Praise to the Lord, who, when darkness of sin is abounding,
   Who, when the godless do triumph, all virtue confounding,
   Sheddeth His light,
   Chaseth the horrors of night,
   Saints with His mercy surrounding.

6. Praise to the Lord! O let all that is in me adore Him!
   All that hath life and breath, come now with praises before Him!
   Let the Amen
   Sound from His people again:
   Gladly for aye we adore Him.

Joachim Neander (1650-80)
Tr. Catherine Winkworth (1829-78) & Percy Dearmer (1867-1936)

471.

Praise ye the Lord

Ps 126:3

Chris Bowater

472.

Praise You, Lord

Is 53:5; 61:1; Lk 4:18; 1 Pet 2:24

Capo 3 (C)

Nettie Rose

With majesty

1. Praise You,— Lord, for the won-der of Your heal—ing.

Praise You,— Lord, for Your love so free-ly given,

out-pour-ing a-noin-ting, flow-ing in to— heal our wounds.

Praise You,— Lord, for Your love for——— me.

2. Praise You, Lord, for Your gift of liberation.
Praise You, Lord, You have set the captives free;
The chains that bind are broken by the sharpness of Your sword,
Praise You, Lord, You gave Your life for me.

3. Praise You, Lord, You have born the depths of sorrow.
Praise You, Lord, for Your anguish on the tree;
The nails that tore Your body and the pain that tore Your soul.
Praise You, Lord, Your tears, they fell for me.

4. Praise You, Lord, You have turned our thorns to roses.
Glory, Lord, as they bloom upon Your brow.
The path of pain is hallowed, for Your love has made it sweet,
Praise You, Lord, and may I love You now.

473.

Prepare the way

Ps 24:7; Is 9:7; Mt 3:3; 21:9;
Mk 1:3; 11:9; Lk 3:4; Phil 2:10–11

Mary Smail
Lk 3:4; Mt 21:9

Brightly
Verse

1. Pre - pare the way of the Lord, — make His paths straight, — o - pen the gates — that He may en - ter free - ly in - to our life, — Ho - sa - nna we cry — to the Lord. ———— *Chorus* And we will fill the earth with the

sound of His praise, — Je - sus is Lord! — Let

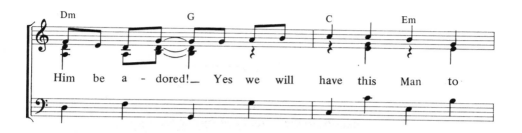

Him be a - dored!— Yes we will have this Man to

reign ov - er us, — Ho - sa - nna! We fol - low the Lord!

2. And He will come to us as He came before,
   Clothed in His grace,
   To stand in our place,
   And we behold Him now our Priest and King,
   Hosanna we sing to the Lord.

3. His kingdom shall increase
   To fill all the earth
   And show forth His worth,
   Then every knee shall bow and every tongue confess
   That Jesus Christ is Lord.

*Ascribe to the Lord the glory due to
his name;
bring an offering and come into
his courts.
Worship the Lord in the splendour
of his holiness;
tremble before him, all the earth.*

PSALM 96:8–9

474.
Prince of Peace You are

Is 9:6; Jn 4:23; Rom 12:1;
Heb 13:15; 2 Pet 1:19;
Rev 22:16

Robert Gay

With strength

Prince of Peace You are, You're the bright and morning star; wondrous royal King,

You have made my heart to sing. I worship You in spirit and in truth;

lifting my praise, Your name in song I raise. I give to You my life, I

offer up my sacrifice, I pledge my love to You, my God _____ and

King. King. My God and ____ King!

475.

Purify my heart
(Refiner's fire)

1 Cor 3:13; 1 Jn 1:7

Brian Doerksen

Capo 2(D)

Prayerfully

Pur - i - fy___ my heart, ___ let me be as
Pur - i - fy___ my heart, ___ cleanse me from with-

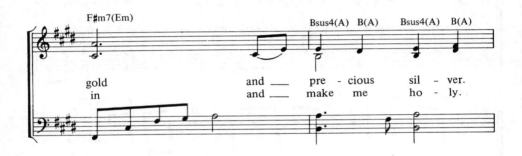

gold and ___ pre - cious sil - ver.
in and ___ make me ho - ly.

Pur - i - fy___ my heart, ___ let me be as
Pur - i - fy___ my heart, ___ cleanse me from my

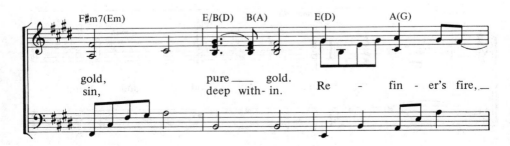

gold, pure___ gold. Re - fin - er's fire, ___
sin, deep with- in.

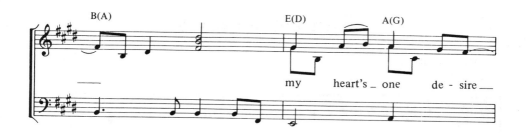

my heart's _ one de - sire _

is to be ho - ly,

set _ a - part _ for _ You _ Lord. _ I choose to be

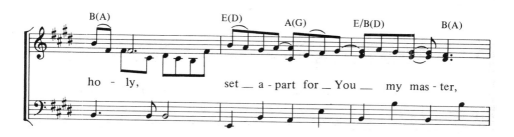

ho - ly, set _ a - part for _ You _ my mas - ter,

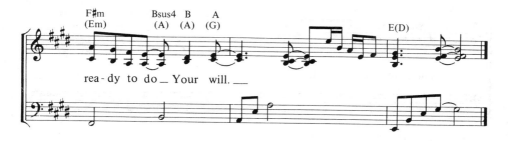

rea - dy to do _ Your will. _

476.

Raise up an army

Josh 5:14

Steve and Vikki Cook

Raise up an ar-my, O God, awake Your peo-ple through-out the earth.

Raise up an ar-my, O God, to pro-claim Your king-dom, to de-clare Your word, to de-clare Your glo-ry, O God.

2. O God, our glorious Maker,
   We marvel at Your grace,
   That You would use us in Your plan.
   Rejoicing at Your favour,
   Delighting in Your ways,
   We'll gladly follow Your command!

477.

Reconciled

Rom 5:9; 10:4; 2 Cor 5:19; Rev 19:8

Mike Kerry

With excitement

1. Re - con - cil'd, I'm re - con - cil'd, I'm re - concil'd to

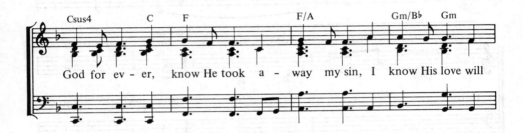

God for ev - er, know He took a - way my sin, I know His love will

leave me ne - ver. Re - con - cil'd, I am His child, I

know it was on me He smil'd, I'm re - con - cil'd, I'm

re - concil'd   to   God. _____ Hal - le -lu-jah I'm _

2. Justified, I'm justified,
    It's just as if I'd never sinned,
    And once I knew such guilty fear,
    But now I know His peace within me.
    Justified, I'm justified,
    It's all because my Jesus died.
    I'm justified, I'm justified by God.

    Hallelujah I'll

3. Magnify, I'll magnify,
    I'll magnify His name for ever,
    Wear the robe of righteousness
    And bless the name of Jesus, Saviour.
    Magnify the One who died,
    The One who reigns for me on high.
    I'll magnify, I'll magnify my God.

478.

Reign in me

Ps 22:3; Mt 6:10; Lk 11:2

Chris Bowater

Reign in me, _____ Sov'reign Lord, reign in me. _____

_____ Reign in me, _____ Sov-'reign Lord,

reign in me. _____ Cap-ti-vate my heart, _____

_____ let Your king-dom come, _____ e-stab-lish there Your

throne, _____ let Your will be done. _____

———————— □ ▢ □ ————————

Do not be anxious about anything, but in everything, by prayer and petition, with thanksgiving, present your requests to God. And the peace of God, which transcends all understanding, will guard your hearts and your minds in Christ Jesus.

PHILIPPIANS 4:6–7

———————— □ ▢ □ ————————

479. Reigning in all splendour

Phil 2:10–11

Capo 5 (Am)

Dave Bilbrough

Reign-ing in all splen - dour, vic - tor - i - ous love,

Christ Je - sus the Sav - iour,

tran - scen-dent a- bove. __ All earth-ly dom-in-

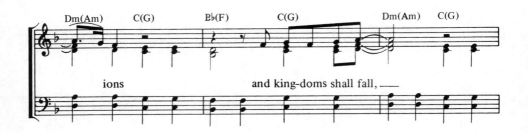

ions and king-doms shall fall, __

480.

Rejoice!

Josh 6:2, 7; Ezek 37:10; Mt 21:7; Mk 11:7;
Lk 19:35–36; Jn 12:14; 1 Cor 4:20; 2 Cor 4:7;
12:10; Col 1:27; Rev 19:11

Graham Kendrick

Re-joice! Re-joice! Christ is in you, the hope of glo - ry in our hearts. He lives! He lives! His breath is in you, a-rise a migh - ty ar - my, we a - rise.

1. Now is the time for us to march u-pon the land, into our

hands He will give the ground — we claim. _____

He rides in ma-jes-ty — to lead us in - to vic - to-ry,—

the world shall see that Christ is Lord! _____ Re -

2. God is at work in us
   His purpose to perform,
   Building a kingdom
   Of power not of words,
   Where things impossible
   By faith shall be made possible;
   Let's give the glory
   To Him now.

3. Though we are weak, His grace
   Is everything we need;
   We're made of clay
   But this treasure is within.
   He turns our weaknesses
   Into His opportunities,
   So that the glory
   Goes to Him.

481.

Rejoice, rejoice, rejoice!

Lk 1:46–47

Chris Bowater

Re - joice, — re - joice, — re - joice! — Re - joice,—

— re - joice, — re - joice! — My soul —

— re - joi - ces in — the Lord! —

Re - joice,— My soul

482.

Rejoice, the Lord is King!

Ps 102:27; Eph 2:22;
1 Thess 4:16; Heb 1:3, 12;
Rev 1:18; 11:15

GOPSAL

Majestically

George Frederick Handel (1685-1759)

1. Re - joice, the Lord is King! Your Lord and King a - dore; mor - tals, give thanks and sing, and tri - umph ev - er - more: lift up your heart, lift up your voice; re - joice! A - gain I say: re - joice!

Chorus

2. Jesus the Saviour reigns,
   The God of truth and love;
   When He had purged our stains,
   He took His seat above:

3. His kingdom cannot fail,
   He rules o'er earth and heaven;
   The keys of death and hell
   Are to our Jesus given:

4. He sits at God's right hand
   Till all His foes submit,
   And bow to His command,
   And fall beneath His feet:

5. Rejoice in glorious hope;
   Jesus the Judge shall come,
   And take His servants up
   To their eternal home:

*We soon shall hear the archangel's voice;
The trump of God shall sound: rejoice!*

Charles Wesley (1707-88)

483.

Restore, O Lord

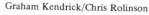

Ps 23:4; 85:4; 102:27; 136:1; Hab 3:2, 6;
1 Cor 3:13; Heb 1:12; 3:12; Rev 11:15

Graham Kendrick/Chris Rolinson

Lk 11:2

2. Restore, O Lord,
    In all the earth Your fame,
    And in our time revive
    The church that bears Your name.
    And in Your anger,
    Lord, remember mercy,
    O living God
    Whose mercy shall outlast the years.

3. Bend us, O Lord,
    Where we are hard and cold,
    In Your refiner's fire
    Come purify the gold.
    Though suffering comes
    And evil crouches near,
    Still our living God
    Is reigning, He is reigning here.

4. *As verse 1*

484.

Revival!

2 Chron 7:14; Mt 6:10; Lk 11:2; Jn 16:13–14

Doug Horley

Re - vi - val! We're pray-ing for re - vi - val,

that Your king-dom may come, Your will may be done through-out this

land. Re - done through-out this

land. Send now Your Spi - rit, Send now Your Spi - rit,

Lord, may He come; __ cause us to glo - ri - fy Je - sus Your Son, that
let truth a - rise; where dark-ness has blind-ed, op - en closed eyes, bring

485.

Ride on, ride on in majesty

Ps 110:1; Mt 21:7;
Mk 11:7; Lk 19:35–36;
Jn 12:14; Acts 2:35;
1 Cor 15:25; Rev 19:11

Capo 3 (G)

From a chorale in *Musikalisch Handbuch*
arr. W.H. Havergal (1793-1870)

WINCHESTER NEW

1. Ride on, ride on in ma - jes - ty! In
low - ly pomp ride on to die! O Christ, Thy tri -umphs
now be - gin o'er cap - tive death and con-quered sin.

2. Ride on, ride on in majesty!
   Hark all the tribes 'hosanna' cry;
   Thine humble beast pursues his road
   With palms and scattered garments strowed.

3. Ride on, ride on in majesty!
   Thy last and fiercest strife is nigh,
   The Father on His sapphire throne
   Expects His own annointed Son.

4. Ride on, ride on in majesty!
   In lowly pomp ride on to die!
   Bow Thy meek head to mortal pain,
   Then take, O God, Thy power, and reign!

H.H. Milman (1791-1868)

I will praise you, O Lord my God,
with all my heart;
I will glorify your name for ever.
For great is your love towards me;
you have delivered my soul from
the depths of the grave.

PSALM 86:12–13

486.

Rise up
(Go forth)

Mt 9:37; 28:19; Lk 10:2; Jn 4:35

Mark Altrogge

1. Rise up, you cham-pi-ons of God, rise up, you roy-al na-tion; rise up, and spread His light a-broad, we'll reach this ge-ne-ra-tion. We've got our march-ing or-ders, we've got our march-ing or-ders; now is the time to car-ry them forth.

2. Feel now the burden of the Lord,
   Feel how He longs to save them;
   Feel now for those who never heard
   About the Son He gave them.
   We've got our marching orders,
   We got our marching orders;
   Now is the time to carry them forth.

487.

River wash over me

Zech 13:1; Jn 4:14; 16:14;
Eph 5:18; Rev 22:1

Capo 3 (C)

Unhurried (with strength)

Dougie Brown

1. Riv - er___ wash ov - er me, ___ Cleanse me and make me new.___ Bathe me, re - fresh me and fill me a - new, Ri - ver___ wash o - ver me. ___

2. Spirit watch over me,
   Lead me to Jesus' feet.
   Cause me to worship and fill me anew,
   Spirit watch over me.

3. Jesus rule over me,
   Reign over all my heart.
   Teach me to praise you and fill me anew,
   Jesus rule over me.

488.

Capo 3 (C)
PETRA

Rock of Ages
(First tune)

Ex 17:6; Ps 18:2; Zech 13:1; Jn 13:8;
19:34; 1 Cor 10:4; Eph 2:8–9; 1 Jn 1:7

Richard Redhead (1820-1901)

1. Rock of Ag - es, cleft for me, let me hide my - self in Thee;
let the wa - ter and the blood, from Thy ri - ven side which flow'd
be of sin the doub - le cure, cleanse me from its guilt and pow'r.

2. Not the labour of my hands
Can fulfil Thy law's demands;
Could my zeal no respite know,
Could my tears for ever flow,
All for sin could not atone:
Thou must save, and Thou alone.

3. Nothing in my hand I bring,
Simply to Thy cross I cling;
Naked, come to Thee for dress;
Helpless, look to Thee for grace;
Foul, I to the fountain fly:
Wash me, Saviour, or I die.

4 While I draw this fleeting breath,
When mine eyes shall close in death,
When I soar to worlds unknown,
See Thee on Thy judgement throne,
Rock of Ages, cleft for me,
Let me hide myself in Thee.

Augustus Montague Toplady (1740-78)

Rock of Ages
(Second tune)

Capo 3 (G)
TOPLADY

Augustus Montague Toplady (1740-78)

1. Rock of Ages, cleft for me, let me hide myself in
Thee; let the wat-er and the blood, from Thy ri-ven side which
flow'd, be of sin the dou-ble cure, cleanse me from its guilt and pow'r.

2. Not the labour of my hands
Can fulfil Thy law's demands;
Could my zeal no respite know,
Could my tears for ever flow,
All for sin could not atone:
Thou must save, and Thou alone.

3. Nothing in my hand I bring,
Simply to Thy cross I cling;
Naked, come to Thee for dress;
Helpless, look to Thee for grace;
Foul, I to the fountain fly:
Wash me, Savoiur, or I die.

4 While I draw this fleeting breath,
When mine eyes shall close in death,
When I soar to worlds unknown,
See Thee on Thy judgement throne,
Rock of Ages, cleft for me,
Let me hide myself in Thee.

Augustus Montague Toplady (1740-78)

———————— □ ◻ □ ————————

*Let the word of Christ dwell in you
richly as you teach and admonish one
another with all wisdom, and as you
sing psalms, hymns and spiritual songs
with gratitude in your hearts to God.*

COLOSSIANS 3:16

———————— □ ◻ □ ————————

489. See amid the winter's snow

Lk 2:4, 7, 14

HUMILITY

John Goss (1800-80)

Steadily

Verse

1. See a - mid the win - ter's snow, born for us on earth be - low, see the Lamb of God ap-pears, pro - mised from e - ter - nal years.

Refrain

Hail, thou ev - er bless - èd morn! Hail re - demp-tion's hap - py dawn! Sing through all Je - ru - sa-lem: Christ is born in Beth - le - hem!

2. Lo, within a manger lies
   He who built the starry skies,
   He who throned in height sublime
   Sits amid the cherubim.

3. Say, ye holy shepherds, say,
   What your joyful news today;
   Wherefore have ye left your sheep
   On the lonely mountain steep?

4. "As we watched at dead of night,
   Lo, we saw a wondrous light:
   Angels, singing peace on earth,
   Told us of the Saviour's birth."

5. Sacred Infant, all divine,
   What a tender love was Thine,
   Thus to come from highest bliss
   Down to such a world as this?

6. Teach, O teach us, holy Child,
   By Thy face so meek and mild,
   Teach us to resemble Thee
   In Thy sweet humility.

Edward Caswall (1814-78)

490.

See Him come
(His body was broken)

Mt 21:7; Mk 11:7; Lk 19:35–36;
Jn 12:14; Phil 2:8

Capo 3(Am)

Hilary Davies

With reverence

1. See Him come, the King up-on a don-key. Where is all His ma - jes - ty and power? He ____ who was glo - ri - ous, yet ___ for my ___ sake put ___ a - way

2. See the people line His path with palm leaves,
   Hear the children shouting out His name.
   He who was glorious, yet for my sake
   Put away power to die upon the cross.
   His body was broken,
   His heart was torn apart for me upon the cross.

491.
See Him lying on a bed of straw
(Calypso carol)

Mt 2:1, 10;
Lk 2:4, 7–8

Michael Perry
arranged Stephen Coates

1. See Him lying on a bed of straw, — a draugh-ty sta-ble with an o-pen door, — Ma-ry cra-dl-ing the babe she bore; — the Prince of glo-ry is His name.

Chorus
O now car-ry me to Beth-le-hem, — to

see the Lord ___ ap - pear to men; ___ just as poor ___ as was the sta - ble then, ___ the Prince of glo - ry when He came.

2. Star of silver, sweep across the skies,
   Show where Jesus in the manger lies;
   Shepherds, swiftly from your stupor rise
   To see the Saviour of the world.

3. Angels, sing again the song you sang,
   Bring God's glory to the heart of man;
   Sing that Bethlehem's little baby can
   Be salvation to the soul.

4. Mine are riches, from Thy poverty,
   From Thine innocence eternity;
   Mine, forgiveness by Thy death for me,
   Child of sorrow for my joy.

492.

See His glory

Ps 136:1; Col 3:4; 1 Pet 5:4

Chris Bowater

Slow and worshipful

See His glo - ry, see His glo - ry, see His glo - ry now ap - pear. See His glo - ry, see His glo - ry, see His glo - ry now ap - pear. God of light,_ ho - li - ness _ and truth, pow'r and might,_ see His

493.

Seek ye first

Prov 3:5–6; Mt 4:4; 5:16; 6:33;
7:7; Lk 4:4; Jn 8:32, 36

Capo 3 (C)

Karen Lafferty

Brightly
Verse

1. Seek ye _ first the _ king - dom of God

and His _ right - eous - ness,

and all these things shall be ad - ded un - to you,

Hal - le - lu, Hal - le - lu - jah!

Chorus

Hal - le - lu - jah!

Hal - le - lu - jah!

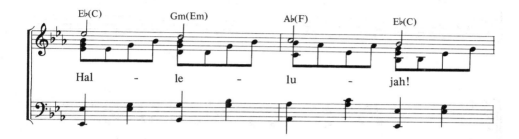

Hal - le - lu - jah!

Hal - le - lu, Hal - le - lu - jah!

2. Man shall not live by bread alone,
   But by every word
   That proceeds from the mouth of God,
   Hallelu, Hallelujah!

3. Ask and it shall be given unto you,
   Seek and ye shall find.
   Knock and it shall be opened unto you,
   Hallelu, Hallelujah!

4. If the Son shall set you free,
   Ye shall be free indeed.
   Ye shall know the truth and the truth shall set you free,
   Hallelu, Hallelujah!

5. Let your light so shine before men
   That they may see your good works
   And glorify your Father in heaven,
   Hallelu, Hallelujah!

6. Trust in the Lord with all thine heart,
   He shall direct thy paths,
   In all thy ways acknowledge Him,
   Hallelu, Hallelujah!

494.

Set my spirit free

Jn 8:32

author unknown
arranged Margaret Evans

Set my spi-rit free that I might wor - ship Thee,

Set my spi-rit free that I might praise Thy Name.

Let all bond-age go and let de - li - v'rance flow,

Set my spi-rit free to wor-ship Thee. _____

─────── □ ☐ □ ───────

In the beginning you laid the
    foundations of the earth,
  and the heavens are the work of your
    hands.
They will perish, but you remain;
  they will all wear out like a
    garment.
Like clothing you will change them
  and they will be discarded.
But you remain the same,
  and your years will never end.

PSALM 102:25–27

─────── □ ☐ □ ───────

495.

Shout for joy

Ps 98:4; Rom 8:19; 10:4; Col 1:26;
Rev 19:8; 21:2–3

Dave Bilbrough

Capo 2(C)

1. Shout for joy and sing,— let your prais-es ring;— see that God is build-ing a king-dom for a King.— His dwell-ing place with men, the new Jer-u-sa-lem; where Je-sus is Lord ov-er all.—

Chorus

And we will wor - ship,— wor - ship,

we will wor – ship Je-sus the

1st time — Lord.   We will Lord.

2nd time — Lord._____ (2. A)

Verse 2

2. A work so long con-ceal'd, in time will be re-veal'd, as the sons of God shall rise and take their stand. *etc*

Verse 3

3. Sov-'reign ov – er all, hail Him ris – en Lord. He a-lone is wor-thy of our praise. *etc*

2. A work so long concealed,
In time will be revealed,
As the sons of God shall rise and take their stand.
Clothed in His righteousness,
The church made manifest,
Where Jesus is Lord over all.

3. Sovereign over all,
Hail Him risen Lord.
He alone is worthy of our praise.
Reigning in majesty,
Ruling in victory,
Jesus is Lord over all.

496. Shout for joy and sing

Gen 22:8, 14; Ex 15:26;
Ps 18:2; 98:4; Jn 10:11, 14

David Fellingham

Shout for joy and sing your prai-ses to the King,

__ lift your voice and let your hal-le-lu-jahs ring;

__ come be-fore His throne to worship and a-dore,__ en-ter joy-ful-ly now__ the

pre-sence of the Lord__ You are my Cre-

497. Show Your power, O Lord

Capo 2(G)

Ps 68:28, 35

Graham Kendrick

Lyrics:

1. Show Your power O Lord, _ dem-on-strate the just-ice of Your king-dom. Prove Your might-y word, _ vin-di-cate _ Your name _ be-fore a watch-ing world.

Awe-some are Your _ deeds, O _

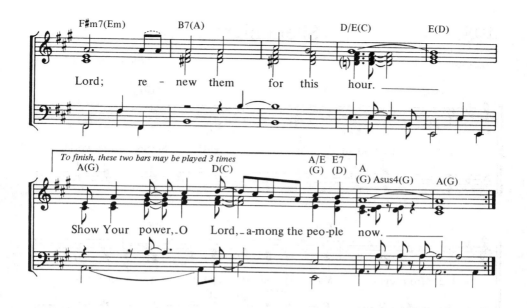

2. Show Your power, O Lord,
   Cause Your church to rise and take action.
   Let all fear be gone,
   Powers of the age to come
   Are breaking through.
   We Your people are ready to serve,
   To arise and to obey.
   Show Your power, O Lord,
   And set the people free.

   Ending last time
   Show Your power, O Lord,
   And set the people —
   Show Your power, O Lord,
   And set the people —
   Show Your power, O Lord,
   And set the people free.

498.

Silent night

Capo 3 (G)

Lk 2:7–8

STILLE NACHT

Franz Gruber (1787-1863)

Gently

1. Si - lent night, ho - ly night! Sleeps the world; hid

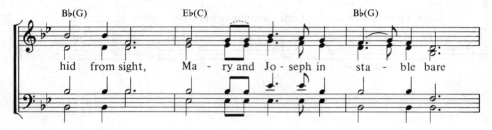

hid from sight, Ma - ry and Jo - seph in sta - ble bare watch

watch o'er the Child _ be - lov - ed and fair, sleep-ing in hea - ven-ly

rest, _____ sleep - ing in hea - ven - ly rest. _____

2. Silent night, holy night!
   Shepherds first saw the light,
   Heard resounding clear and long,
   Far and near, the angel-song:
   "Christ the Redeemer is here,
   Christ the Redeemer is here."

3. Silent night, holy night!
   Son of God, O how bright
   Love is smiling from Thy face!
   Strikes for us now the hour of grace,
   Saviour, since Thou art born,
   Saviour, since Thou art born.

Joseph Mohr (1792-1848)
tr. S. A. Brooke (1832-1916)

499. Sing Hallelujah to the Lord

Mt 28:6; Mk 16:6;
Lk 24:6; Jn 21:14;
1 Cor 15:23, 55

Capo 3 (Am)

Linda Stassen

2.   Jesus is risen from the dead . . . *etc.*

3.   Jesus is Lord of heaven and earth . . . *etc.*

4.   Jesus is living in His church . . . *etc.*

5.   Jesus is coming for His own . . . *etc.*

500. Sing praises unto God

Ps 47:1, 6–7

Capo 2 (G)

Melva Lea

Sing prai-ses un-to God, sing prai - 'ses, __ sing

praises un-to God,, sing prai - ses, _ sing prai-ses un-to God, sing prai-

- ses, Hal - le - lu - jah. ___ Sing

jah.   For God is the King ov - er

501.

Sing to the Lord
(Glory to the Lord)

Capo 3(G)

Joyfully, with a latin rhythm

Noel & Trica Richards

Sing to — the Lord, be joy - ful — in praise, ex-alt His — mag - ni - fi - cent ways.

Sing to — the Lord a - gain and — a - gain, for-ev - er — His glo - ry — pro - claim. Let

an - thems — of wor - ship — as - cend to — the King,

502. Sing unto the Lord a new song

Ps 96:1–2, 10–13

2. Then shall all the trees sing for joy
   Before the Lord, for He comes,
   He will judge the world
   With His righteousness,
   Sing unto the Lord a new song.

503.

So freely

Eph 2:8; 1 Jn 4:10

Dave Bilbrough

Capo 2(G)

With a sense of mystery

1. So free - ly, ___ flows the end - less love ___ You give ___ to me; ___ so free - ly, ___ not de - pen - dent on ___ my part. ___ As I am reach - ing out ___ re - veal the love with - in Your ___

heart, _____ as I am

reach-ing out_ re-veal the love with-in Your_ heart._____

2. Com - __

2. Completely,
   That's the way You give Your love to me,
   Completely.
   Not dependent, on my part.
   As I am reaching out
   Reveal the love within Your heart,
   As I am reaching out
   Reveal the love within Your heart.

3. So easy,
   I receive the love You give to me.
   So easy,
   Not dependent on my part.
   Flowing out to me
   The love within Your heart,
   Flowing out to me
   The love within Your heart.

504.

Soften my heart

Ezek 11:19; 36:26

Cindy Gough

Worshipfully

1. Sof - ten _ my heart, Lord, _ I

want to meet _ You _ here. _

Sof - ten _ my heart, Lord, _

ten - der me _ with _ tears; _ for Your

pre - sence _ is _ be - yond an - y -

thing I __ could __ de - sire. ___

Sof - ten __ my heart, Lord, __ con -

sume me with Your ho - ly

Last time only

fire.

2. Soften my heart, Lord,
   I have made a choice.
   Soften my heart, Lord,
   I want to hear Your voice;
   For Your presence is beyond
   Anything I could desire.
   Soften my heart, Lord,
   Consume me with Your holy fire.

───── □ ▢ □ ─────

He saved us through the washing of rebirth and renewal by the Holy Spirit, whom he poured out on us generously through Jesus Christ our Saviour, so that, having been justified by his grace, we might become heirs having the hope of eternal life.

TITUS 3:5–7

───── □ ▢ □ ─────

505.

Soften my heart, Lord

Ezek 11:19; 36:26

Graham Kendrick

Soften my heart, Lord, soften my heart. From all in dif - f'rence set me a - part. To feel Your com - pas - sion, to weep with Your tears, come sof - ten my heart, O Lord, sof - ten my heart.

Soldiers of Christ, arise

Rom 8:37; Eph 6:10–13;
2 Tim 2:3

Capo 5(C)
ST ETHELWALD

(First tune)

William Henry Monk (1823-89)

1. Sol - diers of Christ, a - rise, and put your arm-our on; strong

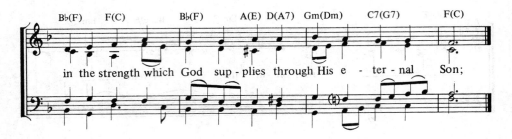

in the strength which God sup - plies through His e - ter - nal Son;

2. Strong in the Lord of hosts,
   And in His mighty power;
   Who in the strength of Jesus trusts
   Is more than conqueror.

3. Stand, then, in His great might,
   With all His strength endued;
   And take, to arm you for the fight,
   The panoply of God.

4. Leave no unguarded place,
   No weakness of the soul;
   Take every virtue, every grace,
   And fortify the whole.

5. From strength to strength go on;
   Wrestle and fight and pray;
   Tread all the powers of darkness down,
   And win the well-fought day.

6. That having all things done,
   And all your conflicts past,
   Ye may o'ercome, through Christ alone,
   And stand complete at last.

Charles Wesley (1707-88)

Soldiers of Christ, arise
(Second tune)

FROM STRENGTH TO STRENGTH

Edward Woodall Naylor (1867-1934)

Triumphantly

1. Sol-diers of Christ, a - rise, and put your ar - mour on; strong in the strength that God supp - lies, through His e - ter - nal Son; strong in the Lord of hosts and in His migh - ty pow'r; who in the strength of Je - sus trusts is more than con - quer - or.

2. Stand, then, in His great might,
   With all His strength endued;
   And take, to arm you for the fight,
   The panoply of God.
   Leave no unguarded place,
   No weakness of the soul;
   Take every virtue, every grace,
   And fortify the whole.

3. From strength to strength go on;
   Wrestle and fight and pray;
   Tread all the powers of darkness down,
   And win the well-fought day.
   That having all things done,
   And all your conflicts past,
   Ye may o'ercome, through Christ alone,
   And stand complete at last.

Charles Wesley (1707-88)

507.

Son of God
(Praise song)

John Wimber

Son of God, this is our {praise / love / praise} song.

Je-sus, my Lord, I sing to You.

Come now, Spi-rit of God, breath life in-

to these words of love; an-gels join from a-bove as we sing our

508.

Sovereign Lord
(Living sacrifice)

Rom 12:1

Capo 3(D)

Noel & Trica Richards

Sov-'reign Lord, I am Yours, now and ev-er-more. You're my King, You're the One I am liv-ing for. I choose to do what pleas-es You, Lord, may my life for-ev-er be a liv-ing sa-cri-fice.

— □ ▢ □ —

Clap your hands, all you nations;
shout to God with cries of joy.
How awesome is the Lord Most High,
the great King over all the earth!

PSALM 47:1–2

— □ ▢ □ —

509.

Spirit, breathe on us

Capo 2(G)

Dave Bilbrough and Graham Kendrick

Spi - rit, breathe on __ us, fall a -

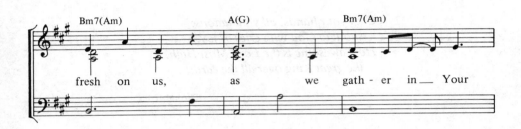

fresh on us, as we gath - er in __ Your

name. __ Bring Your heal - ing __ touch,

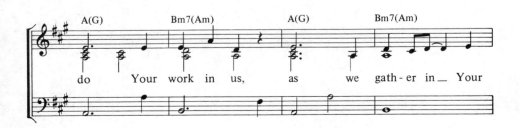

do Your work in us, as we gath - er in __ Your

ho - ly name. Join us to -

geth - er, one to a -

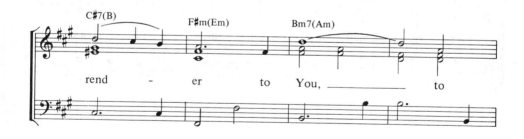

no - ther, as we sur -

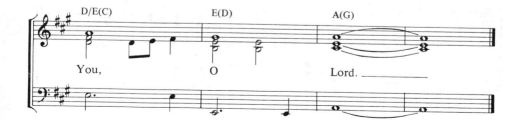

rend - er to You, _____ to

You, O Lord. _____

510.   Spirit of the living God

Eph 5:18

Daniel Iverson

511. Spirit of the living God

Eph 5:18

Paul Armstrong

512.

Stand up, and bless the Lord

Deut 10:8; Neh 9:5;
Ps 118:14; Is 6:6–7

(First tune)

CARLISLE

Lively

Charles Lockhart (1745-1815)

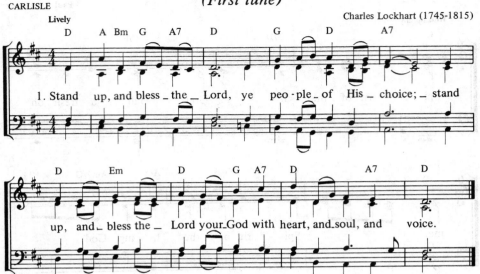

1. Stand up, and bless the Lord, ye peo-ple of His choice; stand up, and bless the Lord your God with heart, and soul, and voice.

2. Though high above all praise,
   Above all blessing high,
   Who would not fear His holy name,
   And laud and magnify?

3. O for the living flame
   From His own altar brought,
   To touch our lips, our minds inspire,
   And wing to heaven our thought!

4. God is our strength and song,
   And His salvation ours;
   Then be His love in Christ proclaimed
   With all our ransomed powers.

5. Stand up, and bless the Lord,
   The Lord your God adore;
   Stand up, and bless His glorious name
   Henceforth for evermore.

James Montgomery (1771-1854)

Stand up, and bless the Lord

(Second tune)

ST MICHAEL

With strength

Composed or adapted by
Louis Bourgeois in *Genevan Psalter* (1551)

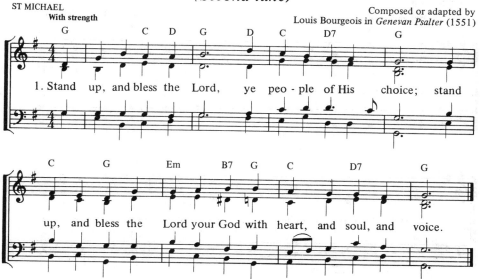

1. Stand up, and bless the Lord, ye peo - ple of His choice; stand up, and bless the Lord your God with heart, and soul, and voice.

2. Though high above all praise,
   Above all blessing high,
   Who would not fear His holy name,
   And laud and magnify?

3. O for the living flame
   From His own altar brought,
   To touch our lips, our minds inspire,
   And wing to heaven our thought!

4. God is our strength and song,
   And His salvation ours;
   Then be His love in Christ proclaimed
   With all our ransomed powers.

5. Stand up, and bless the Lord,
   The Lord your God adore;
   Stand up, and bless His glorious name
   Henceforth for evermore.

   James Montgomery (1771-1854)

513.

Stand up, stand up for Jesus

1 Cor 15:25;
Eph 6:11, 18;
2 Tim 2:3; 1 Pet 5:4; Rev 3:21

MORNING LIGHT

With enthusiasm

George James Webb (1803-87)

1. Stand up, stand up for Je - sus, ye sol - diers of the

cross! Lift high His roy - al ban - ner; it

must not suf - fer loss. From vic - t'ry un - to

vic - t'ry His ar - my He shall lead, _____ till

ev - 'ry foe is van - quish'd, and Christ is Lord in - deed.

2. Stand up, stand up for Jesus!
   The trumpet-call obey;
   Forth to the mighty conflict
   In this His glorious day!
   Ye that are His, now serve Him
   Against unnumbered foes;
   Let courage rise with danger,
   And strength to strength oppose.

3. Stand up, stand up for Jesus!
   Stand in His strength alone;
   The arm of flesh will fail you,
   Ye dare not trust your own.
   Put on the gospel armour,
   Each piece put on with prayer;
   Where duty calls, or danger,
   Be never wanting there.

4. Stand up, stand up for Jesus!
   The strife will not be long;
   This day the noise of battle,
   The next the victor's song.
   To him that overcometh
   A crown of life shall be;
   He with the King of glory
   Shall reign eternally.

George Duffield (1818-88)

———— □ ▢ □ ————

Because Jesus lives for ever, he has a
permanent priesthood. Therefore he is
able to save completely those who come
to God through him, because he always
lives to intercede for them.

HEBREWS 7:24–25

———— □ ▢ □ ————

514.

Such love

Jn 3:16

Capo 4(C)

Graham Kendrick

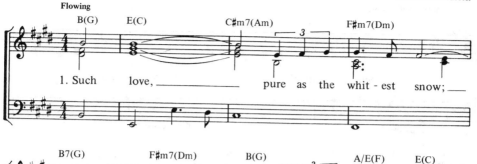

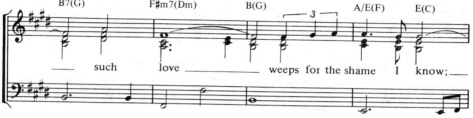

2. Such love, stilling my restlessness;
   Such love, filling my emptiness;
   Such love, showing me holiness;
   O Jesus, such love.

3. Such love springs from eternity;
   Such love, streaming through history;
   Such love, fountain of life to me;
   O Jesus, such love.

515.

Such love, such grace

Rom 8:38–39

Dave Bryant

Such love! Such grace! makes the pie - ces come fall - ing in - to place, breaks through the dark-ness, turns on the light, mak-ing blind - ness give way __ to sight. __ Your love has con-quered, has set us free to be-

516.

Sweet fellowship

Mt 18:20; Jn 4:14

Ronnie Wilson

1. Sweet fel-low-ship, Je-sus in the midst. Life blos-soms in the Church, men by men are blessed When Je-sus is in the midst. I've ne-ver known a time like this, Feel the spi-rit with-in me rise, Come and see what God is doing, Lord, we love You.

2. Peace and harmony — Jesus reigning here;
   The Church moves at His command,
   No room for doubt or fear
   For Jesus is reigning here.

Sequence: verse 1, verse 2, refrain, repeat verse 1.

— □ ▢ □ —

Praise God in his sanctuary;
praise him in his mighty heavens.
Praise him for his acts of power;
praise him for his surpassing
greatness.

PSALM 150:1–2

— □ ▢ □ —

517.
Swing wide the gates

Ps 24:7–8

Chris Bowater

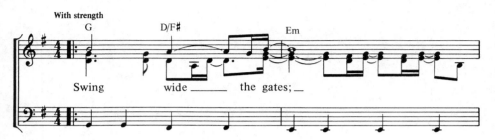

Swing wide _____ the gates; _

let the King _____ come in. ____

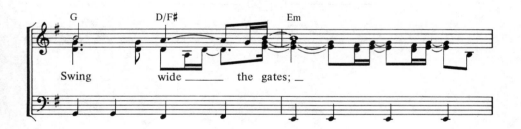

Swing wide _____ the gates; _

make a way _ for Him. _

Here He comes, _____ the King of

glo - ry. Here He comes, _ migh - ty in vic-to-ry. Here He comes,

_____ in splen-dour and ma - jes - ty.

Swing wide the gates, swing wide the gates, let the King come in. __

518.

Take, eat, this is My body

Is 1:18; Mt 26:26;
Mk 14:22; Lk 22:19;
Jn 3:16; 8:36;
1 Cor 11:24

Paul Simmons

Take, eat, this is My bo - dy, bro - ken for you, for I am come that you might have life; eat of My flesh and live, eat of My flesh and live. live.

1. My blood

2. Though your sins be as scarlet
   They shall be white as snow,
   Though they be red like crimson
   They shall be as wool,
   They shall be as wool.

3. For God so loved the world
   He gave His only Son,
   That whosoever believeth on Him
   Might have everlasting life,
   Might have everlasting life.

519.

Take my life, and let it be

Capo 3 (D)

NOTTINGHAM

Rom 12:1

Attributed to
Wolfgang Amadeus Mozart (1756-91)

With feeling

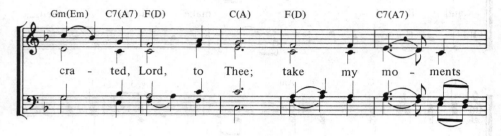

1.Take my life, and let it be con - se -

cra - ted, Lord, to Thee; take my mo - ments and my days, let them flow— in cease - less praise.

2. Take my hands, and let them move
At the impulse of Thy love;
Take my feet, and let them be
Swift and beautiful for Thee.

3. Take my voice, and let me sing
Always, only, for my King;
Take my lips, and let them be
Filled with messages from Thee.

4. Take my silver and my gold,
Not a mite would I withhold;
Take my intellect, and use
Every power as Thou shalt choose.

5. Take my will, and make it Thine;
It shall be no longer mine;
Take my heart, it is Thine own;
It shall be Thy royal throne.

6. Take my love; my Lord, I pour
At Thy feet its treasure store:
Take myself, and I will be
Ever, only, all for Thee.

Frances Ridley Havergal (1836-79)

520.

Tell out, my soul
(First tune)

Lk 1:46–55

Capo 3 (D)
GO FORTH

Michael Baughen

With strength

1. Tell out, my soul, the great-ness of the Lord;
un-num-bered bless - ings give my spi-rit voice;
ten - der to me the pro-mise of His word; in
God my Sa - viour shall my heart re - joice.

2. Tell out, my soul, the greatness of His name!
   Make known His might, the deeds His arm has done;
   His mercy sure, from age to age the same;
   His holy name—the Lord, the mighty One.

3. Tell out my soul, the greatness of His might!
   Powers and dominions lay their glory by;
   Proud hearts and stubborn wills are put to flight,
   The hungry fed, the humble lifted high.

4. Tell out, my soul, the glories of His word!
   Firm is His promise, and His mercy sure;
   Tell out, my soul, the greatness of the Lord
   To children's children, and forever more!

Tell out, my soul
(*Second tune*)

Capo 2 (G)
WOODLANDS

Walter Greatorex (1877–1949)

2. Tell out, my soul,
   The greatness of His name!
   Make known His might,
   The deeds His arm has done;
   His mercy sure,
   From age to age the same;
   His holy name:
   The Lord, the Mighty One.

3. Tell out, my soul,
   The greatness of His might!
   Powers and dominions
   Lay their glory by;
   Proud hearts and stubborn wills
   Are put to flight,
   The hungry fed,
   The humble lifted high.

4. Tell out, my soul,
   The glories of His word!
   Firm is His promise,
   And His mercy sure:
   Tell out, my soul,
   The greatness of the Lord
   To children's children
   And for evermore!

Timothy Dudley-Smith (1926-)

521.

Thanks be to God

1 Cor 10:13; 15:57; Col 1:13;
Heb 2:18; 4:15; Jude 24

Robert Stoodley

Thanks be to God who gives us the vic-to-ry, ___ gives us the vic-to-ry ___ through our Lord Je-sus Christ. ___ our Lord Je-sus Christ. ___

1. He is a-ble to keep us from fall-ing, and to set us free from sin; so let us each live up to our call-ing, and com-mit our way to Him.

2. Jesus knows all about our temptations,
   He has had to bear them too;
   He will show us a way to escape them,
   If we trust Him He will lead us through.

3. He has led us from the power of darkness
   To the kingdom of His blessed Son;
   So let us join in praise together,
   And rejoice in what the Lord has done.

4. Praise the Lord for sending Jesus
   To the cross of Calvary;
   Now He's risen, reigns in power,
   And death is swallowed up in victory.

——————— □ ▢ □ ———————

But you are a chosen people, a royal priesthood, a holy nation, a people belonging to God, that you may declare the praises of him who called you out of darkness into his wonderful light.

1 PETER 2:9

——————— □ ▢ □ ———————

522.
Thank You for the cross
(Oh I love You, Lord)

Ps 18:19; Is 42:1;
Zeph 3:17; Col 1:14;
Heb 7:25; 1 Pet 2:24

Capo 3(G)

Graham Kendrick

1. Thank You for the cross, the price You paid for us, how You
Now our sins are gone, all for - giv - en, cov - er'd

gave Your-self so com-plete-ly, pre-cious Lord. (Pre-cious Lord.) Oh I
by Your blood, all for - got - ten, thank You Lord. (Thank You Lord.)

love You, Lord, real-ly love You, Lord. I will ne-ver un-der-stand why You love

me. You're my deep-est joy, — You're my heart's de-light, — and the

great-est thing of all, O Lord, I see: You de-light in me!

2. For our healing there
Lord You suffered,
And to take our fear
You poured out Your love,
Precious Lord. (Precious Lord.)

Calvary's work is done,
You have conquered,
Able now to save
So completely,
Thank You Lord. (Thank You Lord.)

523.

Thank You Jesus

1 Cor 15:3–4

Author unknown
Arr. Margaret Evans

Verse

1. You went to Cal - va-ry, _____ and there you died for me, _____ thank You Lord _____ for lov-ing me. _____ You went to Cal - va-ry, _____ and there you died for me, thank You Lord _____ for lov-ing me. _____

2. You rose up from the grave,
To me new life You gave,
Thank You Lord for loving me.
You rose up from the grave,
To me new life You gave,
Thank You Lord for loving me.

524. Thank You, Lord, for this fine day

Eph 5:20;
1 Thess 5:18

Diane Davis Andrew

Capo 3 (D)

1. Thank ___ You, Lord, for this fine day, thank ___ You, Lord, for
-le - lu - ia, praise the Lord! Al - le - lu - ia,

this fine day, thank ___ You, Lord, for this fine day,
praise the Lord! Al - le - lu - ia, praise the Lord,

right ___ where we are.
right ___ where we are.

2. Thank You, Lord, for loving us . . .

3. Thank You, Lord, for giving us peace . . .

4. Thank You, Lord, for setting us free . . .

May the praise of God be in their mouths
and a double-edged sword in their hands.

PSALM 149:6

525. The Church's one foundation

1 Cor 3:11;
Eph 2:20; 4:5;
1 Pet 2:6; Rev 6:10

Capo 2 (C)
AURELIA

Samuel Sebastian Wesley (1810-76)

Moderate

1. The Church-'s one found - at - ion is Jes - us Christ, her
Lord; she is His new cre - at - ion by
wat - er and the word; from heav'n He came and
sought her to be His ho - ly bride, with
His own blood He bought her, and for her life He died.

2. Elect from every nation,
   Yet one o'er all the earth,
   Her charter of salvation
   One Lord, one faith, one birth;
   One holy name she blesses,
   Partake one holy food,
   And to one hope she presses
   With every grace endued.

3. Though with a scornful wonder
   Men see her sore oppressed,
   By schisms rent asunder,
   By heresies distressed,
   Yet saints their watch are keeping,
   Their cry goes up, 'How long?'
   And soon the night of weeping
   Shall be the morn of song.

4. 'Mid toil, and tribulation,
   And tumult of her war,
   She waits the consummation
   Of peace for evermore;
   Till with the vision glorious
   Her longing eyes are blessed,
   And the great church victorious
   Shall be the church at rest.

5. Yet she on earth hath union
   With God the Three in One,
   And mystic sweet communion
   With those whose rest is won:
   O happy ones and holy!
   Lord, give us grace that we,
   Like them, the meek and lowly,
   On high may dwell with Thee.

Samuel John Stone

526. The church's one foundation

Jn 4:14; 1 Cor 3:11;
Gal 6:7; Eph 2:20;
1 Pet 2:5–6, 9;
2 Pet 1:19; Rev 22:1

Dave Bilbrough

Majestically

1. The church's one foun - da - tion is Je - sus Christ the
Lord and on that rev - el - a - tion each one of us is
call'd to taste His full sal - va - tion, to know His life with-
- in; a pure and ho - ly na - tion to glor - i - fy the
King. Hal - le - lu - jah, _____ how great You are, _____

reign-ing in glo - ry, _____ en-thron'd in pow'r; _____

Bright Morn-ing Star, _____ how great You are; _____

reign-ing in glo - ry, _____ en-thron'd in

1st & 2nd time | Last time

pow'r. _____ 2. This _____

2. This time of preparation
   Eventually will yield
   The fruit of all His labours;
   His heart will be fulfilled.
   From every tribe and nation
   His people shall be known;
   Drawn to be His kingdom,
   Made out of living stones.

3. See Him and be radiant,
   Taste the Lord and know
   He wants to take us deeper,
   For what we are we sow;
   With streams of living water
   He longs to overflow,
   That out to all creation
   His glory He will show.

527. The day Thou gavest, Lord, is ended

Ps 113:3; Dan 6:26; Mt 24:42; Mk 13:33; Lk 21:36

ST CLEMENT
Peacefully

Clement Cotterill Scholefield (1839-1904)

1. The day Thou gavest, Lord, is ended, the dark-ness falls at Thy be-hest; to Thee our morn-ing hymns as-cend-ed, Thy praise shall sanc-ti-fy our rest.

2. We thank Thee that Thy church unsleeping,
   While earth rolls onward into light,
   Through all the world her watch is keeping,
   And rests not now by day or night.

3. As o'er each continent and island
   The dawn leads on another day,
   The voice of prayer is never silent,
   Nor dies the strain of praise away.

4. The sun that bids us rest is waking
   Our brethren 'neath the western sky,
   And hour by hour fresh lips are making
   Thy wondrous doings heard on high.

5. So be it, Lord! Thy throne shall never,
   Like earth's proud empires, pass away;
   Thy kingdom stands, and grows for ever,
   Till all Thy creatures own Thy sway.

John Ellerton (1826-93)

528.

The earth is the Lord's

Ps 24:1–2

With strength

Graham Kendrick

The earth is the Lord's (and ev'-ry-thing in it.) The earth is the Lord's (the work of His hands.) The earth is the Lord's (and ev'-ry-thing in it;) and all things were made for His glo - ry. _____ The moun-tains are His, the seas and the is-lands, the ci-ties and towns, the hou-ses and

Chorus fourth time:

And all things were made,
Yes all things were made,
And all things were made
For His glory.

*Sequence — Chorus, Verse, Chorus,
Verse, Chorus twice.*

---□ ☐ □---

Worthy is the Lamb, who was
  slain,
to receive power and wealth and
  wisdom and strength
and honour and glory and praise!

REVELATION 5:12

---□ ☐ □---

529.
The first Nowell

Mt 2:1, 10–11; Lk 2:4, 8, 10

2. They lookèd up and saw a star
Shining in the east, beyond them far,
And to the earth it gave great light,
And so it continued both day and night.

3. And by the light of that same star
Three wise men came from country far;
To seek a King was their intent,
And to follow the star wherever it went.

4. This star drew nigh to the north-west;
Over Bethlehem it took its rest,
And there it did both stop and stay
Right over the place where Jesus lay.

5. Then entered in those wise men three
Full reverently on bended knee,
And offered there in His presence
Their gold, and myrrh, and frankincense.

6. Then let us all with one accord
Sing praises to our heavenly Lord,
That hath made heaven and earth of nought,
And with His blood mankind hath bought.

Traditional

530. The God of Abraham praise

Ex 3:6, 14;
Ps 119:57; Is 9:6;
40:31; Jer 23:6; 33:16;
Dan 7:9; Rev 4:8

LEONI

With strength

Adapted from Hebrew melody

1. The God of Ab - r'ham praise, who reigns en-thron'd a - bove. An - cient of ev - er - last - ing days and God of love. Je - ho - vah, Great I AM! By earth and heav'n con - fess'd; I bow and bless the sa - cred name for ev - er bless'd.

2. The God of Abraham praise,
At whose supreme command
From earth I rise, and seek the joys
At His right hand.
I all on earth forsake —
Its wisdom, fame, and power—
And Him my only portion make,
My shield and tower.

3. The God of Abraham praise,
Whose all-sufficient grace
Shall guide me all my happy days
In all my ways.
He calls a worm His friend,
He calls Himself my God;
And He shall save me to the end
Through Jesu's blood.

4. He by Himself hath sworn,
I on His oath depend:
I shall, on eagles' wings upborne,
To heaven ascend;
I shall behold His face,
I shall His power adore,
And sing the wonders of His grace
For evermore.

5. There dwells the Lord our King,
The Lord our Righteousness,
Triumphant o'er the world and sin,
The Prince of Peace;
On Zion's sacred height
His kingdom still maintains,
And glorious with His saints in light
For ever reigns.

6. The God who reigns on high
The great archangels sing;
And, holy, holy, holy, cry,
Almighty King.
Who was and is the same,
And evermore shall be;
Jehovah, Father, Great I AM,
We worship Thee.

7. Before the Saviour's face
The ransomed nations bow;
O'erwhelmed at His almighty grace,
For ever new:
He shows His prints of love,
They kindle to a flame,
And sound through all the worlds above
The slaughtered Lamb.

8. The whole triumphant host
Gives thanks to God on high;
Hail, Father, Son, and Holy Ghost!
They ever cry.
Hail, Abraham's God, and mine!
I join the heavenly lays;
All might and majesty are Thine,
And endless praise.

Thomas Olivers (1725-99)

531. The head that once was crowned with thorns

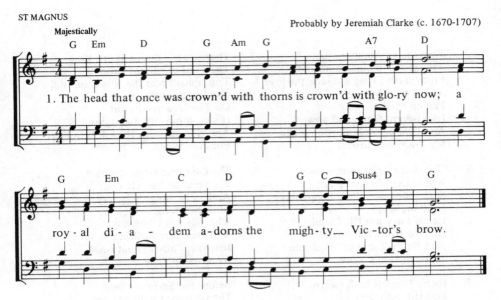

Mt 27:29;
Mk 15:17;
Jn 19:2; 1 Tim 6:15;
Rev 17:14; 19:12, 16; 22:4–5

ST MAGNUS

Probably by Jeremiah Clarke (c. 1670-1707)

Majestically

1. The head that once was crown'd with thorns is crown'd with glo-ry now; a roy-al di-a-dem a-dorns the migh-ty Vic-tor's brow.

2. The highest place that heaven affords
Is His by sovereign right,
The King of kings, the Lord of lords,
And heaven's eternal light.

3. The joy of all who dwell above,
The joy of all below,
To whom He manifests His love,
And grants His name to know.

4. To them the cross, with all its shame,
With all its grace, is given;
Their name an everlasting name,
Their joy the joy of heaven.

5. They suffer with their Lord below,
They reign with Him above;
Their profit and their joy to know
The mystery of His love.

6. The cross He bore is life and health,
Though shame and death to Him;
His people's hope, His people's wealth,
Their everlasting theme.

Thomas Kelly (1769-1854)

532.

The King is among us

Zeph 3:17; Mt 18:20;
Acts 1:4; 1 Cor 12:11

Graham Kendrick

1. The King is a-mong us, His
7.
Spi-rit is here, let's draw near and wor - ship, let songs fill the air.
2. He

2. He looks down upon us,
   Delight in His face,
   Enjoying His children's love,
   Enthralled by our praise.

3. For each child is special,
   Accepted and loved,
   A love gift from Jesus
   To His Father above.

4. And now He is giving
   His gifts to us all,
   For no one is worthless
   And each one is called.

5. The Spirit's anointing
   On all flesh comes down,
   And we shall be channels
   For works like His own.

6. We come now believing
   Your promise of power,
   For we are Your people
   And this is Your hour.

7. *As verse 1*

533.

Capo 2 (F)
DOMINUS REGIT ME

The King of love
(First tune)

Ps 23; Lk 15:20; Jn 10:11, 14

John Bacchus Dykes (1823-76)

Joyfully

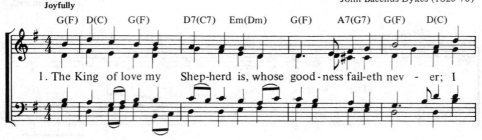

1. The King of love my Shep-herd is, whose good-ness fail-eth nev - er; I

noth- ing— lack if I am — His and He is mine for ev - er.

2. Where streams of living water flow
   My ransomed soul He leadeth,
   And where the verdant pastures grow
   With food celestial feedeth.

3. Perverse and foolish oft I strayed,
   But yet in love He sought me,
   And on His shoulder gently laid,
   And home rejoicing brought me.

4. In death's dark vale I fear no ill
   With Thee, dear Lord, beside me;
   Thy rod and staff my comfort still,
   Thy cross before to guide me.

5. Thou spread'st a table in my sight;
   Thy unction grace bestoweth:
   And O what transport of delight
   From Thy pure chalice floweth!

6. And so through all the length of days
   Thy goodness faileth never;
   Good Shepherd, may I sing Thy praise
   Within Thy house for ever.

Henry Williams Baker (1821-77)

The King of love
(Second tune)

Capo 2 (C)
ST COLUMBA

Traditional Irish melody

1. The__ King of love my__ Shep - herd

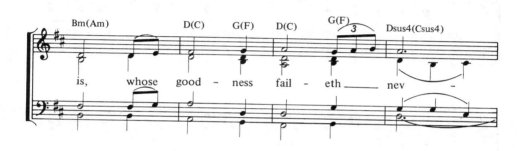

is, whose good - ness fail - eth____ nev -

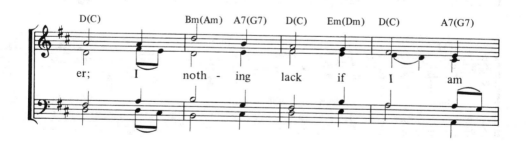

er; I noth - ing lack if I am

His and He is mine for ev - er.

534. The Lord has given

Ps 149:6, 8–9; Eph 6:11

Capo 3(D)

Author unknown
Arr. Margaret Evans

With strength and pace

Verse

1. The Lord has gi - ven ___ a land of good_ things, _ I will press in ___ and make them mine. ___ I'll know His pow - er, ___ I'll know His glo - ry, ___ and in His king - dom I will shine.

Chorus

With the high praises of God in our mouth and a

two - edged   sword — in our hand,   we'll

march   right   on   to   the   vic - tor - y   side, ___

right   in -   to   Can - aan's   land. _____

2. Gird up your armour, ye sons of Zion,
   Gird up your armour, let's go to war.
   We'll win the battle with great rejoicing
   And so we'll praise Him more and more.

3. We'll bind their kings in chains and fetters,
   We'll bind their nobles tight in iron,
   To execute God's written judgement.
   March on to glory, sons of Zion!

535.

The Lord has led forth

Ps 105:43–45

Chris A. Bowater

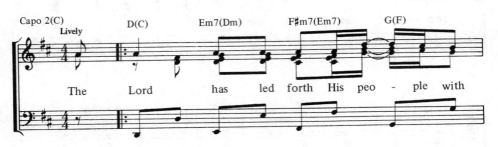

The Lord has led forth His peo - ple with

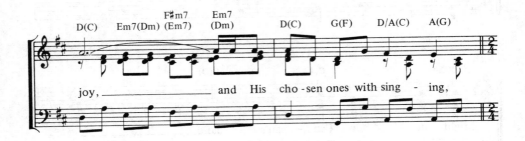

joy, _____ and His cho - sen ones with sing - ing,

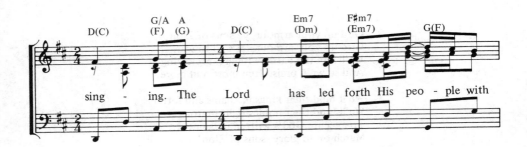

sing - ing. The Lord has led forth His peo - ple with

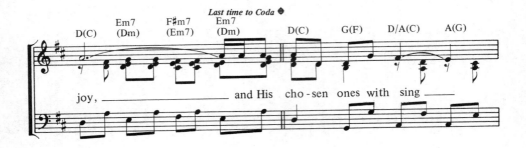

joy, _____ and His cho - sen ones with sing _____

ing. He has giv'n to them the

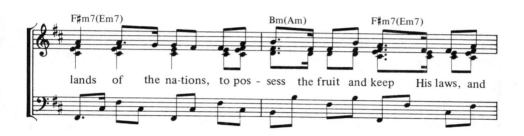

lands of the na-tions, to pos - sess the fruit and keep His laws, and

praise, praise His name._____ The

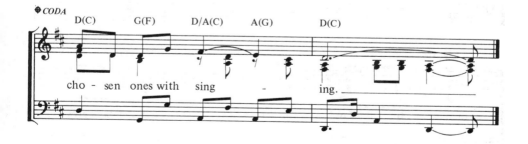

cho - sen ones with sing - ing._____

536.

The Lord is marching out
(O give thanks)

Ps 136:1; Rev 19:11

Graham Kendrick

Capo 2 (Am)

1. The Lord is mar-ching out in splen-dour,
in awe-some ma - jes-ty He rides,
for truth, hu - mil - i - ty and just - ice,
His migh-ty ar-my fills the skies. O give

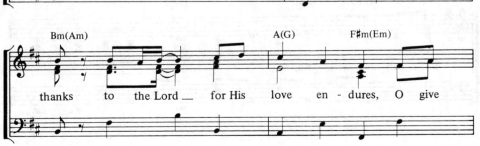

thanks to the Lord — for His love en - dures, O give

thanks to the Lord — for His love en - dures, O give

thanks to the Lord — for His love en - dures for

e - ver, _____ for e - ver. _____

To repeat

To end

_____ _____ for e - ver. _____

2. His army marches out with dancing
    For He has filled our hearts with joy.
    Be glad the kingdom is advancing,
    The love of God, our battle cry!

Sequence: Verse, Chorus, Verse, Chorus.

537.   The Lord's my Shepherd

Capo 3 (D)
CRIMOND

Ps 23; Jn 10:11, 14

Jessie Seymour Irvine (1836-87)

1. The Lord's my Shep - herd, I'll not want; He

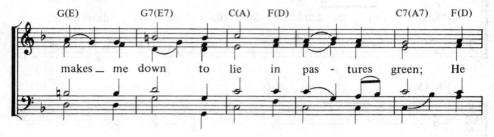

makes me down to lie in pas - tures green; He

lead - eth me the qui - et wa - ters by.

2. My soul He doth restore again;
   And me to walk doth make
   Within the paths of righteousness,
   E'en for His own name's sake.

3. Yea, though I walk in death's dark vale,
   Yet will I fear no ill;
   For Thou art with me; and Thy rod
   And staff me comfort still.

4. My table Thou hast furnishèd
   In presence of my foes;
   My head Thou dost with oil anoint,
   And my cup overflows.

5. Goodness and mercy all my life
   Shall surely follow me;
   And in God's house for evermore
   My dwelling place shall be.

Scottish Psalter (1650)

538. The Lord your God is in your midst

Zeph 3:17

Author unknown

539. The nations are waiting

Ps 20:5; Mt 28:19

Capo 2 (D)

With strength

Mark Altrogge

The na-tions are wait-ing for us, they're dy-ing to hear the song we sing.

The na-tions are wait-ing for us, wait-ing for the gos-pel we will bring

that in each na-tion men might come to know the King.

Je-sus, You lead us,

540.

The price is paid

Is 53:4–5; Mt 28:18; Rom 8:1; 16:20; 1 Cor 7:23; Col 2:15; 1 Pet 2:24; Rev 5:9

Graham Kendrick

1. The price is paid, come let us en-ter in to all that Je-sus died to make our own. For ev'ry sin more than e-nough He gave, and bought our free-dom from each guil-ty stain. The price is paid, A-lle-lu-ia, a-maz-ing grace, so strong and sure and so with all my heart, my life in

ev-'ry __ part, __ I live to thank You for __ the price You paid. __

1st 3 times

__

2.
3. The price is
4.

Last time

paid.

2. The price is paid,
See Satan flee away;
For Jesus crucified
Destroys his power.
No more to pay,
Let accusation cease,
In Christ there is
No condemnation now.

3. The price is paid,
And by that scourging cruel
He took our sicknesses
As if His own.
And by His wounds
His body broken there,
His healing touch may now
By faith be known.

4. The price is paid,
'Worthy the Lamb' we cry,
Eternity shall never
Cease His praise.
The Church of Christ
Shall rule upon the earth,
In Jesus' name we have
Authority.

541. Therefore the redeemed

Is 51:11

Capo 3 (G)

Ruth Lake

With pace and swing

There-fore the re-deemed of the Lord shall re-turn and come with sing-ing __ un-to Zi-on, __ and ev-er-last-ing __ joy shall be up-on their head. There-fore the re-head. They shall ob-tain

*From the lips of children and
     infants
you have ordained praise . . .*

PSALM 8:2

*He said to them, 'Let the little
children come to me, and do not
hinder them, for the kingdom of God
belongs to such as these. I tell you the
truth, anyone who will not receive the
kingdom of God like a little child will
never enter it'.*

*And he took the children in his arms,
put his hands on them and blessed
them.*

MARK 10:14–16

542.

There is a green hill far away

Jn 3:16;
Col 1:14, 20;
Heb 13:12

Capo 3 (C)
HORSLEY

William Horsley (1774-1858)

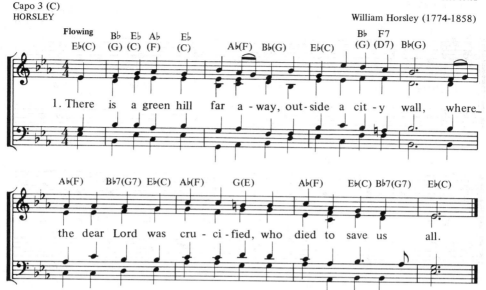

1. There is a green hill far a-way, out-side a cit-y wall, where
the dear Lord was cru-ci-fied, who died to save us all.

2. We may not know, we cannot tell,
   What pains He had to bear;
   But we believe it was for us
   He hung and suffered there.

3. He died that we might be forgiven,
   He died to make us good,
   That we might go at last to heaven,
   Saved by His precious blood.

4. There was no other good enough
   To pay the price of sin;
   He only could unlock the gate
   Of heaven, and let us in.

5. O dearly, dearly has He loved!
   And we must love Him too,
   And trust in His redeeming blood,
   And try His works to do.

Cecil Frances Alexander (1823-95)

543. There is a name I love to hear

1 Kings 19:12;
Col 1:20;
Heb 4:15

SAVIOUR'S NAME

With a lilt

William H. Rudd
(1869-1963)

1. There is a name I love to hear, I love to speak its worth; it sounds like mu-sic in my ear, the sweet-est name on earth:

Chorus

O, how I love the Sav-iour's

name,   O, how I love the Sav - iour's

name,   O, how I love the Sav - iour's

name, the sweet - est name __ on earth. _____

2. It tells me of a Saviour's love,
   Who died to set me free;
   It tells me of His precious blood,
   The sinner's perfect plea.

3. It tells of One whose loving heart
   Can feel my deepest woe;
   Who in my sorrow bears a part
   That none can bear below.

4. It bids my trembling heart rejoice,
   It dries each rising tear;
   It tells me in a still, small voice
   To trust and never fear.

5. Jesus, the name I love so well,
   The name I love to hear!
   No saint on earth its worth can tell,
   No heart conceive how dear!

Frederick Whitfield (1829-1904)

544.
There is a Redeemer

Is 47:4; Jn 1:29; Acts 1:8; Rom 8:32; Phil 2:9; Rev 22:4

Melody Green

Capo 2(D)

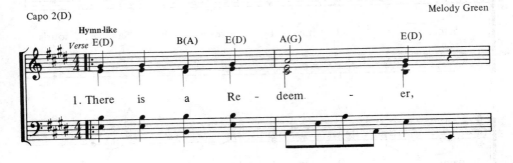

1. There is a Re-deem - er,

Je - sus, God's own Son, _____ Pre - cious Lamb of

God, Mes - si - ah, Ho - ly One.

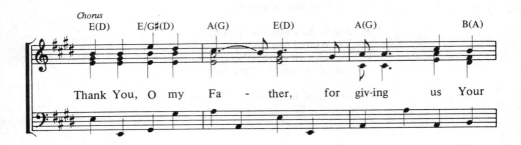

Thank You, O my Fa - ther, for giv-ing us Your

Son, _____ and leav - ing Your Spi - rit till the work _ on _ earth is done. done.

2. Jesus my Redeemer,
   Name above all names,
   Precious Lamb of God, Messiah,
   O for sinners slain.

3. When I stand in glory
   I will see His face.
   And there I'll serve my King for ever,
   In that Holy Place.

545.   There is power in the name of Jesus

Ps 149:6;
Joel 2:32;
Rom 10:13; 16:20; Phil 2:9

Noel Richards

1. There is pow'r___ in the name___ of Je - sus;
we be - lieve___ in His name.___
We have called___ on the name___ of Je - sus;
we are saved!___ We are saved!___
At His name___ the de - mons flee.

2. There is power in the name of Jesus,
   Like a sword in our hands.
   We declare in the name of Jesus
   We shall stand! We shall stand!
   At His name God's enemies
   Shall be crushed beneath our feet.
   For there is no other name that is higher
   Than Jesus!

546. There's a quiet understanding

Ex 16:14–15; Mt 18:20

Tedd Smith

Capo 3 (D)

1. There's a qui-et un-der-stand-ing when we're gath-ered in the Spi-rit, it's a pro-mise that He gives us when we gath-er in His name.

There's a love we feel in Je - sus, that He feeds us, it's a pro-mise that He gives us when we gath-er in His name. thank You, thank You, Lord.

2. And we know when we're together,
   Sharing love and understanding,
   That our brothers and our sisters
   Feel the oneness that He brings.
   Thank You, thank You, thank You, Jesus,
   For the way You love and feed us,
   For the many ways You lead us;
   Thank You, thank You, Lord.

─── □ ▢ □ ───

Praise him with the sounding of the
trumpet,
praise him with the harp and
lyre,
praise him with tambourine and
dancing,
praise him with the strings and
flute,
praise him with the clash of
cymbals.

PSALM 150:3–5

─── □ ▢ □ ───

547. There's a sound on the wind
(Battle hymn)

Phil 2:10;
1 Thess 4:16;
Rev 4:4; 7:14; 21:4

Graham Kendrick

Triumphantly

1. There's a sound on the wind like a vic-tor-y song, lis-ten now, let it rest on your soul. ____ It's a song that I learn'd from a heav-en-ly King, it's the song of a bat-tle royal.

1st and 3rd time ... royal. ____

2nd and 4th times ... sing. / fly! ____ *To refrain*

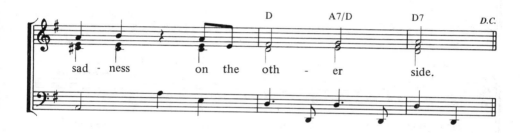

2. There's a loud shout of victory that leaps from our hearts
   As we wait for our conquering King.
   There's a triumph resounding from dark ages past
   To the victory song we now sing.

   Refrain

3. There'll be crowns for the conquerors and white robes to wear,
   There will be no more sorrow or pain.
   And the battles of earth shall be lost in the sight
   Of the glorious Lamb that was slain.

4. Now the King of the ages approaches the earth,
   He will burst through the gates of the sky.
   And all men shall bow down to His beautiful name;
   We shall rise with a shout, we shall fly!

   Refrain

5. *As verse 4.*

548. The Spirit of the Lord

Is 61:1; Lk 4:18

Capo 3(D)

Chris Bowater

1. The Spi-rit of the Lord, the Sove-reign Lord is on me; be-cause He has a-noin-ted me to preach good news to the poor. Pro-claim-ing Je - sus, on-ly Je - sus, it is Je-sus, Sa-viour,

2. And He has called on me
   To bind up all the broken hearts,
   To minister release
   To every captivated soul.

3. Let righteousness arise
   And blossom as a garden,
   Let praise begin to spring
   In every tongue and nation.

549. The steadfast love of the Lord

Lam 3:22–23

Capo 3 (D)

Edith McNeil

Worshipfully

The stead - fast love of the Lord ne - ver cea -

ses, His mer - cies ne - ver come to an end.

They are new ev - 'ry morn - ing, new ev - 'ry

morn - ing, great is Thy faith - ful - ness, O

Lord; great is Thy faith - ful - ness.

550.

The trumpets sound
(The feast is ready)

Ps 23:5; Mt 22:2; Lk 1:53; 14:17

Graham Kendrick

In a 'fiesta' style (♩ = 153)

(Leader speaks:) In Jesus, God has prepared a feast of good things for all who will accept His invitation. Come on: the feast is ready!

1. The trum-pets sound, the an - gels sing, the feast is rea-dy to be-gin; the gates of heav'n are op - en wide, and Je - sus

2. Tables are laden with good things,
   O taste the peace and joy He brings;
   He'll fill you up with love divine,
   He'll turn your water into wine.

3. The hungry heart He satisfies,
   Offers the poor His paradise;
   Now hear all heaven and earth applaud
   The amazing goodness of the Lord.

551.

Thine be the glory

Mt 28:6; Mk 16:6; Lk 24:6;
Jn 20:7, 12; 21:14;
Rom 8:37; 1 Cor 15:55

Capo 2(C)

MACCABAEUS
Triumphant

George Frederick Handel (1685-1759)

1. Thine be the glo-ry, ri-sen con-qu'ring Son,
End-less is the vic-t'ry Thou o'er death hast won.
An-gels in bright rai-ment rolled the stone a-way,
kept the fold-ed grave-clothes where Thy bo-dy lay.

2.   Lo, Jesus meets us, risen from the tomb!
    Lovingly He greets us, scatters fear and gloom.
    Let the Church with gladness hymns of triumph sing,
    For Her Lord now liveth, death hath lost its sting.

3.   No more we doubt Thee, glorious Prince of life;
    Life is naught without Thee: aid us in our strife;
    Make us more than conquerors, through Thy deathless love;
    Lead us in Thy triumph to Thy home above.

Edmond Louis Budry (1854-1932)
Tr. Richard Birch Hoyle (1875-1939)

552. Thine, O Lord, is the greatness

Rev 11:15

Suella Behrns

2. In Thy hand is power and might to make great,
   In Thy hand is power to give strength to all!

3. Now is come salvation and power and might
   For the kingdom of our God has been given to His Christ!

553.

This is the day

Ps 118:24

Les Garrett

Brightly with pace

This is the day, This is the day that the Lord has made, that the Lord has made; We shall re-joice, We shall re-joice and be glad in it, and be glad in it. This is the day that the Lord has made, we shall re-joice and be glad in it; This is the day, this is the day that the Lord has made.

554.

Thou art worthy

Rev 4:11

Pauline Michael Mills

Capo 3 (G)

Thou art wor-thy, Thou art wor-thy, Thou art wor-thy, O Lord, ___

to re-ceive glo-ry, glo-ry and hon-our, glo-ry and hon-our and

power. ___ For Thou hast cre-a-ted, hast all things cre-a-ted,

Thou hast cre-a-ted all things. ___ And for Thy pleasure

they are cre-a-ted, Thou art wor-thy, O Lord. ___

555.

Capo 2 (C)
MARGARET

Thou didst leave Thy throne

Mt 8:20; 27:29;
Mk 15:17; Lk 2:7; 9:58;
Jn 19:2; Phil 2:8; 1 Thess 4:16

Timothy Richard Matthews (1826-1910)

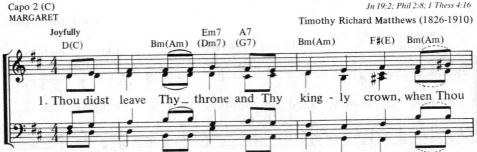

1. Thou didst leave Thy__ throne and Thy king - ly crown, when Thou

ca - mest to earth for __ me; but in Beth - le-hem's home there was

found no__ room for Thy ho - ly nat - i - vi - ty; O __

come to my heart, Lord Je - sus! There is room in my heart_ for Thee.

2. Heaven's arches rang when the angels sang,
   Proclaiming Thy royal degree;
   But of lowly birth cam'st Thou, Lord, on earth,
   And in great humility,
   O come to my heart, Lord Jesus!
   There is room in my heart for Thee.

3. The foxes found rest, and the birds had their nest,
   In the shade of the cedar tree;
   But Thy couch was the sod, O Thou Son of God,
   In the deserts of Galilee.
   O come to my heart, Lord Jesus!
   There is room in my heart for Thee.

4. Thou camest, O Lord, with the living word
   That should set Thy children free;
   But with mocking scorn, and with crown of thorn,
   They bore Thee to Calvary.
   O come to my heart, Lord Jesus!
   Thy cross is my only plea.

5. When heaven's arches shall ring, and her choirs shall sing,
   At Thy coming to victory,
   Let Thy voice call me home, saying, 'Yet there is room,
   There is room at My side for thee.'
   And my heart shall rejoice, Lord Jesus,
   When Thou comest and callest for me.

Emily Elizabeth Steele Elliott (1836-97)

556. Thou, O Lord, art a shield about me

Ps 3:3

Don Thomas and
Charles Williams

Lyrics:
Thou, O Lord, art a shield a-bout me, You're my glo-ry, You're the lift-er of my head. head.

557.

Thou, whose almighty word

Gen 1:2–3; Mt 5:16; Jn 8:12; 1 Jn 1:5–7

MOSCOW

Joyfully

Felice de Giardini (1716-96)

1. Thou, whose al - migh - ty word cha - os and dark - ness heard, and took their flight; hear us, we hum - bly pray, and where the gos-pel day sheds not its glo-rious ray, let there be light!

2. Thou who didst come to bring,
   On Thy redeeming wing,
   Healing and sight,
   Health to the sick in mind,
   Sight to the inly blind,
   O now to all mankind
   Let there be light!

3. Spirit of truth and love,
   Life-giving, holy Dove,
   Speed forth Thy flight;
   Move on the waters' face,
   Bearing the lamp of grace,
   And in earth's darkest place
   Let there be light!

4. Blessèd and holy Three,
   Glorious Trinity,
   Wisdom, love, might;
   Boundless as ocean's tide
   Rolling in fullest pride,
   Through the world far and wide
   Let there be light!

John Marriott (1780-1825)

558.
Through our God
(Victory song)

Capo 3 (Am)

Ps 60:12; 108:13; Rev 19:15

Resolutely with steady pace

Dale Garratt

Through our God — we shall do val-iant-ly, — it is He — who will tread down our e - ne-mies. We'll sing — and shout His vic-tor-y, — Christ is King! For God — has won the vic-tor-y — and set — His peo-ple free, His word — has slain the en-e-my, — the earth shall stand and see that through our Christ is King! Christ is King! Christ is King!

3rd time to Coda

CODA

559.

To God be the glory!

Ps 126:3; Lk 23:43; Jn 3:16;
Heb 2:17; Rev 5:9

TO GOD BE THE GLORY

Fanny J. Crosby (1820-1915)
William H. Doane (1832-1916)

1. To God be the glo - ry! great things He hath done! So

lov'd He the world that He gave us His Son, who

yiel - ded His life an a - tone - ment for sin, and

op - en'd the life - gate that all may go in. Praise the

Lord! Praise the Lord! Let the earth hear His voice! Praise the

Lord! Praise the Lord! Let the peo - ple re - joice! O come to the Fa - ther through Je - sus the Son; and give Him the glo - ry, great things He hath done!

2. O perfect redemption, the purchase of blood!
   To every believer the promise of God;
   The vilest offender who truly believes,
   That moment from Jesus a pardon receives.

3. Great things He hath taught us, great things He hath done,
   And great our rejoicing through Jesus the Son:
   But purer and higher and greater will be
   Our wonder, our worship, when Jesus we see!

560.   To Him who sits on the throne

Rev 5:13

Capo 3 (A)

Debbye Graafsma

With strength

To Him who sits on the throne ____ and un-to the Lamb, ____

____ to Him who sits on the throne ____ and un-to the

Lamb _____ be bless-ing and glo - ry and

hon - our and pow - er for ev - er, _____ be

bless-ing and glo-ry and hon-our and pow-er for ev - er. ____

561   Unto Thee, O Lord

Ps 25:1–4, 7, 14

Capo 5 (C)

Charles F. Munroe

Prayerfully

1. Un-to Thee, O Lord, — do I lift up my soul, —

un-to Thee, O Lord, — do I lift up my soul.

Chorus

— O my God, — I trust in Thee, —

Let me not be a-shamed,_let not mine en-emies tri-umph ov-er me.

2. Yea let none that wait
On Thee be ashamed.
Yea let none that wait
On Thee be ashamed.

3. Show me Thy ways,
Thy ways, O Lord.
Teach me Thy paths,
Thy paths, O Lord.

4. Remember not
The sins of my youth.
Remember not
The sins of my youth.

5. The secret of the Lord
Is with them that fear Him,
The secret of the Lord
Is with them that fear Him.

6. *As verse 1.*

562.

Unto You, O Lord

Phil Townend

563.   We are a chosen people

1 Pet 2:9; Rev 21:2

David J. Hadden

Triumphantly

Chorus

1. We are a cho - sen peo - ple, a roy - al priest-hood, a ho - ly na - tion be-long - ing to God. We are a

1st time

2nd time God.

Verse

You have called us out of dark-ness to de-clare Your praise.

We ex-alt You and en-throne You. Glo-ri-fy Your name.

D.C. al Fine

2. You have placed us into Zion
   In the new Jerusalem.
   Thousand thousand are their voices,
   Singing to the Lamb.

564.

We are all together

(We welcome You)

Mt 6:10; Lk 11:2

Danny Daniels

1. We are all to-geth – er _____ to call up - on Your name. _____ There is no - thing we like _ bet - ter _ than to sing and give You _ praise. _ Lord we wel - come You, _____ we _ wel - come _____ You, we wel - come You, _____ come fill this place. _____ Fa - ther _ come

fill this place, _____ we wel-come_You! Je-sus__ we

seek Your face,_ be-cause _ all we _ want to do _ is give our _

love to You! We wel-come You, __ we _ wel-come You,

_ we wel-come You, __ come fill this place.____ 2. (Bring)

2. Bring healing and salvation,
   Let Your kingdom come;
   Right here just like in heaven,
   May Your will be done.

— □ ▯ □ —

For from him and through him and
to him
are all things.
To him be the glory for ever!
Amen.

ROMANS 11:36

— □ ▯ □ —

565.   We are a people of power

Is 43:21; Jn 1:12

Driving rock

Trevor King

We are a peo-ple of pow-er, we are a peo-ple of praise;
we are a people of pro-mise, Je-sus has ri - sen,— He's
con-quered the grave! Ri - sen, yes, born— again, we walk in the power of His name; po - wer to be— the sons of God, the sons of God! the sons of
God! we are the sons, sons of God!

Final time

566. We are being built into a temple

Eph 2:21–22;
1 Pet 2:5

Ian Traynar

Capo 1 (D)

Freely

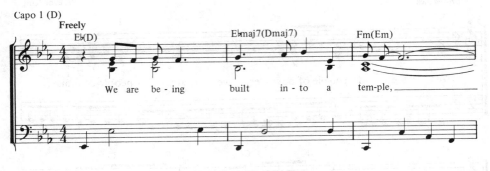

We are be-ing built in-to a tem-ple,

Fit for God's own dwell-ing

place; In - to the house of

God which is the Church, the pill-ar

567. We are here to praise You

Rom 8:15; Gal 4:6;
Heb 13:15

Capo 2(D)

Graham Kendrick

We are here to praise You, lift our hearts and sing.

We are here to give You the best that we can bring.

And it is our love rising from our hearts,
give You pleasure and de - light,

ev - 'ry-thing with-in us cries: 'Ab - ba Fa-ther.'
heart and mind and will that say:

Help us now to 'I love You Lord.'

———————— □ ☐ □ ————————

I will extol the Lord with all my
heart
in the council of the upright and
in the assembly.

PSALM 111:1

———————— □ ☐ □ ————————

568.

We are in God's army

Eph 6:12; 2 Tim 2:3

Ian Smale

We are in God's ar - my, we are in the ar - my of the Lord, yeah, yeah, yeah, we are in God's ar - my. Glo - rie, Glo - rie, Glo - rie, the Glo - rie Com - pan - y.

1. The en - em - y's at - tack - ing, con -

Last time D.C. al Coda

⊕ *CODA*

2. The enemy's regrouping, as he tries another plan,
   He can't pick off an army but he can pick out a man;
   So we'll stay close together, and sing this battle-song —
   We may be weak as soldiers, but as an army we are strong.

3. The enemy's realising that his future's looking poor,
   Though he loves single combat, he's already lost the war;
   United, not divided, together we belong —
   We may be weak as soldiers, but as an army we are strong.

—□ ▢ □—

Now the Lord is the Spirit, and where the Spirit of the Lord is, there is freedom.

2 CORINTHIANS 3:17

—□ ▢ □—

569.

We are standing
(Holy ground)

Ex 3:5

Capo 1 (D)

Geron Davis

We __ are __ stand - ing _____ on ho - ly ground, _____

__ and __ I __ know that there are an - gels all a -

round. _____ Let __ us __ praise _____

__ Je - sus now. _____ We __ are __

stand - ing in His pre - sence on ho - ly ground. _____

570.

We are the hands of God

Mt 16:18; 1 Cor 12:13, 27

(The Church invincible)

John Pantry

Resolutely

1. We are the hands of __ God, our task to do His

will, to lay our hands up on this world, and

by His Spi - rit see it healed. __

Chorus We are __ the Church in - vin - ci - ble, the flesh and

blood of Christ. We are the Gospel visible, our lives the Saviour's light to the world.

2. We are the word of God,
   And by the things we say
   This world will judge the Prince of life
   And be drawn in or turn away.

3. We are the feet of God,
   Who walk the narrow way,
   And every step we take is watched
   By those for whom we fast and pray.

4. Though persecution comes,
   And governments oppose,
   Beneath the crushing weight of law
   The church of Jesus grows and grows.

571.

We are Your people

2 Chron 7:14; Mt 5:14; 6:10;
Lk 11:2; 1 Pet 2:9–10

Capo 4 (D)

David Fellingham

572.

We believe

Is 7:14; Lk 1:34–35; 1 Cor 15:3–4;
Phil 2:10–11; 1 Thess 4:16; Heb 1:3

Capo 2 (Em)

Graham Kendrick

With strength

1. We be-lieve in God the Fa-ther, ma - ker of the

u - ni - verse, and in Christ His Son our Sa-viour,

come to us by vir - gin birth. We be-lieve He died to save us,

bore our sins, was cru-ci-fied. Then from death He rose vic-tor-ious, a-

-scen - ded to the Fa - ther's side.

2. We believe He sends His Spirit,
   On His church with gifts of power.
   God His word of truth affirming,
   Sends us to the nations now.
   He will come again in glory,
   Judge the living and the dead.
   Every knee shall bow before Him,
   Then must every tongue confess.

573.
We break this bread

Mt 26:26–27; Mk 14:22–23;
Lk 22:19–20; 1 Cor 11:23–26

Chris Rolinson

Capo 1 (D)

Thoughtfully

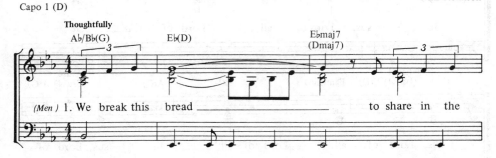

(Men) 1. We break this bread _____ to share in the

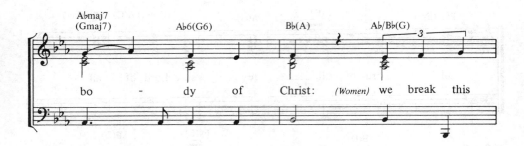

bo - dy of Christ: (Women) we break this

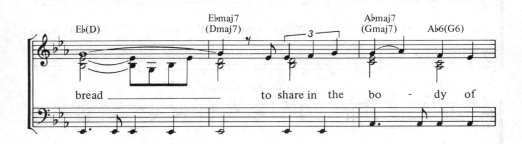

bread _____ to share in the bo - dy of

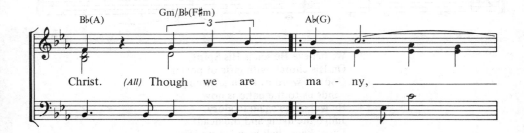

Christ. (All) Though we are ma - ny, _____

2. We drink this cup to share in the body of Christ *(etc.)*

O Lord, open my lips,
  and my mouth will declare your
    praise.
You do not delight in sacrifice, or I
  would bring it;
  you do not take pleasure in burnt
    offerings.
The sacrifices of God are a broken
    spirit;
  a broken and contrite heart,
  O God, you will not despise.

PSALM 51:15–17

574.   We bring the sacrifice of praise

Ps 116:17;
Heb 13:15

Capo 3(C)

Lively

Kirk Dearman

We bring the sac-ri-fice of praise ____ in-to the house of the Lord, we bring the sac-ri-fice of praise ____ in-to the house of the Lord. Lord. And we of - fer up to You ____ the sac-ri-fi - ces of thanks - giv - ing, and we of - fer up to You ____ the sac-ri-fi - ces of joy.

575. We declare that the kingdom of God is here

Mt 11:5; Lk 7:22; 10:9
Graham Kendrick

With strength

Intro

Chorus (Men)

(Women)

We de-clare that the king-dom of God is here.

We de-clare that the king-dom of God is here.

To continue

here. _____ We de-clare that the king-dom of God is

To continue

We de-clare that the king-dom of God is here. _____ A-

To End / *Fine*

_____ here _____ a - mong _ you,

To End / *Fine*

here. _____ - mong _ you, a -

(Women) a - mong you. The mong you.

blind see, the deaf hear, the lame men are walk - ing; sick-ness - es flee at His voice. The dead live a - gain, and the poor hear the good news: Je - sus is King, so re - joice!

Last time Chorus add:

We declare that the Kingdom of God is here, *(men)*
We declare that the Kingdom of God is here, *(ladies)*
We declare that the *(men)*
Kingdom of God is here. *(all)*

Sequence: Chorus twice, Verse,
Chorus, Verse, Chorus twice.

576. We declare there's only one Lord

2 Cor 6:2; Eph 4:5

Capo 2 (D)

Pete Roe

We de-clare there's on-ly one Lord and the earth be-longs to Him, we pro-claim the day of sal-va-tion, it's His king-dom and He's the King. King. There is none like our Migh-ty King, He gave His life to free _ us. There is none more wor-thy of our lives and our al-le-giance. We de-

———— □ ▢ □ ————

*In him we have redemption through his
blood, the forgiveness of sins, in
accordance with the riches of God's
grace that he lavished on us with all
wisdom and understanding.*

EPHESIANS 1:7–8

———— □ ▢ □ ————

577. We declare Your majesty

Mic 5:4; Phil 2:9

Malcolm du Plessis

We de-clare Your maj-es-ty, __ we pro-claim that Your name __ is ex-alt-ed; __ for You reign mag-ni-fi-cent-ly, rule vic-tor-i-ous-ly and Your pow'r is shown through-out the earth. And we ex-

578.

We extol You

Ps 145:1–3, 9–11, 16

David Fellingham

We ex-tol You, _____ our God and King; we bless Your name for-ev-er and for-ev-er, _____ for You o-pen up Your hand and show-er us with good-ness. Your mer-cy and Your grace are free-ly lav-ished on us. So we

——————— □ ▢ □ ———————

*Enter his gates with thanksgiving
and his courts with praise;
give thanks to him and praise his
name.*

PSALM 100:4

——————— □ ▢ □ ———————

579. We have come into this place
(We have come into His house)

Capo 3 (C)

Mt 18:20;
Rom 3:22; 1 Cor 1:30

Worshipfully

Bruce Ballinger

2. So forget about yourself and concentrate on Him and worship Him, *(repeat)*
    So forget about yourself and concentrate on Him and worship Christ the Lord,
    Worship Him, Christ the Lord.

3. He is all my righteousness, I stand complete in Him and worship Him, *(repeat)*
    He is all my righteousness, I stand complete in Him and worship Christ the Lord,
    Worship Him, Christ the Lord.

4. Let us lift up holy hands and magnify His Name and worship Him, *(repeat)*
    Let us lift up holy hands and magnify His Name and worship Christ the Lord,
    Worship Him, Christ the Lord.

580.

We have come to Mount Zion

Capo 6 (C)

Heb 12:19–22

Robert Newey

We have come to Mount Zi - on, — to the ci - ty of the liv - ing God, — to Je - sus our Re - deem - er, — and the sprink - ling of His blood. — We're part of a king - dom that can - not be sha - ken, we've got a found - a - tion that can - not be moved; — so let us praise — Him, hal - le - lu - jah, — let us praise the liv - ing —

God. Now we draw near __ to Him __ by faith, come

through the veil, __ for Je sus brings __ us by His new and

liv - ing way __ in - to His ho - ly place. __ So let us come with bold -

- ness to __ the ve -ry throne of God the Fa - ther, en - ter in __ with

con - fi - dence __ to meet Him face to face. __

581.
We know that all things
(We are more than conquerors)

Capo 3 (D)

Rom 5:9; 8:28–29, 31, 33, 37–39

David J. Hadden

Steadily

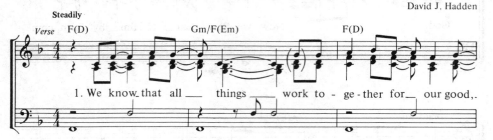

1. We know that all _ things _ work to-ge-ther for _ our good,.

_ for _ good to those _ who love _ the Lord;_

_ for God _ has called_

_ us _ to be just like His Son, _ to _

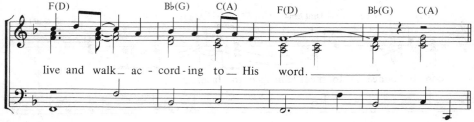

live and walk _ ac-cord-ing to _ His word. _____

2. I am persuaded that neither death nor life,
   Nor angels, principalities, nor powers,
   Nor things that are now, nor things that are to come,
   Can separate us from the love of Christ.

3. If God is for us, who against us can prevail?
   No one can bring a charge against His chosen ones;
   And there will be no separation from our Lord,
   He has justified us through His precious blood.

582.

We'll sing a new song

Is 9:7; Heb 2:9

Diane Fung

Triumphantly

We'll sing a new song ___ of glor-ious tri-umph, ___ For we see the gov-ern-ment of God in our lives.

lives. He is crowned God of the whole world, crowned King of cre-a-tion, Crowned ru-ling the na-tions now.

___ Yes He is crowned God of the whole world, crowned ___ King of Cre-a-tion, crowned ru-ling the na-tions now. ___

583.
We'll walk the land
(Let the flame burn brighter)

Mt 5:16

Capo 3 (D)

Graham Kendrick

With a strong rhythm

1. We'll walk the land with hearts on fire; and ev-'ry

step will be a prayer. Hope is ris-ing, new day

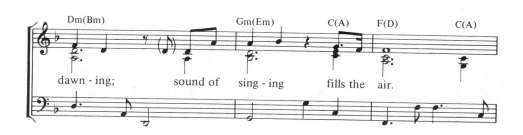

dawn-ing; sound of sing-ing fills the air.

2. Two thou-sand   Let the flame burn

2. Two thousand years, and still the flame
   Is burning bright across the land.
   Hearts are waiting, longing, aching,
   For awakening once again.

3. We'll walk for truth, speak out for love;
   In Jesus' name we shall be strong,
   To lift the fallen, to save the children,
   To fill the nation with Your song.

— □ ▢ □ —

Being confident of this, that he who
began a good work in you will carry
it on to completion until the day of
Christ Jesus.

PHILIPPIANS 1:6

— □ ▢ □ —

584. We place You on the highest place

Heb 4:14

Capo 3(C)

Ramon Pink

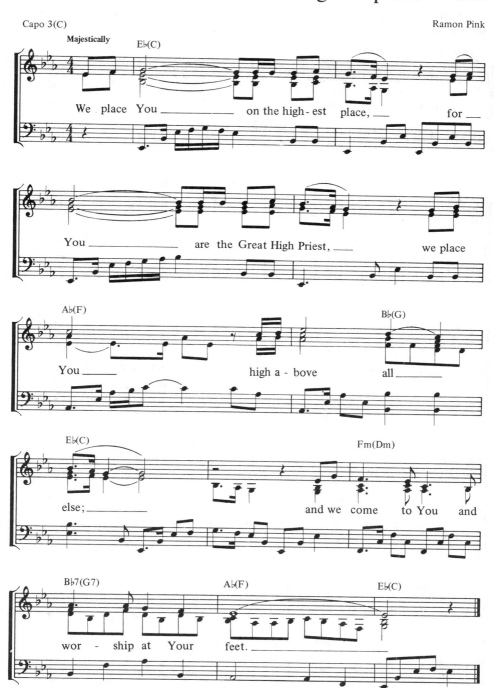

We place You ____ on the high-est place, ___ for ___

You ____ are the Great High Priest, ___ we place

You ____ high a-bove all ___

else; ____ and we come to You and

wor - ship at Your feet. ____

585.

We plough the fields

Mt 8:27; Mk 4:41; Lk 8:25

Capo 2 (G)

WIR PFLÜGEN

J. A. P. Schultz (1747-1800)

1. We plough the fields and scat - ter the good seed on the land, but it is fed and wa - tered by God's al - migh - ty hand; He sends the snow in win - ter, the warmth to swell the grain, the breez - es and the sun - shine, and soft re - fresh - ing

rain. All good gifts a-round us are sent from heav'n a-bove; then thank the Lord, O thank the Lord for all His love.

2. He only is the Maker
   Of all things near and far;
   He paints the wayside flower,
   He lights the evening star;
   The winds and waves obey Him,
   By Him the birds are fed;
   Much more to us, His children,
   He gives our daily bread.

3. We thank Thee, then, O Father,
   For all things bright and good;
   The seedtime and the harvest,
   Our life, our health, our food.
   No gifts have we to offer
   For all Thy love imparts,
   But that which Thou desirest,
   Our humble, thankful hearts.

Matthias Claudius (1740-1815)
tr. Jane Montgomery Campbell (1817-78)

586. We really want to thank You Lord

Capo 2(C)

Ed Baggett

With pace

Chorus

We real-ly want to thank You Lord,— we real-ly want to bless Your name,— Hal-le-lu-jah! Je-sus is— our King!— 1. We thank You Lord,— for Your

Last time to Coda

1st time

2nd time

Verse

to us, ___ Your life so rich be -
yond com - pare, ___ the gift of Your bo - dy
here on earth of which we sing and share. ___
King! ___

2. We thank You Lord for our life together,
   To live and move in the love of Christ,
   Tenderness which sets us free
   To serve You with our lives.

587.

Capo 5 (C)
FINLANDIA

We rest on Thee, our Shield and our Defender!

Josh 5:14;
2 Chron 14:11;
Ps 18:2; Mt 11:28;
1 Cor 1:30

Jean Sibelius (1865-1957)

(Alternative Words)

1. We rest on Thee, our Shield and our De-fend-er! We go not forth a-lone a-gainst the foe; strong in Thy strength, safe. in Thy keep-ing ten-der, we rest on Thee, and in Thy name we

His name, His name shall be called Won-der-ful; His name, His name shall be called Coun-sell-or, The Might-y God, the Ev-er-last-ing Fath-er, The Prince of Peace through all e-tern-it-

Chords above the staff, top line:
F(C) · Dm(Am)

go. _____ Strong in Thy strength, safe
y; _____ The Might - y God, the

F(C) · C(G) · Gm(Dm) · D7(A7) Gm(Dm)

in Thy keep - ing ten - der, _____ we rest on
Ev - er - last - ing Fath - er, _____ The Prince of

F(C) · C7(G7) · F(C)

Thee, and in Thy name we go. _____
Peace through all e - tern - it - y. _____

2. Yes, in Thy name, O Captain of salvation!
   In Thy dear name, all other names above,
   Jesus our Righteousness, our sure Foundation,
   Our Prince of glory and our King of love.
   Jesus our Righteousness, our sure Foundation,
   Our Prince of glory and our King of love.

3. We go in faith, our own great weakness feeling,
   And needing more each day Thy grace to know:
   Yet from our hearts a song of triumph pealing;
   We rest on Thee, and in Thy name we go.
   Yet from our hearts a song of triumph pealing;
   We rest on Thee, and in Thy name we go.

4. We rest on Thee, our Shield and our Defender!
   Thine is the battle, Thine shall be the praise;
   When passing through the gates of pearly splendour,
   Victors, we rest with Thee, through endless days.
   When passing through the gates of pearly splendour,
   Victors, we rest with Thee, through endless days.

Edith Gilling Cherry (d. 1897)

Ascribe to the Lord the glory due to
his name;
bring an offering and come into
his courts.
Worship the Lord in the splendour
of his holiness;
tremble before him, all the earth.

PSALM 96:8–9

588. We shall be as one

Jn 13:35; 17:21; 1 Jn 4:19

Joan Parsons

Smoothly

1. We shall be as one,_____ We shall be as one,_____
He the Fa - ther of us all,_____ We His cho - sen sons;_____
And by His com - mand _____ Take each oth - er's hand,_____
Live our lives in u - ni - ty,_____ We shall be as one._____

2.   We shall be as one,
    We shall be as one;
    And by this shall all men know
    Of the work He has done.
    Love will take us on
    Through His precious Son;
    Love of Him who first loved us
    We shall be as one.

589.

We shall stand

Is 50:7; Lk 9:51; Jn 15:16; 2 Cor 3:18;
Eph 6:13; Rev 22:4

Capo 3(D)

Graham Kendrick

We shall stand, _____ with our feet on the Rock. _____

_____ What-ev-er men may say _____ we'll lift Your name _____ up high. _____

_____ And we shall walk _____

_____ through the dark - est _____ night; _____ set-ting our fa-

- ces like flint we'll walk in-to _____ the _____ light. _____

Verse

1. Lord You have cho - sen me _ for _ fruit - ful -ness, _____

to be trans-formed _ in - to _ Your _ like -

ness. _____ I'm gon-na fight on through_ 'till I see You_ face _

_ to _ face. _____

CODA

2. Lord as Your witnesses
   You've appointed us.
   And with Your Holy Spirit
   Anointed us.
   And so I'll fight on through
   'Till I see You face to face.

590.

We will glorify

1 Tim 6:15; Rev 17:14; 19:16

Capo 1 (D)

Twila Paris

2.   Lord Jehovah reigns in majesty,
      We will bow before His throne;
      We will worship Him in righteousness,
      We worship Him alone.

3.   He is Lord of heaven, Lord of earth,
      He is Lord of all who live;
      He is Lord above the universe,
      All praise to Him we give.

4.   Hallelujah to the King of kings,
      Hellelujah to the Lamb;
      Hallelujah to the Lord of lords,
      Who is the great 'I Am.'

——————————— □ ☐ □ ———————————

He is the image of the invisible God,
the firstborn over all creation. For
by him all things were created: things
in heaven and on earth, visible and
invisible, whether thrones or powers
or rulers or authorities; all things
were created by him and for him.

COLOSSIANS 1:15–16

——————————— □ ☐ □ ———————————

591.

We will honour You

Ex 15:11; Ps 22:3; 2 Cor 6:16;
Phil 2:10; Rev 1:8; 21:6; 22:13

Philip Lawson Johnston

Triumphantly

Chorus

We will hon - our You, we will hon - our You,

we will ex - alt the Ho - ly One of Is - ra - el. We will

hon - our You, yes, we will hon - our You, we will en -

throne You in our ___ praise.

Verse

1. You are the Al - pha and ___ O - me -

ga; You are the be - gin - ning and the end. _____ There is no oth- - er we __ can turn to, no oth - er rock _ on which we can _ de - pend. We will

2. You will not share Your praise with idols;
   All glory belongs to You alone.
   Who in the skies can be compared with
   The Lord Almighty Father God and King?

3. All the earth will bow before You;
   They will be left no place to hide.
   No longer Satan's rule of darkness,
   But the name of Jesus ever glorified.

592.

We worship and adore You

Ge Baas

Gently

We— wor - ship and a - dore You, Christ ____ our King. ____ (Christ_our_ King.) We— wor - ship and a - dore You, Christ ____ our King. ____ (Christ_our_ King.) And we fol - low You to - geth - er, we fol - low You to - geth - er, and we fol - low You to - geth - er, Christ ____ our King. ____ (Christ_our_ King.)

(Main group hold note;)
(small group sing response.)

593.
What a friend we have in Jesus

Capo 3 (D)
CONVERSE

Mt 11:28;
Jn 15:15;
1 Cor 10:13; Eph 6:18; Phil 4:6; 1 Pet 5:7
Charles Crozat Converse (1832-1918)

Peacefully

1. What a friend we have in Je - sus, all our sins and griefs to bear!

What a priv - i -lege to car - ry ev - 'ry-thing to God in prayer!

O what peace we of-ten for - feit! O what need-less pain we bear!

All be-cause we do not car - ry ev - 'ry-thing to God in prayer.

Alternative tune: BLAENWERN

2. Have we trials and temptations?
   Is there trouble anywhere?
   We should never be discouraged;
   Take it to the Lord in prayer.
   Can we find a friend so faithful
   Who will all our sorrows share?
   Jesus knows our every weakness;
   Take it to the Lord in prayer.

3. Are we weak and heavy-laden,
   Cumbered with a load of care?
   Precious Saviour, still our refuge,
   Take it to the Lord in prayer.
   Do thy friends despise, forsake thee?
   Take it to the Lord in prayer;
   In His arms He'll take and shield thee,
   Thou wilt find a solace there.

Joseph Medlicott Scriven (1819-86)

594.

When I feel the touch

Keri Jones & David Matthew

— □ ▢ □ —

I will praise you, O Lord my God,
with all my heart;
I will glorify your name for ever.
For great is your love towards me;
you have delivered my soul from
the depths of the grave.

PSALM 86:12–13

— □ ▢ □ —

595. When I look into Your holiness

Ps 27:4

Wayne & Cathy Perrin

When I look in-to Your ho - li-ness, ___ when I gaze in-to Your love - li -

ness, when all things that sur-round be-come sha-dows in the light of

You; ___ when I've found the joy of reach - ing Your

heart, ___ when my will be-comes en-thrall'd in Your love, when all

things that sur-round be-come shad-ows in the light of You: ___

596. When I survey the wondrous cross

Mt 27:29;
Mk 15:17; Jn 19:2;
Rom 12:1; Gal 6:14

ROCKINGHAM

Peacefully

18th Century melody
Adapted by Edward Miller (1731-1807)

1. When I ___ sur - vey the won - drous cross on
which the Prince of glo - ry died, ___ my
rich - est gain I count ___ but loss, and
pour con - tempt on all ___ my pride.

2. Forbid it, Lord, that I should boast,
   Save in the death of Christ my God:
   All the vain things that charm me most,
   I sacrifice them to His blood.

3. See from His head, His hands, His feet,
   Sorrow and love flow mingled down:
   Did e'er such love and sorrow meet,
   Or thorns compose so rich a crown?

4. Were the whole realm of Nature mine,
   That were an offering far too small,
   Love so amazing, so divine,
   Demands my soul, my life, my all.

Isaac Watts (1674-1748)

When morning gilds the skies

Ps 148:2, 4, 7

Brightly

Joseph Barnby (1838-96)

1. When morn-ing gilds the skies ___ my heart a - wa - king cries: 'May Je - sus Christ be prais'd!' A - like at work and prayer to Je - sus I re - pair: 'May Je - sus Christ be prais'd!'

2. Does sadness fill my mind?
   A solace here I find:
   'May Jesus Christ be praised!'
   When evil thoughts molest,
   With this I shield my breast:
   'May Jesus Christ be praised!'

3. To God, the Word, on high
   The hosts of angels cry:
   'May Jesus Christ be praised!'
   Let mortals, too, upraise
   Their voice in hymns of praise:
   'May Jesus Christ be praised!'

4. Let earth's wide circle round
   In joyful notes resound:
   'May Jesus Christ be praised!'
   Let air, and sea, and sky,
   From depth to height, reply:
   'May Jesus Christ be praised!'

5. Be this while life is mine
   My canticle divine:
   'May Jesus Christ be praised!'
   Be this the eternal song,
   Through all the ages long:
   'May Jesus Christ be praised!'

Author unknown
Tr. Edward Caswall (1814-78)

Be joyful always; pray continually; give thanks in all circumstances, for this is God's will for you in Christ Jesus.

1 THESSALONIANS 5:16–18

598.
When the Spirit of the Lord

2 Sam 6:14

Author unknown
Arr. Margaret Evans

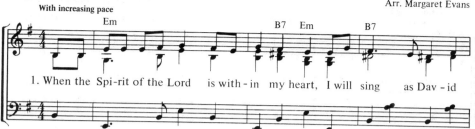

With increasing pace

1. When the Spi-rit of the Lord is with-in my heart, I will sing as Dav-id

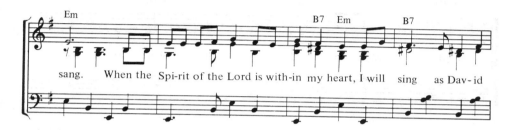

sang. When the Spi-rit of the Lord is with-in my heart, I will sing as Dav-id

sang. I will sing,___ I will sing, ___ I will sing as Dav-id

sang. I will sing,___ I will sing, ___ I will sing as Dav-id sang.

2. When the Spirit of the Lord is within my heart,
   I will clap as David clapped . . . *etc.*

3. When the Spirit of the Lord is within my heart,
   I will dance as David danced . . . *etc.*

4. When the Spirit of the Lord is within my heart,
   I will praise as David praised . . . *etc.*

599.

When we walk with the Lord
(Trust and obey)

Ps 119:105;
Is 26:3–4; Jn 14:1, 23;
Rom 12:1; 1 Pet 5:7

Capo 3 (D)
TRUST AND OBEY

Daniel Brink Towner (1850-1919)

1. When we walk with the Lord in the light of His Word, what a glo-ry He sheds on our way! While we do His good will He a-bides with us still, and with all who will trust and o - bey!

Chorus

Trust and o - bey! For there's no o - ther way to be

hap - py in Je - sus, but to trust and o - bey.

2. Not a shadow can rise,
   Not a cloud in the skies,
   But His smile quickly drives it away;
   Not a doubt nor a fear,
   Not a sigh nor a tear,
   Can abide while we trust and obey!

3. Not a burden we bear,
   Not a sorrow we share,
   But our toil He doth richly repay:
   Not a grief nor a loss,
   Not a frown nor a cross,
   But is blessed if we trust and obey!

4. But we never can prove
   The delights of His love
   Until all on the altar we lay;
   For the favour He shows,
   And the joy He bestows,
   Are for those who will trust and obey.

5. Then in fellowship sweet
   We will sit at His feet,
   Or we'll walk by His side in the way;
   What He says we will do,
   Where He sends we will go;
   Never fear, only trust and obey!

John Henry Sammis (1846-1919)

600.

Where you go I will go

Ruth 1:16

Capo 3 (C)

Author unknown
Arr. Margaret Evans

Steadily

Eb(C)   Cm(Am)   Fm(Dm)   Bb7(G7)

Where you go   I will go,   where you lodge   I will lodge,

Eb(C)   Cm(Am)   Fm(Dm)   Bb7(G7)

do not ask   me to   turn a-way,   for I will   follow   you. __ We'll

Ab(F)   Gm(Em)   G(E)   Cm(Am)

serve the Lord   to-ge-ther __   and praise Him day to   day,   for He

Eb(C)   Cm(Am)   Fm7(Dm7)   Bb7(G7)   Eb(C)

brought us   to-ge-ther __   to love Him and serve   Him al - ways. __

601.

Whether you're one

Jn 3:16

Capo 4(C)

Graham Kendrick

1. Whe-ther you're one or whe-ther you're two or three or four or five, six or se-ven or eight or nine it's good to be a - live. It real-ly does-n't mat-ter how old you are, Je-sus loves you who-ev-er you are.

Chorus

La la la la la la la la la — Je-sus loves us all. all.

2. Whether you're big or whether you're small
Or somewhere in between,
First in the class or middle or last
We're all the same to Him.
It really doesn't matter how clever you are,
Jesus loves you whoever you are.

602.

While shepherds watched

Lk 2:8–14

Capo 3 (D)

Este's Psalter (1592)

WINCHESTER OLD

1. While shep - herds watched their flocks by night, all

seat - ed on the ground, the an - gel of the

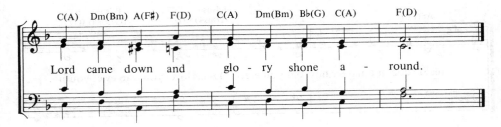

Lord came down and glo - ry shone a - round.

2. "Fear not" said he, for mighty dread
   Had seized their troubled mind;
   "Glad tidings of great joy I bring
   To you and all mankind.

3. "To you in David's town this day
   Is born of David's line
   A Saviour, who is Christ the Lord,
   And this shall be the sign:

4. The heavenly babe you there shall find
   To human view displayed,
   All meanly wrapped in swaddling bands,
   And in a manger laid."

5. Thus spake the seraph; and forthwith
   Appeared a shining throng
   Of angels, praising God, who thus
   Addressed their joyful song:

6. "All glory be to God on high
   And on the earth be peace;
   Goodwill hence forth from heaven to men
   Begin and never cease."

Nahum Tate (1652-1715)

— ☐ ☐ ☐ —

In the beginning you laid the
  foundations of the earth,
  and the heavens are the work of your
  hands.
They will perish, but you remain;
  they will all wear out like a
  garment.
Like clothing you will change them
  and they will be discarded.
But you remain the same,
  and your years will never end.

PSALM 102:25–27

— ☐ ☐ ☐ —

603. Who can ever say they understand
(Forever more)

Phil 2:10–11;
Rev 4:4; 5:13

Dave Bilbrough

1. Who can ever say they understand all the wonders of His master plan? Christ came down and gave Himself to man forever more.

2. He was

Forever more we'll sing the story of love come down. Forever more

2. He was Lord before all time began,
   Yet made Himself the sacrificial lamb,
   Perfect love now reconciled to man
   Forever more.

3. He is coming back to earth again,
   Every knee shall bow before His name,
   'Christ is Lord', let thankful hearts proclaim
   Forever more.

4. (*As verse 1*)

604. Who can sound the depths of sorrow

Capo 1(A)

Lev 18:21; Ps 85:4–7; Is 53:3; Jer 32:35; 1 Jn 1:7

Graham Kendrick

With feeling

1. Who can sound the depths of sor-row in the Fa-ther heart of God, for the child - ren we've re-ject-ed, for the lives so deep-ly scarred? And each light that we've ex-tin-guished has brought dark-ness to our land: u - pon our na -tion, u - pon our na -tion have

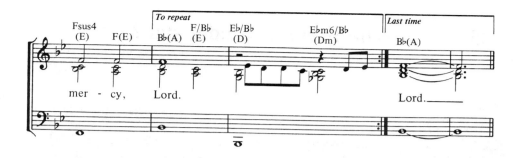

mer - cy,   Lord.   Lord._____

2. We have scorned the truth You gave us,
    We have bowed to other lords.
    We have sacrificed the children
    On the altars of our gods.
    O let truth again shine on us,
    Let Your holy fear descend:
    Upon our nation, upon our nation
    Have mercy Lord.

     (Men)
3. Who can stand before Your anger?
    Who can face Your piercing eyes?
    For You love the weak and helpless,
    And You hear the victims' cries.
    (All)
    Yes, You are a God of justice,
    And Your judgement surely comes:
    Upon our nation, upon our nation
    Have mercy, Lord.

     (Women)
4. Who will stand against the violence?
    Who will comfort those who mourn?
    In an age of cruel rejection,
    Who will build for love a home?
    (All)
    Come and shake us into action,
    Come and melt our hearts of stone:
    Upon Your people, upon Your people
    Have mercy, Lord.

5. Who can sound the depths of mercy
    In the Father heart of God?
    For there is a Man of sorrows
    Who for sinners shed His blood.
    He can heal the wounds of nations,
    He can wash the guilty clean:
    Because of Jesus, because of Jesus
    Have mercy, Lord.

*N.B. Some congregations may wish to add to the effectiveness of this song
by transposing the final verse up a semitone, into B major.*

605.

Who is He in yonder stall?

Mt 27:50; 28:6; Mk 15:37; 16:6; Lk 2:15–16;
5:15; 23:46; Jn 11:35; 19:30; 21:14;
Acts 1:5; 1 Thess 4:16; Rev 19:12

WONDROUS STORY

Benjamin Russell Hanby (1833-67)

1. Who is He in yon-der stall, at whose feet the shep-herds fall? 'Tis the Lord! O won-drous sto-ry! 'Tis the Lord, the King of glo-ry! At His feet we hum-bly fall. Crown Him! Crown Him, Lord of all!

2. Who is He to whom they bring
   All the sick and sorrowing?

3. Who is He that stands and weeps
   At the grave where Lazarus sleeps?

4. Who is He on yonder tree
   Dies in pain and agony?

5. Who is He who from the grave
   Comes to rescue, help, and save?

6. Who is He who from His throne
   Sends the Spirit to His own?

7. Who is He who comes again,
   Judge of angels and of men?

Benjamin Russell Hanby (1833-67) Alt.

606.
Who is like unto Thee?

Ex 15:11

Judy Horner-Montemayor

Worshipfully

Who is like un-to Thee, O Lord a-mongst gods? Who is like un-to Thee, glo-rious in ho - li - ness, fear-ful in prais - es, do - ing won - ders? Who is like un - to Thee?

607.

Who is on the Lord's side?

Ex 32:26; Josh 24:15;
Is 6:8; Rom 8:31;
Eph 6:11; 1 Tim 1:18; 2 Tim 2:3

ARMAGEDDON

German melody
Adapted by John Goss (1800-80)

1. Who is on the Lord's side? Who will serve the King?
Who will be His help - ers oth - er lives to bring?
Who will leave the world's side? Who will face the foe?
Who is on the Lord's side? Who for Him will go?
By Thy call of mer - cy, by Thy grace di - vine,

we are on the Lord's side, Sav-iour, we are Thine.

2. Jesus, Thou hast bought us
   Not with gold or gem,
   But with Thine own life-blood,
   For Thy diadem.
   With Thy blessing filling
   Each who comes to Thee
   Thou hast made us willing,
   Thou hast made us free.
   By Thy grand redemption,
   By Thy grace divine,
   We are on the Lord's side
   Saviour, we are Thine.

3. Fierce may be the conflict,
   Strong may be the foe,
   But the King's own army
   None can overthrow;
   Round His standard ranging
   Victory is secure;
   For His truth unchanging
   Makes the triumph sure.
   Joyfully enlisting,
   By Thy grace divine,
   We are on the Lord's side,
   Saviour, we are Thine.

4. Chosen to be soldiers
   In an alien land,
   Chosen, called, and faithful,
   For our Captain's band;
   In the service royal
   Let us not grow cold,
   Let us be right loyal
   Noble, true, and bold.
   Master, Thou wilt keep us,
   By Thy grace divine,
   Always on the Lord's side,
   Saviour, always Thine.

Frances Ridley Havergal (1836-79)

608.

Who is this?

Ps 20:5; Song 6:4, 10; Rev 7:14; 19:8

Phil Rogers

Capo 3 (C)

With strength

1. Who is this that grows like the dawn, as bright as the sun, as fair as the moon? Who is this that grows like the dawn, as awe - some as an ar - my, as an ar - my with

————— □ □ □ —————

I pray that you may be active in sharing your faith, so that you will have a full understanding of every good thing we have in Christ.

PHILEMON 6

————— □ □ □ —————

609.

Wind, wind, blow on me

Jn 3:8; 14:16–17;
16:7, 14; Acts 2:2

Capo 3 (D)

Jane Clowe & Betsy Clowe

Wind, wind, blow on me,— wind, wind, set me free,—

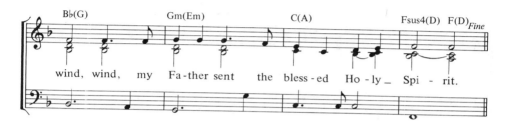

wind, wind, my Fa-ther sent the bless-ed Ho-ly— Spi - rit.

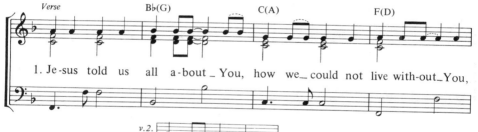

1. Je-sus told us all a-bout — You, how we— could not live with-out— You,

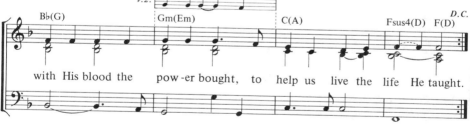

with His blood the pow-er bought, to help us live the life He taught.

2. When we're weary, You console us;
When we're lonely You enfold us;
When in danger You uphold us,
Blessed Holy Spirit.

3. When unto the Church You came
It was not Your own but Jesus' name,
Jesus Christ is still the same,
He sends the Holy Spirit.

4. Set us free to love our brothers;
Set us free to live for others,
That the world the Son might see,
And Jesus' name exalted be.

610. With all my heart

Mt 26:26–27; Mk 14:22–23;
Lk 22:19–20; 1 Cor 11:23–26

Paul Field

Steadily

1. With all my heart I thank You Lord. _____ With all my

heart I thank You Lord, _____ for this

bread and wine we break, for this sac - ra - ment we

take, for the for - give - ness that You make, I thank You Lord.

2. With
3. With

2. With all my soul I thank You Lord.
   With all my soul I thank You Lord,
   For this victory that You've won,
   For this taste of things to come,
   For this love that makes us one,
   I thank You Lord.

3. With all my voice I thank You Lord.
   With all my voice I thank You Lord,
   For the sacrifice of pain,
   For the Spirit and the flame,
   For the power of Your name,
   I thank You Lord.

611.

With my whole heart

Song 5:10; Rev 22:17

Graham Kendrick

Joyfully with swing

1. With my whole heart I will praise You, hold-ing no-thing back, Hal - le - lu - jah! You have made me glad and now I come with op - en arms to thank You, with my heart em - brace, Hal - le - lu - jah! I can see Your

face is smil - ing. With my whole life I will serve You

cap-tur'd by Your love, Hal - le - lu - jah!

O a-maz-ing love, O a-maz-ing love!

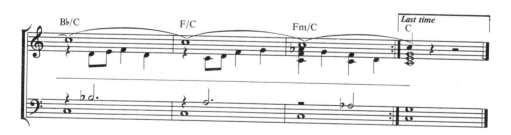

2. Lord, Your heart is overflowing
With a love divine, Hallelujah!
And this love is mine for ever.
Now Your joy has set You laughing
As You join the song, Hallelujah!
Heaven sings along, I hear the
Voices swell to great crescendos,
Praising Your great love, Hallelujah!
O amazing love! O amazing love!

3. Come, O Bridegroom, clothed in splendour,
My Beloved One, Hallelujah!
How I long to run and meet You.
You're the fairest of ten thousand,
You're my life and breath, Hallelujah!
Love as strong as death has won me.
All the rivers, all the oceans
Cannot quench this love, Hallelujah!
O amazing love! O amazing love!

612.

Wonderful love

I Cor 7:23

Capo 2 (G)

David Fellingham

Won - der-ful love _____ com - ing to me, _____

_____ won - der-ful grace, _____ free - dom and

mer - cy; _____ bought with a price, _____

_____ death on a cross, _____

won-der-ful love   Je - sus You've gi-ven to me. _____

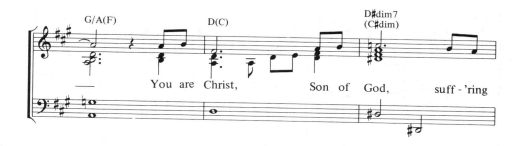

_____ You are Christ,   Son of God,   suff - 'ring

Lamb, pour-ing out Your life,   You've con-quered death,   and You're

reign - ing su - preme in my   life. _____

613.

Worship the Lord

2 Cor 9:8; Phil 1:9; 1 Pet 5:7

John Watson/Vinesong

Additional choruses: Faithful, faithful, faithful is the Lord.
Mighty, mighty, mighty is the Lord.

614.

Worthy art Thou

Rev 4:11; 5:13

Dave Richards

Worthy art Thou O Lord our God of honour and power,

For You are reigning now on high, Halle-lu-jah.

Jesus is Lord of all the earth, Halle-lu-jah, Halle-lu-jah, Halle-lu-jah.

615. Worthy is the Lamb seated on the throne

Rev 5:12–13

David J. Hadden

Wor - thy is the Lamb seat - ed on the throne, wor - thy is the Lamb who was slain, to re-ceive po-wer and rich - es, and wis - dom and strength, hon - our and glor-y, glor - y and praise, for ev - er and ev - er - more.

---□ ▢ □---

Clap your hands, all you nations;
shout to God with cries of joy.
How awesome is the Lord Most High,
the great King over all the earth!

PSALM 47:1–2

---□ ▢ □---

616.
Worthy is the Lamb who was slain
(Glory and praise)

Rev 5:12–13

Andy Park

Capo 2(D)

Slowly, with awe

2. Now to Him who sits on the throne
   And to the Lamb who was slain,
   Now be praise and honour
   And glory and power forever,
   And power forever.
   > *Worthy of power and wealth,*
   > *Worthy of wisdom and strength,*
   > *Worthy of honour and glory,*
   > *Worthy of glory and praise.*

(Final Chorus)
Unto the Lamb be power and wealth,
Unto the Lamb be wisdom and strength,
Unto the Lamb be honour and glory,
Unto the Lamb be glory and praise.

617. Worthy, O worthy are You Lord

Capo 3(C)

Rev 4:11;
5:12–13

Mark S. Kinzer

Wor-thy, O wor-thy are You Lord, wor-thy to be thank'd and prais'd and wor-shipp'd and a-dor'd. Wor-thy, O wor-thy are You Lord, wor-thy to be thank'd and prais'd and wor-shipp'd and a-dor'd.

618.
Worthy, the Lord is worthy

Ps 145:3, 8, 13, 17–18, 21

Ian White

1. Wor - thy, the Lord is wor - thy, and no one un - der-stands the great-ness of His name. Gra - cious, so kind and gra - cious, and slow to an - ger, and rich, so rich in love. My mouth will speak in praise of my Lord, let ev-er-y

crea - ture praise His ho-ly name. For ev - er, and ev - er - more. For ev - er, and ev - er - more. For ev - er, and ev - er - more. For ev - er, and ev - er - more.

2. Faithful, the Lord is faithful
   To all His promises, and loves all He has made.
   Righteous, in all ways righteous,
   And He is near to all who call on Him in truth.

—— □ ▢ □ ——

*Through Jesus, therefore, let us
continually offer to God a sacrifice
of praise—the fruit of lips that
confess his name.*

HEBREWS 13:15

—— □ ▢ □ ——

619.

Ye holy angels bright

Ps 103:20–21

DARWALL'S 148th

Joyfully

John Darwall (1731-89)

1. Ye ho-ly an-gels bright, who wait at God's right hand, or through the realms of light fly at your Lord's com-mand, as-sist our song, or else the theme too high doth seem for mor-tal tongue.

2. Ye blessèd souls at rest,
   Who see your Saviour's face,
   Whose glory, e'en the least
   Is far above our grace,
   God's praises sound,
   As in His sight
   With sweet delight
   Ye do abound.

3. Ye saints who toil below,
   Adore your heavenly King,
   And onward as ye go,
   Some joyful anthem sing;
   Take what He gives,
   And praise Him still
   Through good and ill,
   Who ever lives.

4. My soul, bear thou thy part,
   Triumph in God above,
   And with a well-tuned heart
   Sing thou the songs of love.
   Let all thy days
   Till life shall end,
   Whate'er He send,
   Be filled with praise.

Richard Baxter (1615-91)
Altered by John H. Gurney (1802-62) &
Richard R. Chope (1830-1928)

620.

Ye servants of God

Capo 3 (G)

LAUDATE DOMINUM (PARRY)

Rev 7:9–12

Charles Hubert Hastings Parry (1848-1918)

Grandly

1. Ye ser - vants of God, your Mas - ter pro -
claim, and pub - lish a - broad His
won - der - ful name; the name all vic -
tor - ious of Je - sus ex - tol; His
king - dom is glor - ious, and rules ov - er all.

Alternative tune: LAUDATE DOMINUM (GAUNTLETT)

2. God ruleth on high,
   Almighty to save;
   And still He is nigh,
   His presence we have;
   The great congregation
   His triumph shall sing,
   Ascribing salvation
   To Jesus our King.

3. Salvation to God,
   Who sits on the throne!
   Let all cry aloud,
   And honour the Son;
   The praises of Jesus
   The angels proclaim,
   Fall down on their faces,
   And worship the Lamb.

4. Then let us adore,
   And give Him His right,
   All glory and power,
   All wisdom and might,
   All honour and blessing,
   With angels above,
   And thanks never ceasing,
   And infinite love.

Charles Wesley (1707-88)

621.
You are beautiful
(I stand in awe)

Ps 27:4

Capo 2 (G)

Mark Altrogge

Majestically

You are beau-ti-ful be-yond de-scrip-tion, _____ too

mar - vel - lous _____ for words, _____ too

won-der-ful for com - pre-hen - sion _____ like

no - thing ev - er seen or heard. _____ Who can

grasp Your in - fi-nite wis - dom? Who can

fa - thom the depth of Your love? _____ You are

beau - ti - ful be-yond de-scrip - tion, Ma-jes-ty, ___ en-thron'd a - bove.

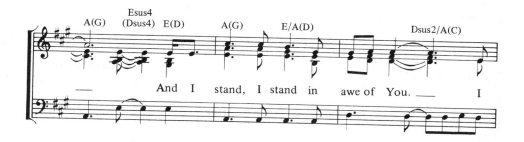

_____ And I stand, I stand in awe of You. ___ I

stand, I stand in awe of You. ___ Ho - ly God, to whom all

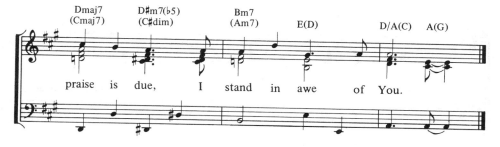

praise is due, I stand in awe of You.

622.

You are compassionate
(Higher than the heavens)

Ps 103:8, 11–12

Capo 1 (D)

Mark Altrogge

623. You are crowned with many crowns

Heb 1:3; 2:9; Rev 19:12

John Sellers

With a strong rhythm

You are crowned with ma-ny crowns, — and
rule all things in right-eous-ness. —
You are crowned with ma-ny crowns, — up
hold-ing all things by Your word. —
You rule — in pow-er — and reign — in

624.
You are here

Is 6:1; Mt 18:20

Patty Kennedy

1. You are here — and I be-hold Your beau-ty, _____ Your glo-ry fills this place. _____
2. I lift my voice — to wor-ship and ex-alt You _____ for You a-lone are wor-thy.

625.

You are my hiding place

Ps 32:7; 2 Cor 12:10

Michael Ledner

Round **Slowly with feeling**

You are my hid-ing place, ___ You al-ways fill my heart with
songs of de-liv-er-ance when-ev-er I am a-fraid. I will trust in
You, ___ I will trust in You; ___ let the weak say
I am strong in the strength of my God.

Last time only

————————— □ ▢ □ —————————

Praise God in his sanctuary;
  praise him in his mighty heavens.
Praise him for his acts of power;
  praise him for his surpassing
    greatness.

PSALM 150:1–2

————————— □ ▢ □ —————————

626.

You are the Holy One
(We exalt Your name)

Phil 2:9; 1 Tim 6:15;
Rev 5:9–10; 17:14; 19:16

Andy Park

With strength

Verse

You are the Ho - ly One, the Lord most _ High.

You reign in ma - jes-ty, You reign on high.

You are the Wor - thy One, Lamb that was _ slain.
You are the King of kings, the Lord of _ lords.

You bought us with Your blood and with You we'll reign.
All men will bow to You, be - fore Your throne.

Chorus

We ex - alt Your

627.

You are the King of Glory
(Hosanna to the Son of David)

Is 9:6; Mal 4:2;
Mt 21:9, 15;
Mk 11:9–10;
Lk 19:38; Jn 12:13

Mavis Ford

With majesty

You are the King of Glo-ry, You are the Prince of Peace, You are the Lord of heav'n and earth, You're the Son of righteousness. An-gels bow down be - fore You, Wor - ship and a - dore, for You have the words of e - ter-nal life,_You are Je-sus Christ the Lord._ Ho - san-na to the Son of Da-vid!_ Ho - san-na to the King of _ kings! Glo-ry in the high-est hea - ven, for Je - sus the Mes-si - ah reigns.

628.

You are the Mighty King

Is 9:6

Capo 3(C)

Eddie Espinosa

1. You are the Might-y King, the liv-ing Word; Mas-ter of ev-'ry-thing, You are the Lord. And I praise Your name, and I praise Your name.

2. You are Almighty God,
   Saviour and Lord;
   Wonderful Counsellor,
   You are the Lord.

   And I praise Your name,
   And I praise Your name.

3. You are the Prince of Peace,
   Emmanuel;
   Everlasting Father,
   You are the Lord.

   And I love Your name,
   And I love Your name.

4. *Repeat verse 1.*

629.

You are the Vine

Jn 15:5

Capo 2(C)

Danny Daniels
& Randy Rigby

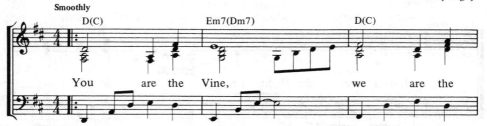

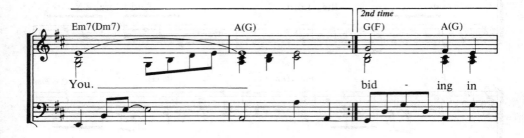

630.

You are worthy

Rev 4:11

John Daniel Lawtum

With breadth

You are wor-thy,_____ Lord, You're wor-thy,_____ — so I lift my heart, I lift my voice and cry 'Ho-ly'._____ You have sav'd_____ me,_____ and I_____ love_____ You,_____ Je-sus ev-er-more I live to praise Your _ name._____

631.

You did not wait for me
(I'm forever grateful)

Lk 15:20; 19:10; Phil 2:7

Capo 2 (G)

Mark Altrogge

With wonder

You did not wait for me — to draw near to You — but You cloth'd Yourself — in frail hu-man-i-ty.— You did not wait for me — to cry out to You — but You let me hear Your voice call-ing me. And I'm for-ev-er grate-ful — to You, — I'm for-ev-er grate-ful — for the cross, I'm for-ev-er grate-ful — to You — that You came ——— to seek and save the lost.

632.

You have been given

Phil 2:9; 1 Pet 2:9; Rev 7:9

Bob Kauflin

1. You have been giv-en __ the Name a-bove all names, and we wor - ship You, yes we wor - ship You. You have been giv-en __ the Name a-bove all names, and we wor - ship You. Yes, we wor - ship You.

To next verse

Last time only

2. We are Your people, made for Your glory,
And we worship You, yes we worship You.
We are Your people, made for Your glory,
And we worship You,
And we worship You.

3. You have redeemed us from every nation,
And we worship You, yes we worship You.
You have redeemed us from every nation,
And we worship You,
And we worship You.

———————— □ ☐ □ ————————

How great is the love the Father has lavished on us, that we should be called children of God! And that is what we are!

1 JOHN 3:1

———————— □ ☐ □ ————————

633. You laid aside Your majesty

(I really want to worship You, my Lord)

Is 53:5; Phil 2:6–9

Noel Richards

You laid a-side Your maj-es-ty, gave up ev-'ry-thing for me, suf-fer'd at the hands_ of those You had cre-a-ted. You took all my guilt and shame, when You died_ and rose a-gain; _ now to-day_ _ You reign,_ in heav'n and earth ex-alt-ed.

I real-ly want to wor-ship You, my Lord, You have won my

heart and I am Yours for ev-er and ev-er; I will

love You. You are the on-ly one who died for me, gave Your life

to set me free, so I lift my voice to You in ad-or-

a - tion.

634.
You make my heart feel glad

Ps 8:1; 92:4

Patricia Morgan
and Sue Rinaldi

Copyright © 1990 Thankyou Music, P.O. Box 75, Eastbourne, East Sussex BN23 6NW, UK

2. When I look around around me, and I see the life You made,
   All creation shouts aloud in praise;
   I realise Your greatness, how majestic is Your name,
   O Lord, I love You more each day.

635.

You, O Lord

Eph 2:4–6

Mark Veary & Paul Oakley

Majestically

You, O — Lord, rich in mer - cy, be - cause of Your great love. You, O — Lord, so — lov'd — us, ev-en when we were dead in our sins. — You made us a - live to -ge - ther with Christ, _____ and rais'd us up to - (Men) / (Women) Christ, _____ and rais'd us — up,

geth - er with Him and seat - ed us with Him in heav'n-ly pla - ces and

C   D7   G   D   C   D7

_____ and seat - ed ___ us, _____ and

rais'd us up to - geth - er with Him and seat - ed us with

G   D   C   D7   G   D

rais'd us ___ up, _____ and seat - ed ___ us ___

Him in heav'n-ly pla - ces in Christ. _____ ___

C   D7   G   D   C   D

Last time

_____ in Christ. _____ ___

Last time
G

636.

You purchased men
(Worthy is the Lamb)

Gal 5:1; Rev 4:8; 5:9, 12

John G. Elliot

With strength

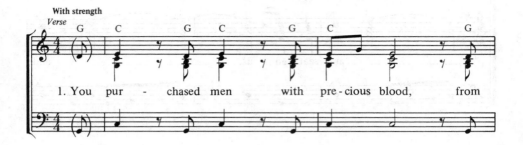

1. You pur - chased men with pre - cious blood, from

ev - 'ry na - tion, tribe and tongue; brought from sla-v'ry, freed from

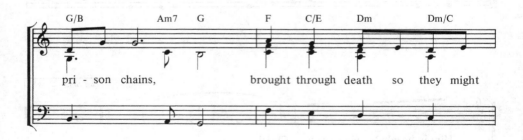

pri - son chains, brought through death so they might

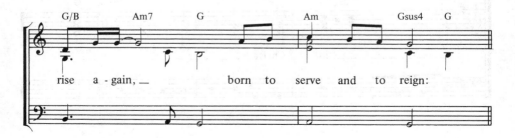

rise a - gain, __ born to serve and to reign:

Wor-thy is the lamb _ that was slain, to re-ceive _ high-est

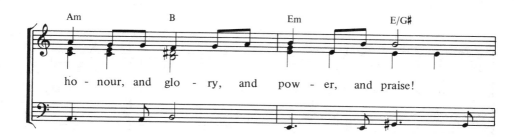

ho - nour, and glo - ry, and pow - er, and praise!

Wor-thy is the lamb _ that was slain, to re-ceive high-est

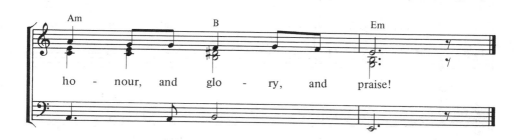

ho - nour, and glo - ry, and praise!

2. Holy, holy to our God,
   Who was, and is, and is to come;
   Let us join the throng who see His face,
   Bowing down to Him both night and day,
   Lost in wonder and praise:

637.
Your mercy flows

Ps 46:4; 85:4–7

Wes Sutton

Majestically

Verse

1. Your mer - cy flows u - pon us like a ri - ver. Your mer - cy stands un - shak - a - ble and true. Most ho - ly God, of all good things the gi - ver, we turn and lift our

(Ladies)
fer - vent prayer to You. Hear our cry, _____

(Men) *Chorus*
fer - vent prayer to You. Hear our cry, _____ O

O Lord, _____ be mer - ci - ful _____

Lord, _____ be mer - ci - ful _____ once

_____ once more. _____ Let Your love _____ Your an-ger

more. _____ Let Your love _____ Your an-ger stem, _____

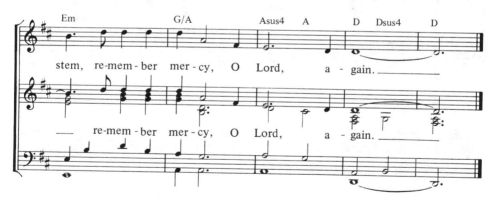

stem, re-mem - ber mer - cy, O Lord, a - gain. _____

_____ re-mem - ber mer - cy, O Lord, a - gain. _____

2. Your church once great, though standing clothed in sorrow,
   Is even still the bride that You adore;
   Revive Your church, that we again may honour
   Our God and King, our Master and our Lord.

3. As we have slept, this nation has been taken
   By every sin, ever known to man;
   So at its gates, though burnt by fire and broken,
   In Jesus' name we come to take our stand.

638.

Your works, Lord
(Great are Your works)

Rev 15:3–4

Andy Park

2. You will reign (*echo*) ⎫
   Forever (*echo*) ⎬ *x2*
   In power (*echo*) ⎪
   You will reign. (*all*) ⎭

3. Because of (*echo*) ⎫
   Your greatness (*echo*) ⎬ *x2*
   All the earth (*echo*) ⎪
   Will sing (*all*) ⎭

— □ ▯ □ —

Great and marvellous are your
deeds,
Lord God Almighty.
Just and true are your ways,
King of the ages.
Who will not fear you, O Lord,
and bring glory to your name?
For you alone are holy.
All nations will come
and worship before you
for your righteous acts have been
revealed.

REVELATION 15:3–4

— □ ▯ □ —

639.

You sat down

Heb 1:3; 2:9

Mark Altrogge

You sat down at the right hand of the Father in majesty. You sat down at the right hand of the Father in majesty. You are crown'd Lord of all, You are faithful and righteous and true, You're my Master, You're my Owner, and I love serving You.

640. You shall go out with joy

(The trees of the field)

Is 55:12

Steffi Geiser Rubin & Stuart Dauermann

You shall go out with joy ___ and be led forth with peace, ___

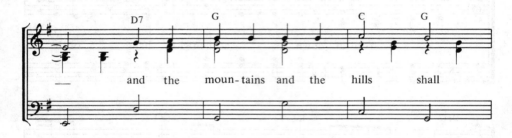

___ and the moun-tains and the hills shall

break forth be - fore you. There'll be shouts of joy ___

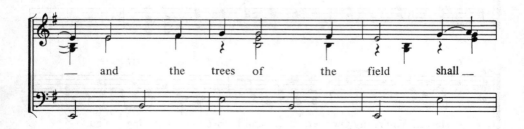

___ and the trees of the field shall ___

Index of Titles and First Lines

Authors' titles, where different from first lines, are shown in *italics*.

1140

1141

1142

1144

Scripture Index

This index lists the *key* Bible passages quoted or echoed in the songs, and not every *passing* reference. In many cases the whole Bible passage will repay further exploration, beyond the verses given here.

1148

1151

Thematic Index

The following index is designed to help church leaders, worship leaders and musicians find songs and hymns appropriate for various themes, settings or occasions. It should be noted that this is by no means an exhaustive listing, and many of these inevitably overlap. If looking for a particular theme, therefore, it is recommended that one looks at several associated categories, rather than just one.

The "seasonal" section has deliberately been kept short. Apart from Easter and Harvest (Christmas songs and carols can be found under the "Jesus: Nativity" section), most other occasions in the church calendar will be covered by themes already listed below.

A. GOD THE FATHER

1. General
2. Creation
3. God's love and faithfulness
4. Salvation and protection
5. God's grace
6. Forgiveness
7. Thirst for God
8. His presence

B. JESUS

1. Kingship
2. Nativity
3. The cross and redemption
4. Sacrifice (the Lamb)
5. Second coming
6. His name
7. Resurrection

C. HOLY SPIRIT

1. Love
2. Joy
3. Peace
4. Holiness
5. Faith
6. Hope
7. Power

D. CHURCH

1. General
2. Call to worship
3. Praise and thanksgiving
4. Proclamation and evangelism
5. Worship and adoration
6. Confession and repentance
7. Communion
8. Commission and revival
9. Commitment
10. Unity
11. Healing and personal renewal
12. Spiritual warfare
13. Justice
14. Prayer
15. Church eternal

E. CHILDREN

F. SEASONAL

1. Easter
2. Harvest

A. GOD THE FATHER

1156

B. JESUS

C. HOLY SPIRIT

3. Praise and thanksgiving

5. Worship and adoration

4. Proclamation and evangelism

F. SEASONAL

Index of Tunes

1171

GUITAR CHORD CHART

The following chord diagrams show the fingering for many of the guitar chords in this songbook.

Key

o = *play open string*   2 = *index finger*   5 = *little finger*

x = *don't play string*   3 = *middle finger*   ▨ = *index finger bar*

1 = *thumb*   4 = *ring finger*   **3** = *fret number*

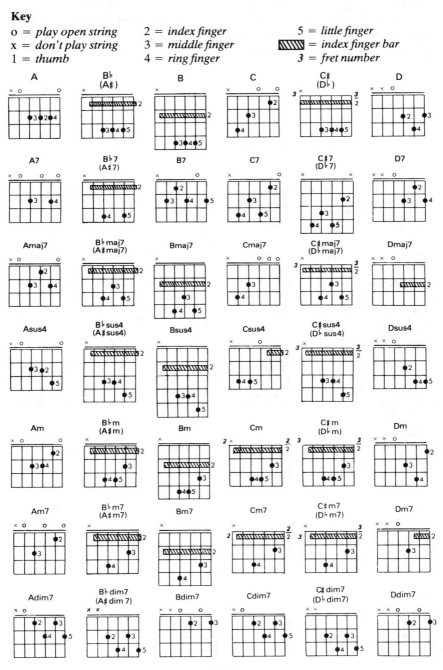

1173

The chords which have been used throughout the book have been carefully chosen with the elementary guitarist in mind. Capo markings, in the left hand corner of many of the songs, allow simple chord shapes to be played with a capo in position. *Capo 3 (C)*, for example, means place the capo at the third fret and play the simple chords in brackets, which you will find are in C rather than E♭. If you use these capo markings you will find that you are able to play almost all of the songs using just ten chords: C, D, Dm, E, Em, F, G, A, Am, B7. If you do see a chord which you don't know, you will probably find that it is playable by mentally stripping it of all its 'extras' e.g. Gmaj7, just play G; Dm9, just play Dm; Csus4, just play C.

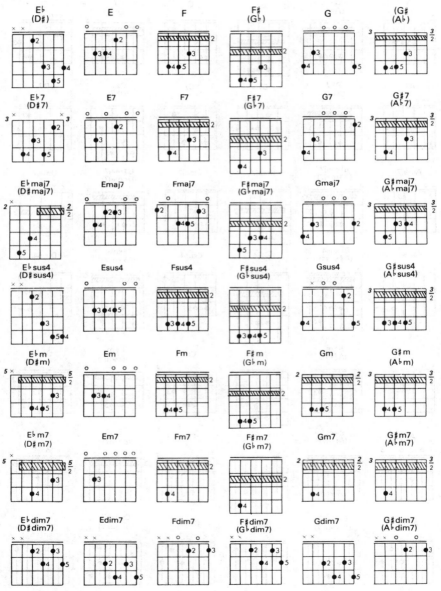

More unusual chords

In this songbook you will come across some more unusual chords—mainly chords with different bass notes. If you see D/A, for example, this means play the chord of D with the note A in the bass. For a guitarist who is strumming, this bass note isn't too important and he can just play an ordinary chord of D, but the A bass note is useful for bass and keyboard players, and for guitarists who are picking and want to add colour to their playing.

The diagram on the right above shows the position of bass notes

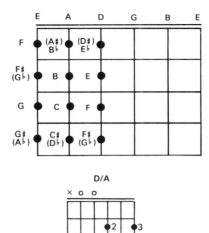

on the guitar for those who want to learn them. Looking at the diagram you can work out that a D/A is simple (see second diagram).

As already stated, when *strumming*, the bass note (as long as it is a note from the chord) isn't too important as it doesn't sound above the other guitar strings. Because one requires as loud and full a sound as possible when strumming it is best to play chords which use all six strings. This can be achieved by incorporating a different bass note. Use the following full sounding versions of common chords when strumming. For—

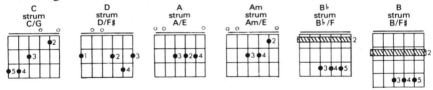

The following are some of the more complex chords you will find in the songbook:

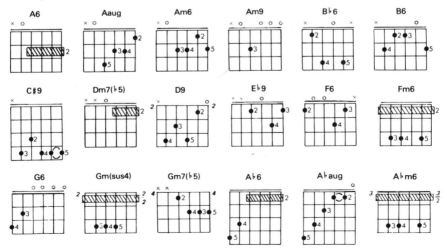

Mice unusual chords.

In this song-book you will sometimes see more unusual
chords—mainly chords with different bass notes. If you see D/A,
for example, this means play the
chord of D with the note A in the
bass. For a guitarist who is strumming, this bass note isn't too important and he can just play an
ordinary chord of D. But the A
bass note is useful for bass and
keyboard players and for guitar
picking, and for guitar
players who the picking and want to
add colour to the voicing.

The diagram on the right above
shows the position of bass notes
on the guitar for those who want to learn them. (Ignore for the diagram
you can work out that A.) (As a guide to the second diagram.)

As for the slated, when strumming, the bass or C (as long as it's a root
from the chord) isn't too important as it doesn't change the other
note strings. Basically this is quite easy to find and play as most is
when strumming, just to play chords which usually strum that this can
be achieved by incorporating different bass notes. Use the following
sounding combinations of chord when strumming. For—

The following are some of the more complex changes you will find in the
song-book:

Copyright Addresses

Karen Barrie, 511 Maple, Wilmette, IL 60091, USA

Bob Kilpatrick Music, P.O. Box 2383, Fair Oaks, CA 95628, USA

Central Board of Finance of the Church of England, Church House, Great Smith Street, London SW1P 3NZ, UK

Kay Chance, Glaubenszentrum 3353, Bad Gandersheim, Germany

Christian Fellowship of Columbia, 4600 Christian Fellowship Road, Columbia, Missouri 65203, USA

David Higham Associates Limited, 5–8 Lower John Street, Golden Square, London W1R 4HA, UK

Timothy Dudley-Smith, Rectory Meadow, Bramerton, Norwich, Norfolk NR14 7DW, UK

Far Lane Music Publishing, P.O. Box 2164, Florence, Alabama 35630, USA

Franciscan Communications, 1229 South Santee Street, Los Angeles, CA 90015, USA

G.I.A. Publications, Inc., 7404 S. Mason Avenue, Chicago, Illinois 60638, USA

HarperCollins Publishers, 77–85 Fulham Palace Road, Hammersmith, London W6 8JB, UK

Hope Publishing, 380 South Main Place, Carol Stream, IL 60188, USA

Integrity's Hosanna! Music, P.O. Box 101, Eastbourne, East Sussex BN21 3UX, UK

Josef Weinberger Limited, 12–14 Mortimer Street, London W1N 7RD, UK

Jubilate Hymns, 61 Chessel Avenue, Southampton, Hampshire SO2 4DY, UK

Len Magee Music, Tweed Heads Christian Life Centre, P.O. Box 242, Tweed Heads, NSW 2485, Australia

Larry Lea Ministries, P.O. Box 414, Rockwall, Texas 75087, USA

Leosong Copyright Management Limited, 7–8 Greenland Place, London NW1 0AP, UK

Lifestyle Music Limited, P.O. 356, Leighton Buzzard, Beds LU7 8WP, UK

Little Misty Music Ltd, P.O. Box 8, Perth PH2 7EX, UK

Meadowgreen Music Co., 54 Music Square East, Suite 305, Nashville, TN 37203, USA

Make Way Music, Glyndley Manor, Hailsham Road, Stone Cross, East Sussex BN24 5BS, UK

Mike and Clair McIntosh, 645 Southcentre, Suite 9, Seattle, Washington 98188, USA

Moody Bible Institute of Chicago, 820 North La Salle Street, Chicago, IL 60610, USA

Mustard Seed Music, P.O. Box 356, Leighton Buzzard, Beds, LU7 8WP, UK

New Song Ministries, P.O. Box 11662, Costa Mesa, CA 92627, USA

Oxford University Press, 7–8 Hatherley Street, London SW1P 2QT, UK

Overseas Missionary Fellowship, Belmont, The Vine, Sevenoaks, Kent TN13 3TZ, UK

Pete Sanchez Jr., 4723 Hickory Downs, Houston, Texas 77084, USA

C Simmonds, School House, 81 Clapham Road, Bedford MK41 7RB, UK

Mary Smail, 100 Prince of Wales Drive, By All Saints Church, London SW11 4BD, UK

Songs for Today Limited, P.O. Box 130, Hove, East Sussex BN3 6QU, UK

Sovereign Music UK, P.O. Box 356, Leighton Buzzard, Beds LU7 8WP, UK

Thankyou Music, P.O. Box 75, Eastbourne, East Sussex BN23 6NW, UK

The Word of God Music, P.O. Box 8617, Ann Arbor, Michigan 48107, USA

United Nations Music Publishers, Boosey & Hawkes Music Publishers Ltd, 295 Regent Street, London W1R 8JH, UK

Word Music (UK), 9 Holdom Avenue, Bletchley, Milton Keynes, MK1 1QR, UK

Australia and New Zealand

Trevor King, 22 Baroona Street, Rochedale, Queensland 4123, Australia

Seam of Gold International, Unit 11/9–13, Winbourne Road, Brookvale, NSW 2100, Australia

Scripture in Song (Celebration, Maranatha! Music, Mercy Publishing, Thankyou Music), P.O. Box 17–161, Greenlane, Auckland 5, New Zealand

Word Australia Ltd (Straightway Music), 140 Canterbury Road, Kilsyth, Victoria 3137, Australia

France

Ateliers et Presses de Taizé, F–71250 Taizé-Communauté, Cluny, France

USA and Canada

BMG (LCS Songs, Charlie Monk Music), One Music Circle North, Nashville, TN 37203, USA

Benson Company, The (Lion of Judah Music, Singspiration, Stamps Baxter Music) 365 Great Circle Road, Nashville, TN 37228 USA

Catacombs Productions Ltd, Management Services, P.O. Box 4124, Station A, Victoria BC, V8X 3X4, Canada

Copyright Management Inc. (Ed Grant Inc., Lexicon), 1102 – 17th Avenue South, Suite 400, Nashville, TN 37212, USA

Fairhill Music, P.O. Box 933, Newbury Park, CA 91320, USA

The Fred Bock Music Company, P.O. Box 333, Tarzana, California 91357, USA

Gaither Copyright Management (Friends First Music, Dawn Treader Music, Straightway Music), P.O. Box 737, Alexandria, IN 46001, USA

Hope Publishing Company (Timothy Dudley-Smith, Jubilate Hymns), 380 South Main Place, Carol Stream, IL 60188, USA

Integrity's Hosanna! Music, P.O. Box 16813, Mobile, Alabama 36616, USA

Lillenas Publishing Company, P.O. Box 419527, Kansas City, MO 64141, USA

Mackenzie & Associates (Samsongs/Coronation) 23 Music Square East, Suite 101, Nashville, TN 37203, USA

Manna Music Inc., 25510 Avenue Stanford, Suite 101, Valencia, CA 91355, USA

Maranatha! Music (Celebration, Scripture in Song, Thankyou Music), P.O. Box 31050, Laguna Hills, CA 92654-1050, USA

Mercy Publishing P.O. Box 65004, Anaheim, CA 92815, USA

Music Services (CA Music), 2021 N Brower, Simi Valley, CA 93065, USA

People of Destiny, 7881-B Beechcraft Avenue, Gaithersburg, MD 20879, USA

Rocksmith Music, c/o Trust Music Management 6255 Sunset Blvd, Suite 1000, Irving, TX 75039, USA

Sparrow Corporation (Birdwing Music, Cherry Blossom Music, Cherry Lane Music, His Eye Music, Latter Rain Music), P.O. Box 2120, 9255 Deering Avenue, Chatsworth, CA 91311, USA

Randy Spier, 2222 Clearview Circle, Dallas, Texas 75224, USA

Tempo Music Pub. Inc. (Glory Alleluia, Sound III Music), 2712 W 104th Terrace, Leawood, Kansas, Missouri 66206, USA

Whole Armor Publishing, 2821 Bransford Avenue, Nashville, TN 37204, USA

Word Inc. (Spoone Music, Word Music), East Tower – Williams Square, 5221 N. O'Connor Blvd, Ste 1000, Irving, TX 75039, USA

Rest of the World

EMI Music Publishing (Acts Music, Ampelos Music), 32 Steele Street, Steeldale 2197, Johannesburg, Republic of South Africa

Kempen Music 12 Surrey Road, Kensington, Johannesburg 2094, South Africa

This new songbook represents the best of the old mixed with the best of the new. Over 600 songs featuring the latest from *Graham Kendrick, Noel Richards, Chris Bowater* and others. Seasonal hymns and songs for Easter, Christmas, etc have been included for the first time.

Compiled by a team of editors from various denominations and across the country this new songbook will appeal to a wide range of people. As well as a full music edition with Scripture, thematic and chord indexes there is an ordinary words edition and a large print words edition available.

Simultaneously two albums on cassette and CD will be released featuring some of the best and most popular songs from the songbook. These exciting albums will capture the live feel of God's people worshipping and praising Him.

MUSIC EDITION
0 86065 935 6

WORDS EDITION
0 86065 936 4

LARGE PRINT EDITION
0 86065 937 2

Cassette Vol. 1 - *SFC280*
CD Vol. 1 - *SFCD280*

Cassette Vol. 2 - *SFC281*
CD Vol. 2 - *SFCD281*

*Songs of Fellowship
for the '90s*

Worship

Worship draws together some of the finest new songs of praise and worship from different parts of the globe - from John Wimber's California-based Vineyard Fellowship, to the UK's own writers, including Graham Kendrick, Dave Fellingham, Noel Richards, Dave Bilbrough and others.

Here is a rich resource of worship songs, from joyful celebration to quiet intimacy, that should prove invaluable to churches everywhere for whom variety and creativity is a vital part of their worship.

 Exalted on High
SFC251

 Reign in Me
SFC252

 **Combined words edition Includes 130 songs**

 **65 Songs**

 **Faithful One**
SFC265

Spirit Breathe on Us
SFC266

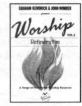 **65 Songs**

Order from your local Christian Bookshop, or in case of difficulty direct from: The Rainbow Company, Lottbridge Drove, Eastbourne, East Sussex, BN23 6NT

Around the world God is building His church, very often in spectacular and dramatic ways. This is resulting in many churches developing vibrant and energetic forms of worship whilst others are becoming more majestic and awesome in their worship. The "Worshipping Churches" series will bring you a selection of this tapestry of praise and worship from around the world.

The first volume "Our God Is Good" is from Kensington Temple, London. This dynamic fellowship is caught on tape worshipping God in a powerful and contemporary way.

 **OUR GOD IS GOOD**
Kensington Temple
SFC251

"Stand" is the second Worshipping Churches album and features the Christian City Church, Sydney, Australia. This album is different, even radical, it's praise and worship with the lid blown off! But this fellowship is real, it's vibrant, it's reaching people and causing them to praise God.

 STAND
Christian City Church, Australia
SFC251

Order from your local Christian Bookshop, or in case of difficulty direct from: The Rainbow Company, Lottbridge Drove, Eastbourne, East Sussex, BN23 6NT

Songs of Fellowship Resources

SONGS OF FELLOWSHIP BACKING TRACKS

Backing tracks are available for a number of songs from the Songs of Fellowship range. These are recorded to professional studio standard, and are idealy suited for public performance or congregational accompaniment.

Write for current available selection to:

Songs of Fellowship Trax, Gap Music, 15 Trueman Place
Aldbrook, Milton Keynes MK6 2HE, UK.

SONGS OF FELLOWSHIP ARRANGEMENT SERVICE

Apart from the fully scored music editions, individual instrumental and vocal arrangements are available for most of the songs in the Songs of Fellowship range from:

The Songs of Fellowship Arrangement Service,
PO Box 4, Sheffield, South Yorkshire D1 1DU.

Please send an A4 stamped addressed envelope (100 grammes postage) for song list and prices.
Please state what vocal or instrumental arrangements you are interested in.

Keep up to date with the best new worship songs, using the convenient THANKYOU MUSIC UPDATE - drawn from the resources of Britain's leading worship publisher. Savour the best new songs from Songs of Fellowship, and use them to enrich the life and witness of your church.

THANKYOU MUSIC UPDATE has several helpful features which will help you as a worship leader or musician.

* 6 new songs - every three months.

* A professionally recorded cassette containing a musical and vocal version of each song.

* A 'backing track' version of the song on the same cassette. This can help the worship group and the church learn the song. You can also use it in situations where you might not have musicians readily available, such as housegroups.

* Fully scored sheet music for every song.

* A helpful teaching article on an aspect of worship.

Songs from the leading Worship Leaders of Britain and America plus other new song writers.

Available from: Thankyou Music, Lottbridge Drove, Eastbourne, East Sussex, BN23 6NT